"This book is descriptive,
prescriptive, visionary
and brutally honest.
It is one of the half-dozen
indispensable texts
for informing the emerging
shape of the church."

GEORGE G. HUNTER
School of World Mission & Evangelism
Asbury Theological Seminary

ChurchNext

Quantum *Changes* in How
We Do Ministry

Eddie Gibbs

InterVarsity Press
Downers Grove, Illinois

InterVarsity Press
P.O. Box 1400, Downers Grove, IL 60515
World Wide Web: www.ivpress.com
E-mail: mail@ivpress.com

InterVarsity Press® is the book-publishing division of InterVarsity Christian Fellowship/USA®, a student
movement active on campus at hundreds of universities, colleges and schools of nursing in the United States
of America, and a member movement of the International Fellowship of Evangelical Students. For information about local and regional activities, write Public Relations Dept., InterVarsity Christian Fellowship/
USA, 6400 Schroeder Rd., P.O. Box 7895, Madison, WI 53707-7895.

All Scripture quotations, unless otherwise indicated, are taken from the New Revised Standard Version of
the Bible, copyright 1989 by the Division of Christian Education of the National Council of the Churches of
Christ in the USA. Used by permission. All rights reserved.

Cover photograph: SuperStock

ISBN 0-8308-2261-5

Printed in the United States of America ∞

Library of Congress Cataloging-in-Publication Data

Gibbs, Eddie.
 ChurchNext : quantum changes in how we do ministry / Eddie Gibbs.
  p. cm.
 Includes bibliographical references and indexes.
 ISBN 0-8308-2261-5 (paper : alk. paper)
  1. Church renewal. I. Title: Church Next. II. Title.
BV600.2.G46 2000
262'.001'7—dc21

                                                                          99-086867

15 14 13 12 11 10 9 8 7 6 5 4 3 2 1
11 10 09 08 07 06 05 04 03 02 01 00

c o n t e n t s ....

Acknowledgments

First, my thanks go to Rodney Clapp who, having heard me speak on the topic of the challenges churches in the West are currently facing, encouraged me to develop those thoughts for publication. I am also indebted to Andrew T. Le Peau, the editorial director at Inter-Varsity Press, and to his outside readers for their many perceptive comments.

I also benefited from my critical interaction with my esteemed colleague Wilbert Shenk and the group of students that meets at Fuller Theological Seminary to discuss the pervasive impact of postmodernity on Western societies. The group includes Ryan Bolger, Gwen Fleming, Alison Houghton-Kral, Karen Kuchan, Randy Hines, Mike Patterson, Shawn Redford and Barry Taylor.

In addition I have been enriched and kept current by the pastoral experience of the pastors in the Doctor of Ministry program and by master's level students. They have helped shape this material by their contributions in classroom discussions. In exploring the impact of popular culture, our students are often our teachers in that the reality we older generations seek to describe from a detached standpoint is the culture in which the students have been totally immersed all their lives.

I am so thankful for the work of Kristin Kvaalen, who straightened out the grammar and spelling and gave meticulous attention to checking references and hunting up misplaced sources. Ben Penner also has been of great help to me in collecting and preparing reference information.

Yet I must absolve all of the above from any inaccuracies that remain and for the continuing limitations in my own understanding of the complexities and confusion of a society in the midst of profound changes and transition. I confess to being a slow learner and that this is still very much a work in progress. It is difficult to think clearly when aftershocks continue to rumble through and shake the ground under your feet.

Introduction

Behind this book lies a story, which in this case has been a long time in taking shape. In some ways it is the story of my life, in that I came into the church in the midst of a time of profound cultural transition in England during the years following World War II. My parents were not churchgoers, although the ministry of the Salvation Army influenced my mother in her early years. Yet despite their own lack of church involvement, they had me baptized in a Methodist church when I was just a few days old and followed this up by sending me to Sunday school as a young child, and encouraging me to graduate to the boys' Bible class.

My home life was characterized by a high moral tone. I never heard bad language and was taught to be truthful at all times. My parents were strict in their Sunday observance: my mother would never consider doing the washing on Sundays; and I was not allowed to play ball on that day, which was reserved for quieter activities. I never heard the Lord's name taken in vain in my home and seldom among the kids in our inner-city neighborhood. It was a society undergirded and permeated by what some call "implicit religion," or "culture Christianity." A high percentage of my school friends went to Sunday school or sang in a church choir, while, as in my own case, their parents never attended church or attended only on special occasions.

Having left school at sixteen years of age to spend two years in the laboratories of a pharmaceutical company, two years in military service and five years in seminary, I was eventually ordained into the ministry of the Church of England thirty-six years ago as of this writing. Looking back to those formative years I realize that I have been trained for a world that has changed beyond all recognition, not just in terms of technological progress but in cultural climate.

Many of these changes have overwhelmed local churches with the force of alpine avalanches. Church buildings are derelict or have been converted to other uses. Others are maintained but now house ever-dwindling and aging congregations. It is sad and painful to go past these monuments to faithful ministry that did not have the needed crosscultural mission insights and experience to engage a society in transition.

The church in which my wife and I came to a personal faith in Christ and that had a wide reputation for being faithful to the gospel, for being committed to evangelism and for having a dynamic youth ministry has now been amalgamated with another parish. The church building has been converted into apartments for the elderly. The population surrounding that church today is racially mixed and religiously pluralistic, with significant numbers of Muslims and Sikhs. Given the changing demographics, was its future made inevitably untenable?

But the challenge is not simply that presented by increasing ethnic diversity and the migration of people of other religions. For at the same time, the indigenous population has become increasingly distanced from the church. During the past four decades, churches have found themselves increasingly marginalized and their influence on society considerably weakened. The church's loss of social strength has revealed its spiritual impoverishment so that there is a loss of nerve. Most mainline churches have experienced serious numerical decline to the point that the continuing viability of increasing numbers of churches, especially in rural and inner-city areas, is a matter of growing concern.

Sociologists of religion have continued to affirm the observation Alexis de Tocqueville made in the 1830s that the United States is an anomaly in Western societies. The United States is one of the most technologically advanced countries, yet with the single exception of Ireland it has the highest percentage of its population going to church. However, in recent years it has become increasingly evident that even this part of the world is not immune from the erosion of Christian influence so evident in most of the Western world.

We are reminded that any church is potentially just one generation away from extinction. Now we are faced with a generation of under-thirty-five-year-olds who are turning away from institutional expressions of Christianity, opting to define their own spiritual journey. Therefore, churches in the West must recognize that they face a missionary challenge that is more urgent and radical than it has been for many generations. Whereas just a decade ago younger people were saying no to church but yes to Jesus, increasing numbers are now in search of a transcendent spirituality in which Jesus no longer occupies a central place.

Yet in the midst of moral uncertainties and spiritual confusion there are encouraging signs of spiritual vitality and examples of Christian communities engaging the challenges of a new day. It has always been the case that new wine must be poured into new wineskins. But those new wineskins cannot simply be freshly made versions of the old models. Neither can they be cut from a template made from blueprints provided by a handful of high-profile churches that have succeeded in bucking the national trends.

Indeed we may find that the most helpful models might be drawn from the first 150 years of the Christian church, when it began as a movement with neither political power nor social influence within a pluralist environment. Furthermore, churches in the West are discovering that they have much to learn from growing churches in the Majority World,[1] which are thriving in the midst of pluralistic environments without either the social influence or the material resources that the churches of the West enjoyed for so many centuries.

The purpose of the following chapters is to attempt to identify some of the major storm centers through which churches have to navigate. These storm fronts do not simply represent a short-term threat churches must survive in order to return to the familiar and more tranquil conditions that they have previously known. Rather, these storm fronts represent boundary lines that separate two very different worlds. The major themes covered include the church's mission, its structures, leadership emergence and mentoring, worship, spirituality and evangelism.

The nine chapter headings identify key areas in which churches need to undergo transforming transitions in the midst of the seismic shifts that are happening in our cultural contexts. Pastors and other church leaders are well aware that significant changes in the life of the local church (or insignificant ones for that matter!) are seldom made smoothly or neatly. For within most local churches, especially those in existence for thirty years or more, there will be groups of individuals who think with traditional, modern and postmodern assumptions. Each group has a legitimate perspective and deep concerns. Furthermore, they have been so shaped by cultural influences that have permeated their thinking and fueled their attitudes that they have seldom paused to examine critically their positions and reactions to the issues that so inflame their passions.

Pastors and church leaders have a responsibility to serve each group, as well as to acknowledge their own particular cultural and generational biases that may be conveniently masked by theological and ecclesiological rationales. In order for the range of highly emotive issues to be addressed in a fair and positive manner, deeply embedded assumptions must be brought to the surface.

The purpose of the following chapters is to begin such a conversation. It offers no blueprint for the shape of the church in the twenty-first century. The author claims no prophetic insight adequate for such a task. Furthermore, so unpredictable is the future and the trends are so diverse that blueprints galore would need to be rapidly produced and just as quickly shredded! Welcome to the twenty-first century.

Eddie Gibbs
Pasadena, California

one

From Living in the Past
to Engaging with the Present

T*he longer a person lives, the more he or she tends to dwell on* the past rather than live in dynamic interaction with the present or be inspired by the hope of future possibilities. If this is true for the individual, it also holds true for institutions that have an inherited corporate culture reinforced by each succeeding generation. Furthermore, when changes in society are occurring at a rapid rate and in an unpredictable manner, the desire to resort to a protective entrenchment becomes even stronger. In this opening chapter we will examine evidence that reveals the extent of this mentality among the churches, assess its impact and explore some of the megatrends that are threatening the survival of tens of thousands of churches across North America as they have throughout much of Europe.

During the past decade there has been a glut of books analyzing the growing crisis that has engulfed the Christian churches of North America since the mid-1960s. In much of Europe this crisis has been brewing over a much longer period, dating from the aftermath of World War I. On that continent its progress has been at a slower pace, yet with devastating long-term consequences. The decline in active membership and of influence of the state churches and mainline denominations has also been experienced by many independent congregations, which found that they were just as vulnerable to the adverse social forces causing the retrenchment.

The current state of affairs across Europe has now become a warning flag to churches of every theological and ecclesiastical tradition in North America. North Americans had long considered themselves immune from such a fate because the United States had for so many decades been an anomaly in the Western world. Americans, it appeared, were incurably religious, reflected in both the orthodoxy of their religious beliefs and the high percentage of the population that attended church each Sunday.

Some mission agencies and independent, mission-minded churches "with a burden for Europe" were eager to assume the role of rescuers. They sent missionaries to plant churches with a germ-resistant, "made in America" seed with a high-yield potential. They confidently felt they could provide a viable alternative to the struggling and sterile European varieties. However, those missionaries soon found that the soil was harder than they had anticipated. The new, imported models simply contributed to the further fragmentation of the church, failing to stimulate growth through significant numbers of new conversions.

At the present time there is a refreshing new humility spreading among church and mission leaders in the face of the challenges presented by a post-Christian and postmodern Western culture confronting them on both sides of the Atlantic Ocean. The writings of the late Lesslie Newbigin have become obligatory reading for perplexed and discouraged pastors searching for new insights to apply to the challenges which they face.[1]

Here we may cite a few significant writers on the subject of churchgoing trends whose voices are contributing to the siren being sounded. Mike Regele, whose company, Percept Group, Inc., provides sophisticated demographic data gathering and mapping for anywhere in the United States, is keenly aware of the extent of the challenge facing the churches. He believes that the institutional church in America will look very different twenty-five years from now and that several denominations may no longer exist.

Mike Regele has no doubt that hundreds of local congregations will close their doors for the last time. Most of the reasons for this pessimistic prognosis are to be found within society and the tragic fact that so many churches are failing to discern the signs of the times and neglecting to seek the spiritual discernment and vitality to meet the challenges. "The forces reshaping our culture are too many and too strong. We see signs of social fragmentation and collapse everywhere."[2]

Regele's views are reinforced through his widespread contacts with church leaders at conferences and consultations. Having analyzed data on churchgoing trends and attitudes toward the churches held by each of the five generations alive today, he comes to the following sobering conclusion:

> At the brink of the twenty-first century, the king who knew not Joseph is the collective culture of which we are a part. The combined impact of the Information Age, postmodern thought, globalization, and racial-ethnic pluralism that has seen the demise of the grand American story also has displaced the historic role the church has played in that story. As a result, we are seeing the marginalization of the institutional church.[3]

The Decline of Mainline Denominations

Mike Regele does not stand alone in this assessment. Pollster and marketing analyst George Barna reinforces his somber message. While we may take comfort from the many inspiring exceptions to Barna's generalizations, the overall picture he presents of the spiritual barrenness and consequent unattractiveness of many churches to visitors is disturbingly accurate.

Those who have turned to Christianity and churches seeking truth and meaning have left empty-handed, confused by the apparent inability of Christians themselves to implement the principles they profess. Churches, for the most part, have failed to address the nagging anxieties and deep-seated fears of the people, focusing instead upon outdated or secondary issues and proposing tired or trite solutions.[4]

Lyle Schaller, the church consultant with probably the longest record and widest experience regarding the churches in North America, also shares their pessimism as to the future of the mainline denominations. Throughout his career Schaller has demonstrated a strong commitment to denominational churches, but he now recognizes that unless they make some drastic changes, their future looks bleak. In his book *Innovations in Ministry* he identified fifteen serious problems facing mainline denominations.[5] Two years later he described the dysfunction that characterizes the majority of traditional denominations in his book entitled *Tattered Trust,* in which he particularly addressed the United Methodist Church, his own denomination (see figure 1.1). The data of numerical decline speaks for itself.

Denomination	1968		1995	
	No. of Congreg.	Inclusive Mbship.	No. of Congreg.	Inclusive Mbship.
Chr. Church (Disciples)	5,862	1,592,609	4,036	929,725
Episcopal Church	7,137	3,373,890	7,415	2,536,550
Reformed Ch. in Am.	939	383,166	903	306,312
United Ch. of Christ	6,866	2,032,648	6,145	1,472,213
United Methodist Ch.	41,901	10,990,720	36,361	8,538,662

Figure 1.1. Numerical decline in a sample of mainline denominations (*Yearbook of American Churches,* 1970 and 1997)

In the face of such statistics some researchers are predicting that if present trends continue, sixty percent of all existing Christian congregations in America will disappear before the year 2050.[6] Congregations whose average member is over fifty years of age are especially vulnerable, bearing in mind that the average American is in his or her mid-thirties.

Smaller congregations are finding increasingly that they are no longer economically viable. They struggle to meet the rising costs of maintaining property, paying insurance, and meeting the salary and compensation needs of seminary-trained pastors, many of whom have outstanding loans. These struggling churches will be forced to close, to amalgamate with other churches or to radically restructure and redefine their ministries in order to meet the demands of a new day.[7]

The Growth of "New Paradigm" Churches

The drastic decline in membership across the denominations that has occurred in the four decades of the sixties through the nineties has resulted in religious demographers renaming the mainline denominations "old-line." These denominations have become increasingly sidelined not only within the wider culture but within the churchgoing population of North America. However, during the same period in which many churches have been declining, others have experienced phenomenal growth. Also, increasing numbers of Westerners are attracted to Islam and to New Age adaptations of Hinduism, Buddhism, Native American spirituality and paganism. So decline in church attendance cannot entirely be attributed to the influence of secularization.

A number of non-Christian religions are growing due to the change in immigration patterns in North America, with more people coming from areas of the world where Islam, Confucianism, Taoism and Buddhism prevail. Furthermore, Muslim and Hindu families tend to have a higher-than-average birth rate, and these religions are seeing conversions from former churchgoers and people with no prior church allegiance.

Those churches that are experiencing growth, in defiance of the national downward trends, are usually located in new suburban areas. They are acutely market-sensitive and base their strategy on attracting the nonchurchgoer into "seeker-sensitive" worship services. They have a laid-back approach while emphasizing excellence in all that they do. They empower their laity for manifold ministries both within the church and out in the community and are in close touch with their target populations. Some seeker-sensitive churches work within a modern worldview, while alongside them is an increasingly significant, more radical wing that engages postmodernity with a transformational message and lifestyle.

These churches are called by a variety of titles. Lyle Schaller terms them "New Reformation," Donald Miller describes them as "New Paradigm," and George Hunter and Peter Wagner label them "New Apostolic," each applying the term with a different emphasis. As these growing networks are not more than twenty years old, it is still too soon to assess their long-term significance. It is by no means certain that they will be able to buck the trend by maintaining their growth over the long haul. And any voice of triumphalism from among their ranks needs to be moderated by the fact that these new movements have not as yet exerted sufficient influence to reverse the overall decline in churchgoing. Until this happens, it is an open question whether they represent a reconfiguration of existing churchgoers or a significant expansion into the unchurched population through effective evangelistic outreach.

In response to the challenge and inspiration provided by these "New Paradigm" churches, some visionary leaders within traditional denominations are asking what lessons can be learned from their vitality and popular appeal. Addressing the Episcopal Church, Richard Kew and Roger White call for radical changes for the revitalization of a declining denomination.[8] Tony Campolo raises the question for his own American Baptist denomination, "Can mainline denominations make a comeback?" in a book by that title.[9] It must be emphasized that these writers have not given up on their denominations. They remain as committed as ever, for within most denominations churches can be found that demonstrate renewed spiritual vitality and a commitment to mission, resulting in both transformed lives, numerically growing churches and the planting of new churches.

A Cultural Shift of Seismic Proportions

Churches can become so traumatized by their internal problems that they fail to notice that society at large is in the midst of a cultural shift of seismic proportions, which affects every area of society. William Easum describes this shift in terms of a transition from the Industrial Age to the Quantum Age. He observes that "established Protestantism was born into the Industrial Age, a world of slow, incremental change."[10] By about the middle of the twentieth century the rate of change quickened and became increasingly complex. Today a momentum has been generated to such a degree that change has become discontinuous and chaotic.

Mike Regele issued a wake-up call to American Christianity in *The Death of the Church,* in which he alerts church leaders to the fact that they minister in a world out of control, characterized by stress and uncertainty.[11] He believes that "if we do not understand the forces of change, we will be overwhelmed by them."[12] The transition from modernity to postmodernity represents a seismic shift that can result in churches becoming paralyzed in the midst of the shock waves. The changes are deep-rooted, comprehensive, complex, unpredictable and global in their ramifications.

Unlike most institutions the church cannot confine its attention to certain groups of people. Rather it endeavors to respond sensitively to all comers, caring for them from the cradle to the grave. At the same time it must also give high priority to reaching beyond its ranks to meet people in every walk of life, to demonstrate the love of Christ in practical ways and invite them to join their ranks in following Christ as Lord and Savior.

In some areas of the country, such as rural locations and small towns, churches continue to minister in traditional societies, where they still occupy a central place. In other settings churches find themselves marginalized by modernity, a mindset represented by self-assertive secular presuppositions that allow no place for the transcendent. In yet other areas they find themselves grappling with a different set of challenges posed by postmodernity. This is especially true of churches located near university campuses or in locations where the media and entertainment industries are influential.

Furthermore, within many congregations, groups exist that represent each of these three mindsets: traditional, modern and postmodern. It is no wonder that church leaders find it hard to secure consensus and set a clear direction. And they are not alone because the cultural shifts represented by these three worldviews run throughout society. Leaders in many institutions—educational, religious, commercial and medical—face similar conflicts as they try to deal with differing and oftentimes conflicting assumptions.

Churches Ministering Within Traditional Societies

In a traditional setting, society assigns places for religious faith to be expressed within its institutions. It reserves a central location to the most prestigious or numerically strong churches. Church buildings occupy pride of place in the town square, next to the city hall and along Main Street. Pastors drawn from the mainline denominations or largest churches fulfill civic responsibilities as chaplains to the mayor members of hospital boards and school boards. They are active in Rotary and other social and business fraternities and country clubs. Their wisdom is valued, and they are frequently consulted on a range of community issues.

Churches in such contexts are called to bear witness to the gospel of the kingdom of God within the social structures, while resisting being subverted by them. In order to retain their privileged place in society, church leaders can easily lose their distinctive witness and prophetic stance. They mirror society's values instead of acting as salt, light and yeast—the salt to savor and sanitize, the light to expose and guide, and the yeast to unobtrusively permeate. One common feature of salt, light and yeast is that they are capable of exerting influence far beyond their size.

Church leaders must resist becoming subverted by patronage, for it is all too easy to mistake social strength for spiritual vitality.

Within contemporary American evangelicalism there is a loud and influential voice calling for a return to a past era of privilege and prestige when there was a more broadly accepted Protestant Christian ethic and culture. However, there is no going back along tracks that have been obliterated by the windstorms and rock falls created by the contemporary social and cultural context, with its religious pluralism, philosophical skepticism and ethical relativism. Not only are we prevented from retracing our steps, we also discover that there is scant possibility of further advance along this particular road. Of course, exceptions may still be found in those Christian groups located in isolated communities or that have isolated themselves in the midst of their multicultural, urban settings.

Although traditional settings are becoming increasingly rare, traditional mindsets still prevail in many churches of all denominations, whether liberal or evangelical, mainline or independent. This is because the church is an inherently conservative institution, and the average age of people who attend mainline churches is twenty years older than the general population.

The Church's Responses to Modernity

The *modern worldview* represents the apex of the Enlightenment paradigm. It is humankind in its most self-confident pose: proud of its achievements and feeling in control of its own destiny. It is the self-contained and exclusionary world of the secularist. Arrogance is a dangerous state of mind in that it is prone to produce tunnel vision and a stubborn reluctance—if not outright refusal—to face issues that threaten the collapse of the tunnel. James Hunter defines modernity in the following terms:

> As *both* a mode of social life *and* moral understanding more or less characterized by the universal claims of reason and instrumental (or means/ends) rationality; the differentiation of spheres of life-experience into public and private; and the pluralization and competition of truth claims.[13]

Modernity is an understanding of the world through an autonomous and human rationality. Evangelicalism arose within that context, which meant that it had to confront the challenges of humanism and rationalism. In so doing it was itself influenced, more than it realized, by the modernism it combated. In response to the questionable assumptions and reductionist explanations of Darwinian evolutionists and Freudian psychologists, Christian apologists had to employ the tools of their opponents in order to engage in meaningful debate. In so doing they became unwittingly subverted by the assumptions they made in debating with their opponents. Christian apologists argued for the reliability of biblical texts based on their consistency and inerrancy defined in terms of modern "scientific" criteria.

There was no place for revelation; such was the confidence in self-evident, universal truths available to all through unaided reason. There was little place for the "mystery" of the gospel of Jesus Christ. For it was beyond the powers of human reason to reconcile a holy God with sinful humankind. That message could only be known through God's revelation in Jesus Christ and through the proclamation of those who had encountered the truth and linked their personal stories with God's salvation story.

The separation of life into public and private spheres and its compartmentalization into specialized areas resulted in religious faith becoming marginalized from society and reduced to a privatized matter for like-minded individuals to pursue without imposing their views on the public sphere. Religious faith becomes relativized, helpful as a resource for coping with the crises of life, but having no legitimacy in claiming public truth. James Hunter describes the resulting crisis in the following terms; "What was 'known' with a taken-for-granted certitude becomes, at best, a 'belief.' Further along in this process it becomes a 'religious opinion' or a 'feeling.'. . . The emphasis shifts from a concern with the proclamation of an objective and universal truth to a concern with the subjective applicability of truth."[14]

The emergence of postmodernity. Postmodernity is a term used with different meanings arising out of a variety of contexts. The term cannot escape becoming a casualty of the fragmented world it seeks to describe! It appears that the term *postmodern* was first coined by Frederico de Onis in the 1930s but did not achieve prominence until it was used to describe reactive tendencies to modernism in art and literature in the 1960s and in architecture in the 1970s. Then in the 1980s its meaning was stretched to cover an emergent, comprehensive worldview embracing philosophy, the arts, politics and certain branches of science, theology and popular culture. Postmodernism has been labeled as "pessimistic wishful thinking," and as "nihilism with a smile."[15]

As the modern secular version of the ancient "Tower of Babel," modernity began to crumble and topple when it became increasingly evident that technological advances created as many problems as they were solving. There was a growing realization that human progress bore within it the prospect of self-destruction. There were unseen consequences that threatened to render the planet uninhabitable as a consequence of nuclear, chemical and biological warfare; industrial pollution of the atmosphere and rivers, lakes and oceans; and deforestation. New technologies designed to free the human spirit and remove physical drudgery created new dependencies and enslavement.

We find ourselves caught in the vortex of the need to know and to achieve on an ever-increasing scale and at an accelerating pace. Our technical knowledge has advanced far beyond our wisdom to know when to refrain from applying what we know in humble recognition of the limitations of our knowledge. We lack the moral courage to restrain our compulsive urges to do what we know how to do with reckless disregard for the human and environmental consequences.

The optimism that characterized much of the liberal, humanist tradition has given way to pessimism and skepticism. In a pervasive atmosphere of cynicism, postmodernists look for the motives behind truth claims. Philip Sampson interprets the postmodern mindset in the following terms: "Reason is displaced by reasons, each within its own discourse and for its own public. None is privileged. The rational project begun in the seventeenth century has collapsed, leaving a field of competing rationalities. But then there is no privileged rationality to adjudicate and therefore no rational basis for judgment."[16] In the arena of liberal education, Roger Lundin observes that educators "do not desire that their students seek truth, justice, or righteousness—unless one defines truth as the process of uncovering the biases of others, justice as the protection of personal preferences, and righteousness as the pursuit of desire."[17]

Postmodernists have abandoned the illusive search for truth, or more accurately, they have redefined truth in terms of consensus and "whatever works for you." They reject propositional certainty as the ploy of the powerful, who exert their influence by disempowering those who hold to a divergent view. Rather, they claim we should celebrate diversity and regard ambiguity as providing the fertile soil for continuing creativity. There is no "metanarrative," no grand story to inspire a people, no explanation of everything, no meaning or purpose to life awaiting discovery at either the cosmic or the personal level.

Each individual has to create his or her own meaning and associate with others to increase his or her power base in a fragmented society of competing interests. Everyone is entitled to his or her point of view, because for the perspectivilist, what you see depends on where you stand. The world of the postmodernists is a world of image rather than substance. They are concerned with the immediate rather than the long term because history is meaningless and the future is too scary and unpredictable to contemplate. Meanwhile the present is lived out as a tumble and tangle of fleeting experiences.

But postmodernists do not live in isolation. On the contrary, they are computer-savvy people connected by the World Wide Web of the electronic global village. This virtual community provides a marketplace of ideas. It represents a virtual reality that is paradoxically both anonymous and intimate. It is a world in which you can invent yourself and create multiple personalities. Consequently, you can never be sure of the identities of the persons with whom you are free to communicate the most intimate details of your life.[18]

Modern	Postmodern
Centralized hierarchies	Decentralized networks
Predictable world and long range strategic planning and goal setting	Unpredictable world requiring a rapid response of "plan-do"
Confidence regarding human ability to manage the present and face the future	Uncertainty in dealing with the present, and pessimism and paranoia in considering the future
Change initiated at the center	Change initiated at the periphery

Figure 1.2. Contrasting modern and postmodern worldviews

The challenges are daunting because the traditional, modern and postmodern phases are not sequential but exist side by side. If the tensions created by these conflicting worldviews are significant for Christians engaging in mission within the Western world, they are even more so in many parts of Asia. Japan and South Korea have experienced the successive waves of modernity and postmodernity pounding over their ancient cultures within a much shorter time period.

Loss of a sense of self. Self is fragmented into splintered images and momentary "selves." The deconstruction of the first person singular means that I have to reinvent myself each new day. There is no ultimate meaning, and there are no abiding relationships, only transient encounters. Against such a background Bob Dylan revealed not so much an embarrassed evasiveness as a thoroughly postmodern attitude in the course of an interview with David Gates for *Newsweek* magazine in 1997. Gates comments that

> [Dylan] seems near the edge of his comfort zone talking about why he's not talking about one of his most illegible back pages: that conservative, born-again-Christian phase that blindsided his liberal, secular fan base some 15 years ago. "It's not tangible to me," he says, "I don't think I'm tangible to myself. I mean, I think one thing today and I think another thing tomorrow. I change during the course of a day. I wake and I'm one person, and when I go to sleep I know for certain I'm somebody else. I don't know *who* I am most of the time.

It doesn't even matter to me." This cracks him up.

Then he says, "Here's the thing with me and the religious thing. This is the flat-out truth: I find the religiosity and philosophy in the music. I don't find it anywhere else. Songs like 'Let Me Rest on a Peaceful Mountain' or 'I Saw the Light'—that's my religion. I don't adhere to rabbis, preachers, evangelists, all of that. I've learned more from the songs than I've learned from any of this kind of entity. The songs are my lexicon.[19]

In this deconstructed world there is no place for God. The search for truth has been abandoned, life is meaningless, there is no correspondence between words and what they signify, and the self has disintegrated. What are the implications of this depressing scenario for the Christian church?

Marginalizing the church. As our culture lurches from modernity to postmodernity, the church finds itself pushed out to the wings of the social stage. Secular society only allows the church's representatives back on stage on its own terms. They may serve as therapists, as chaplains of civil religion in the United States or as celebrants of ceremonial religion in Europe. But the secular world allows no place for the prophet or the priest. In the Romantic period the poet replaced the priest.[20] Evangelicals need a greater appreciation for the role of the poet and the lyricist in raising the questions and providing the prologue and platform necessary for the prophet to gain a hearing in a secular society. Our age has more regard for the artist than for the orator.

This crumbling of modernity presents an increasingly urgent challenge to successful megachurches, which grew through the return of the baby boomers in the mid-1980s. The megachurch phenomenon, which represents evangelicalism's media-hyped response to modernity, will need to make the transition from an invitational strategy to one of dispersal, with a sustained commitment to infiltrating each segment of this fragmenting world. In order to release its people for their God-assigned tasks, the megachurch must be prepared to dismantle a great number of its centralized programs dependent upon professional staff specialists and aided by an army of volunteers. This transformation is so radical and its challenges so complex that we will return to this theme in the following chapters to work out the far-reaching implications for church structures, leadership, spirituality, worship and evangelization. The modern world that is now falling apart is unlikely to be reassembled around any new unifying vision in the foreseeable future.

The Need for Missiological Training

The majority of church leaders throughout the Western world find themselves ministering in a rapidly changing cultural context that is both post-Christian and pluralistic. Consequently their outreach ministries are as crosscultural as those of their more traditional missionary counterparts seeking to make Christ known in other parts of the world. Consequently they are in as much need of missionary training to venture across the street as to venture overseas. The renowned Scottish missiologist Andrew Walls emphasizes both the gravity and urgency of the challenge:

> It is now too late to treat Western society as in some sort of decline from Christian standards, to be brought back to church by preaching and persuasion. Modern Western society, taken as a whole, reflects one of the great non-Christian cultures of the world. There is one department of the life of the Western church that spent centuries grappling with non-Christian cultures, and gradually learned something of the processes of comprehending, penetrating, exploring, and translating within them. That was the task of the missionary movement.[21]

Cultures permeate every aspect of life, and each culture provides its own lens through which the people within that culture view the world around them. A culture defines what is normative and plausible among a group of people according to its worldview. It also constructs their internal world. None of us is free from the all-pervasive influence of culture. It influences our theological thinking and our missiological endeavors no less than our social interaction.

Due to the fact that culture's presence is so pervasive and that we are all shaped by the culture in which we are nurtured, we are often unaware of the extent to which our culture influences our thinking, attitudes and actions. No theological tradition is immune from the influence of culture. Every person, to a greater or lesser extent, is shaped by his or her own cultural context. The evangelical movement has been as much influenced by culture as has the liberal tradition within Christianity. For the most part we remain unaware of our cultural biases until someone from another culture is sufficiently frank or angry to confront us with the issues that we have either chosen to ignore or have been unable to see.

The Missiological Challenge of Postmodernity

The loss of confidence in previously entrenched certainties, coupled with a growing suspicion of the institutions built around those certainties, has led to a new openness to explore alternative explanations of the world of experience. However, for Christians to engage people who are earnestly seeking alternative explanations that are more convincing and comprehensive requires a commitment to listen patiently and discerningly. It necessitates an unconditional acceptance of those who are content to live with ambiguity, and it requires the humility to communicate in open dialogue with those who hold a pluralistic worldview. The confidence of the witness must be in Christ alone and not in religious institutions or in the impregnability of a Christian apologetic. Any hint that the witness is motivated by a desire to enhance an institution or to monopolize conversation will cause the people with whom he or she is in contact to turn away uttering expletives as they go!

The witness must be prepared to be questioned at every point, not only in the area of basic beliefs but also in relation to obedience based on those beliefs. Does our *orthodoxy* translate into *orthopraxis?* Do we practice what we preach? Are we seeking to live by an unconditional and radical commitment to our beliefs, whatever the personal cost? The postmodernist is prepared to live adventurously as an individual, constructing his or her own "reality" as an autonomous self, discovering fulfillment independent of the restraints of precedent and of community.[22] Only in so far as Christians are prepared for their own position to be scrutinized at close quarters will they be in a position to persuade postmodernists to critique their own assumptions.

Despite the ultimately self-destructive tendencies of nihilistic postmodernism, Christians need to appreciate the valuable contribution it makes in criticizing modernism, rather than defensively assuming a denunciatory stance. Roger Lundin strikes a healthy balance when he writes:

> Deconstruction questions the claims to truth made by unaided reason and thus may appear to have much in common with Christian convictions about the noetic effects of sin; it judges the pretensions and abuses of moral systems and so may seem to echo the prophetic voice of judgment in Jewish and Christian faith; and in breaking with rigid forms of scientific discourse, deconstruction may appear to present itself as a potent ally for Christians who wish to reintroduce mystery into the human experience.[23]

In the area of literary criticism, Jewish scholar George Steiner sets a brilliant example. He attacks the postmodern "deconstruction" approaches to literature that have sought to negate altogether the correspondence between human discourse and the "reality" or correspondence of the world. " 'In the beginning was the Word.' There was no such beginning, says deconstruction; only the play of sounds and markers amid the mutations of time."[24]

Steiner points out, "It is this break of the covenant between word and world which constitutes one of the very few genuine revolutions of spirit in Western history and which defines modernity itself."[25] In "modernity" he establishes the connection between the dissolution of self, that is, the deconstruction of forms, which leads to the destabilization of meaning. The postmodern psyche, which he describes as a "vacant heart of consciousness," results in "splintered images of others" and "momentary 'selves.' "[26]

The response of a Christian witness to a person enmeshed in postmodern categories must be that of the fellow traveler. The witness walks with his companion to the rim of the abyss to face his "final nothingness" and "midnight of absence."[27] There, as an intercessor, the witness cries out to God to graciously intervene for postmodernists to realize their true destinies as unique beings within all of creation because they are made in the image of God. The witness bears the good news that in Jesus people encounter God who was made flesh and who dwelt among us.

No prepackaged "gospel presentations" and "seeker-sensitive" worship services will constitute adequate responses to the challenge presented by the post-Christian, neopagan, postmodern generation. Witness must be self-evidently altruistic among people shaped by a culture that is profoundly suspicious. For the postmodernist "all principles are preferences—and only preferences—they are nothing but masks for the will to power, which is the ultimate source of what we call 'values.'"[28]

The church in the postmodern era must be prepared to witness with vulnerability and humility from the margins of society, much as it did in the first two centuries of its existence. The part of its past that truly liberates is that which is rooted in the gospel and the community life of the people of faith throughout the centuries and in multiple cultural contexts. On the other hand, the part of the church's past that is associated with the politics of power and the compromises of self-interest must be jettisoned. Our ongoing dialogue with those who have been shaped by the popular culture of postmodernism will sharpen our discernment of the difference between these two.

The gospel of God's grace is the only message with the power to radically liberate. It must be clearly distinguished from that "other gospel," the gospel of traditionalism and legalism, which in reality is bad news that enslaves (Gal 1:6-9; 2:4-5). Postmodernists and Christians stand side by side in recognizing that neither has the power to determine the future, nor even to see it with complete clarity and unrestricted vision. Yet the Christian walks with an assured hope based on an unshakable faith, while at the same time acknowledging that our knowledge is indeed partial and readily confessing that our obedience is prone to be selective and inconsistent. Such frank admissions will strengthen rather than weaken our testimony among postmodernists who look for honesty and authenticity.

Challenges to Leadership in an Era of Discontinuous Change

Most churches are conservative by nature, which has both a positive and a negative aspect. On the one hand, the long history of the church has built a store of experiences that cautions the present generation from simply riding every cultural wave that comes along for fear of being overwhelmed by it. Yet the church is also called to relate the gospel to each cultural context in which it seeks to bear witness.

In traditional and "modern" contexts it was possible to engage in long-term strategic planning because either society was stable, or change was predictable and evolutionary. However, in the culture of postmodernity, change is discontinuous rather than incremental. It comes rapidly and without warning. This culture has been described as a "plan-do" environment. The challenge, calling for flexibility and rapid response, is by no means confined to the church but is experienced in many areas of life such as business, politics and education. The great multinational corporations developed by the "builder" generations must now undergo radical restructuring. They have flattened their hierarchical structures by removing layers of middle managers and separated their operations into semiautonomous divisions in order to become more market sensitive and able to respond to opportunities and challenges in a timely manner.

If evangelical churches struggled to relate to *modernity* without becoming subverted by it, the challenges posed by *postmodernity* will be even greater. Church leaders will need to acquire a mission-based theology enabling them to theologize in the crosscultural settings of Western urban societies. In response to the challenges of modernity, churches that made a significant appeal to the baby boomer generation did so through applying marketing strategies rather than mission insights. This shortsighted strategy has contributed to shallow discipleship, short-term commitments and compartmentalized living. Tom Beaudoin aptly describes boomer religion as "religion-as-accessory," resulting in Gen X children taking the next step to "religion-as-unnecessary."[29]

There is an urgent need to engage in *critical contextualization* through ongoing dialogue with popular culture, which will bring questions, old and new, to the Scriptures. Such engagement will enable us to read the Bible in a new light as we seek insights in response to the challenges of ministry and mission in postmodern contexts. Pastors must be equally skilled in exegeting both Scripture and culture, bringing the understanding derived from this interplay to the task of applying biblically grounded insights to the issues of postmodernity. They are challenged not just to be able to think clearly but to have the nerve and faith to act decisively in navigating through stormy and uncharted waters.

Churches Poised at the "Strategic Inflection Point"

The church in the Western world, I believe, is located at present on the midpoint of an S-curve. Andrew Grove, former CEO of Intel, terms this a "strategic inflection point."[30] He defines this as "a time in the life of a business when its fundamentals are about to change."[31] Leaving the fundamentals unattended will prove not only detrimental but ultimately deadly to the organization. Local churches and entire denominations must not assume that they have divine immunity from the consequences of failing to move at the "kairos" moment, which is a special God-appointed time when significant factors converge to provoke the need for decisive action. The configuration of the S-curve does not allow for a plateaued, continuing existence. In times of seismic change you will either tumble into a steep declining curve from which it is extremely difficult to recover, or you will begin another upward trajectory. Grove labels this seismic shift the "10X force." Things happen to the organization that didn't happen before. The organization no longer responds to the actions of the leaders as it used to.[32]

What is the evidence of the 10X force impacting the church? With only slight rewording Andrew Grove's list can be transferred from the business world to the church. The 10X force present when churches of other traditions are going through the same experiences. When denominational hierarchies and seminaries are facing turbulence and sudden loss of "altitude." When there is a growing dissonance between what is being said through official church channels and what is happening at the grass roots level. When leaders say one thing and then do another. When there is a loss of confidence in or respect for one another. When new movements such as megachurches, new apostolic networks and alternative religions emerge, further destabilizing traditional institutions, and disaffected members go elsewhere.[33]

Who Are the Change Agents?

Generally, those most aware of the cultural shift from modernity to postmodernity are people who are not locked into the power structures. Those who shoulder the responsibility for the functioning and survival of hierarchies and local churches tend to be too preoccupied in bailing out the boat to be setting a new course. Change agents are most likely to be pioneering church planters who have no congregational history to deal with and who are immersed in the cultures of the people they endeavor to reach. In the case of established churches, they tend to be those who are arriving fresh to the task. According to Andrew Grove, "People who have no emotional stake in a decision can see what needs to be done sooner." We must also recognize that God may have important things to say to the church through the complete outsider. Whether in secular business or in the church, new leaders are more able to see things with fresh eyes.

> I suspect that the people coming in are probably no better managers or leaders than the people they are replacing. They have only one advantage, but it may be crucial: unlike the person who has devoted his entire life to the company and therefore has a history of deep involvement in the sequence of events that led to the present mess, the new managers come unencumbered by such emotional involvement and therefore are capable of applying an impersonal logic to the situation. They can see things much more objectively then their predecessors did.[34]

In any anxiety-producing situation the worst response is a conspiracy of silence produced by corporate denial. Another destructive response is mutual blame, where first the leadership is blamed and then retaliates by blaming the members. To move in the right direction from a "strategic inflection point" requires the participation of people at all levels, as well as a willingness to listen to voices from outside the local congregation or denomination.

Leading a church beyond a "strategic inflection point" requires a clear sense of vision for a desired future that is significantly different from the present. It also requires an equally clear understanding of where the church is now. For the only place to start is where we are. Otherwise the vision is never brought down to earth and consequently remains in fantasyland.

Moving a church through the stormy waters of change requires an understanding of the different ways in which systems work in both modern and postmodern cultural contexts. It requires a team-building ability to group people according to vision, and the gifts and competencies to express the vision in the many pieces of the fractured postmodern world. It requires skills in confidence building and mentoring. It requires strong faith in the guiding and protecting presence of the Lord in the midst of the storm. It requires gaining freedom to fail with dignity by ensuring that lessons are learned and lives are put back together again after defeat and disappointment. In a culture of chaos, experimentation and risk taking are the order of the day.

Finally, leading a church beyond a "strategic inflection point" requires the reallocation of resources to facilitate experimentation, the development of pilot projects and the consolidation of gains. Such a challenge cannot be faced with the self-assured know-how that modern church technocrats have often possessed. It must be tackled with the humble spirit of pilgrim adventurers prepared to put themselves to the test by having the courage to take God at his word. The wisdom of Andrew Grove regarding the need to replace strategic planning with strategic actions is as applicable to the church as it is to high-tech industry.

Implementation

1. Analyze your congregation to determine the significant groupings: by generation, lifestyle, employment or whatever other categories are

relevant to your local church.

2. Determine the major concerns that characterize each group and how the ministry of your church relates to each of the concerns you have listed.

3. Identify people who have joined your church within the last five years. Are they significantly different from those who have been in the church for a longer period of time? Conduct a survey among them to discover their characteristics (e.g., marital status, ethnicity, socioeconomic bracket), what initially attracted them to the church, to what extent their expectations have been realized and what has disappointed or frustrated them.

4. Undertake the same analysis for your community. What are the significant groupings in the community, and which people do you feel called to work among?

two

From Market Driven
to Mission Oriented

n the previous chapter we reviewed the challenges presented by
the megatrends affecting Western society. Now we turn our attention to the ways in which the churches are responding to those
challenges. Churches throughout the Western world find themselves
increasingly marginalized from society as they endeavor to relate
the good news to people whose assumptions and attitudes have been
shaped by modernity and postmodernity. Our post-Christian, neopagan, pluralistic North American context presents crosscultural missionary challenges every bit as daunting as those we would face on
any other continent.

Unfortunately most pastors and church leaders have had no missiological training. Consequently they resort to marketing strategies in
place of missionary insights in their attempts to reach out to a population that is becoming increasingly distanced from the church. In
this chapter we will examine the assumptions inherent in the marketing mentality, which we will then critique theologically and missio-
logically. I will argue that while valuable lessons can be learned

from marketing, those lessons must be carefully evaluated from a theological perspective and that marketing insights and tools will prove increasingly inadequate as North America moves still further into its postmodern, post-Christian and neopagan phase.

In the United States, as distinct from most other Western nations, the majority of the population has identified in some way with a particular church denomination or Christian tradition as a matter of personal choice. Most people have been involved in a church at some time in their lives or are not more than one generation removed from active participation in a local congregation.

This state of affairs has determined the way in which most congregations have understood their evangelistic task. Their first step has been to build a "prospect" list of individuals. They have then profiled the segment of the population that is most likely to respond positively to an invitation to attend a special worship function or outreach activity. It is a strategy designed to reconnect with and reactivate previously churched segments of the community.

Churches realize that when they advertise their presence and promote their programs through print and electronic media, they are in a competitive market. So they must strive for prominence by featuring some distinctive feature designed to attract potential visitors. George Barna, who has consistently applied marketing theory to church ministry, explains it in the following terms, "For several decades, the Church has relied upon greater sums of money, better techniques, bigger numbers and facilities, and more impressive credentials as the means to influence society at large. These elements have failed us; in our efforts to serve God, we have crowded out God Himself."[1]

The Nature of the Marketing Approach
Marketing strategies begin by identifying the unfulfilled wants and needs of the total population or a population segment. Next they measure the extent and intensity of those needs and desires. Then

the organization asks itself which of those needs it has the vision and resources to meet. On the basis of this analysis it decides which needs it will respond to, explores ways in which they may be addressed and develops programs and delivery systems to meet the target group at its point of need.[2]

At first glance this approach seems to have much in common with the incarnational approach to ministry as modeled by Jesus. Both approaches recognize the need to begin where people are and to help them see that the gospel does address their concerns and aspirations, that God is speaking to *them* and not to a distant people in the remote past.

The value of the marketing perspective. In their explanation of marketing strategies Philip Kenneson and James Street provide the following criteria:

☐ *Measurement*—data are really clusters of concealed "values."

☐ *Accessibility*—not a characteristic of a particular targeted populations as much as it is a characteristic of those who target them.

☐ *Substantiality*—cost-benefit analysis.

☐ *Responsiveness*—there is little reason to exert too much effort if the segment has a history of being unresponsive.[3]

The entrepreneurship that has characterized evangelicalism has also made it more "market sensitive." Consequently evangelical churches gave high priority to the new suburban areas where potentially responsive people were relocating. The boomers' search for relevance and excellence led to the emergence of a new generation of megachurches that for the most part replaced the large downtown "first churches" that were the flagships of the denominations from 1945 to 1965.

G. A. Pritchard, in his in-depth analysis of Willow Creek Community Church in Barrington, Illinois, draws attention to the positive factors displayed by the "seeker-sensitive" church's marketing approach to ministry. First, it emphasizes the importance of a clear vision to replace the blurred, panoramic outlook that results in churches trying to do everything without doing anything either effectively or consistently. Second, it has important implications for stewardship, which Pritchard defines as the church taking "responsibility for its resources and being faithful stewards." Third, it is a strategic approach by which the church deploys its people appropriately. Fourth, it employs persuasive communication, using concepts and vocabulary that make sense and relate to the life situations of the intended audience.[4]

In more homogeneous, traditional societies a message can be conveyed using concepts and language that are relevant to everybody. This is not the case in multiethnic and socially stratified urban societies impacted by modernity and postmodernity, where there is increasing differentiation and fragmentation. Society is splintered into a complex range of groups that collide with one another and reconfigure like the colored glass shapes in a kaleidoscope. Furthermore, individuals find their own lives compartmentalized among the workaday world, home, leisure pursuits and participation in voluntary organizations.

Commercial interests divide the world into a plethora of narrowly segmented and precisely defined markets. If the message and services one wishes to extend only relate to certain segments, then the marketing task is to discover the location, size and accessibility of that market. However, the gospel is not a "product" developed for a restricted market. The church is mandated to pass on the message that has brought it into being to all peoples everywhere. This cannot be undertaken by a simple "blanket-cover" approach but has to be contextualized for each people group. In order to "broadcast" the message effectively a much more sophisticated approach must be adopted. No one individual or team can hope to reach everybody using one standardized method.

Churches cannot stand apart from society and invite people to come to them on their terms. Rather, churches must go to people where they are and communicate in terms that will make sense to them, addressing the issues that shape their lives and speaking their language. Donald McGavran emphasizes the point that people should not be required to cross racial, linguistic or class barriers in order to become Christians.[5] Messengers of the gospel are called to immerse themselves in the host culture rather than endeavoring to extract those who respond from their own culture. In his study of churches that are reaching unchurched people in California, Donald E. Miller also recognizes the reality that fragmented populations require diverse approaches.

> Here it is important to recognize that different generations and different subcultures contend with different meaning issues, and as we have moved from primitive, to modern, to postmodern societies the gaps between generations and various subcultures have increased. In this regard, leaders of religious institutions who do not understand their church's market niche and the particular audience to whom they are communicating will typically fail in their mission. Although this market-place language may seem jarring, the point is not to commercialize religion, but rather to underline that society is not homogeneous and all people's needs are not the same. A diffuse message will not be heard, especially in contemporary society, because while the desire for ultimate meaning may be universal, beliefs and values are contextualized and experienced quite differently depending on one's age, education, race or ethnicity, and cultural background.[6]

Some critics who denounce the use of marketing insights seem to be so focused on their theological presuppositions that they fail to engage the missionary challenges presented by Western societies. They are more skilled in exegeting the message than in exegeting the culture, or in the case of urban societies, the plurality of cultures.

Attitudes churches display toward the world around them. Christians can become so unnerved by all that is happening in the world around them or so hardhearted toward the plight of the lost that they simply withdraw from the world in a Jonah-like attitude of *judgmental isolation.* They believe that the world is under divine judgment and that the church must call it to repentance. In actuality this is an unrealistic strategy, as the church cannot achieve its desired degree of isolation. The vast majority of its members are firmly ensconced in the world for most of their lives whether they like it or not.

The second option is for the church to exist within culture taking a stance of *protective separation,* in which the church positions itself in the world and engages it in an ongoing basis. However, in order to guard its own integrity it builds a high wall around its fellowship. Before individuals are permitted to enter, they must not only clean up their lives and but also undergo cultural indoctrination and initiation.

The third option is one of *missionary engagement,* in which the church recognizes not only its distinctive identity in the gospel but also its calling within a specific culture. There is no escaping this divine-human tension in the nature of the church. As the body of Christ, the church continues the incarnational witness of its Lord and Savior. The complicating factor is that the human nature within the church remains vulnerable to sin. The church is compromised by the world to which it seeks to bring the saving message. Withdrawal from its mission obligations is no answer to this vulnerability. Rather, the church goes into the world with the same degree of dependence as Jesus demonstrated toward his heavenly Father, and also with humility and repentance in communicating its message.

Critique of the Marketing Mentality

Evangelistic and church growth strategies developed out of marketing insights also present particular dangers that must not be ignored. In the first place, measuring results in terms of increased attendance at worship services and other church-related activities creates a premature sense of achievement. We always have to ask who the new people are and where they are coming from. Is one church winning people simply at the expense of other congregations that do not have the resources to compete on equal terms in the religious marketplace?

More than numbers. A distinction needs to be made between those "seeker-sensitive" churches that represent new growth (returning "de-churched" and "never-churched" people), and the "market-driven" churches that have grown at the expense of the smaller community churches around them. In the latter case, one is left wondering what will happen to these market-driven churches when their small-church feeder systems dry up. Furthermore, large congregations that lack a shared memory are unstable communities. A significant percentage of their members drift from church to church and are especially vulnerable during a time of leadership transition. If such churches eventually collapse and the churches around them are so depleted or have already been driven out of business, will they have produced a spiritual wilderness?

Also, we must examine what happens to those individuals who have been enticed out of one church into another or who have opted to make the transition on their own, believing that the grass would be greener on the other side? Are they now more fully involved in the life of the church, or have they withdrawn into a more passive stance? Is there greater or less evidence of the grace of God making a transforming impact on their lives? What percentage of a growing congregation is finding support and being held accountable in face-to-face relationships that are so essential to discipleship? What percentage is moving from a passive, consumer-oriented mentality to one of sacrificial and fruitful Christian service? While some megachurches display an impressive track record in these areas, this is not always the case. So we must always look beyond numbers. The issue is not who can attract the biggest crowd but who is making the biggest impact on society.

Marketing is not value-neutral. The most strident and penetrating criticisms of the marketing approach to ministry are presented in Os Guinness's *Dining with the Devil: The Megachurch Movement Flirts with Modernity,* Philip D. Kenneson and James L. Street's *Selling Out the Church,* and Bruce and Marshall Shelley's *The Consumer Church.*

Os Guinness expresses the concerns of a growing number of observers who are prepared to look beneath the surface to assess the significance of the numerical strength of the church in the United States. Social strength should never be confused with spiritual vitality. The presence of the one does not guarantee the existence of the other.

The impact of modernity in the United States means that the Christian faith has lost much of its integrity and effectiveness in shaping the lives of believers. The statistical indicators of faith are still high, but its social influence is down. A central fact of modern times is faith's search for its own lost authority. A central challenge of modern times is faith's need to recover its integrity and effectiveness.[7]

In reflecting on the causes of so much nominality in the church and its increasing marginalization, Guinness lays much of the blame on the church's marketing mentality. He believes that the church's mission is being driven by marketing considerations rather than by its missional calling. For him the key question is, "In implementing its vision of church growth, is the church of Christ primarily guided and shaped by its own character and calling—or by considerations and circumstances alien to itself?"[8]

The questionable nature of marketing values and assumptions. G. A. Pritchard highlights the danger of a market-driven mission strategy. It distorts how Christians view unbelievers as well as the process of telling others the gospel with the allure of success—the bottom line in marketing is numbers. "A church may be completely devoid of spiritual life and still be increasing in numbers and influence."[9] Marketing makes the audience sovereign, propagating the attitude that "the customer is always right." Such an attitude might provide an impressive boost to sales but is disastrous when applied outside of the realm of commerce.

No doctor can operate on the principle that "the patient is always right" or that the patient is the best judge of his or her physical well-being. This is because a correct diagnosis of the patient's condition depends not only on the symptoms described by the patient but on how the doctor interprets that information and the further tests that are carried out.

Moving from the medical to the spiritual realm, the argument is even stronger, for as sinners we are frequently unaware of the seriousness of our spiritual condition and are "dead" in terms of ability to respond to exhortation. Like skillful doctors, discerning pastors listen with great care to what a person is saying. They probe more deeply by framing clear and carefully worded questions as they bring their knowledge and discernment to bear upon each case. Pastors and doctors alike have to acknowledge the limits of their knowledge and expertise. In the spiritual realm, pastors recognize that it requires miracles of divine revelation and the work of the Holy Spirit in the heart of an individual for the truth of God to penetrate a sinner's defenses and dispel the darkness within.

A second and yet more serious criticism of market-driven thinking is that it turns the gospel message into a means for personal fulfillment. Pritchard contends that "to teach Christianity as a means to fulfillment eventually teaches that it is superfluous."[10] If the gospel is reduced to a means to an end, then as soon as that fulfillment is achieved, the gospel can be dispensed with. Emphasizing freedom and fulfillment to the exclusion of the need for the breaking of our prideful self-reliance and the crucifying of our rebellious spirit loses the essential paradox that is at the heart of the message. For the Jew the good news proclaimed by Christ was one of freedom from the law. Preached by Paul among the Gentiles, it was freedom from idolatry, debauchery and the power of evil spirits that inhabited their world. Yet at the same time, it was a freedom in *servitude,* not as slaves of an uncaring and overdemanding tyrant but as servants of a self-giving Lord who treated them as sons and daughters. To the Philippians, Paul wrote,

> Let each of you look not to your own interests, but to the interests of others. Let the same mind be in you that was in Christ Jesus,
> > who, though he was in the form of God,
> > > did not regard equality with God
> > > as something to be exploited,
> > but emptied himself,
> > > taking the form of a slave,
> > > being born in human likeness.
> > And being found in human form,
> > > he humbled himself
> > > and become obedient to the point of death—
> > > even death on a cross.

> Therefore God also highly exalted him
> and gave him the name
> that is above every name. (Phil 2:4-9)

Christianity is a "going down" kind of religion before it is a "going up" kind of religion. In communicating this message we do not attract people as though they were customers, but we address them as fellow sinners, confessing together that we have only one answer to our common need. Unless and until we are prepared to die to self, we will never be in a position to live for Christ.

A third issue concerns the consequences of basing one's message on meeting human needs. When meeting the needs of individuals is made the determining factor, then there is a serious danger that the message itself will become distorted and edited down in the interest of relevance and immediacy. Kenneson and Street bring out this point:

> If the church's goal is to meet felt needs, then the danger arises that the entire enterprise will be shaped primarily by those needs that the consumer desires to have satisfied. This consumer orientation in the church echoes the retailing industry's maxim: The customer is always right. Some Christians might legitimately worry that this emphasis on consumer sovereignty might undermine the integrity of the church's witness.[11]

In response to such an approach, Guinness argues that basing a gospel presentation on meeting human needs not only results in a shallow identification of the nature of the human predicament, but it leads to an escalation of demands that eventually overwhelm. "Meeting needs does not always satisfy needs; it often stokes further ones and raises the pressure of eventual disillusionment. Modernity has expanded and corrupted the very notion of need by creating a 'need on command' society."[12] Generating a climate in which people demand to have their needs met creates an addictive situation, with people becoming increasingly strident and unreasonable in their demands. The marketers, for their part, work to stimulate fresh needs and thereby create new markets. An obsession with need results in consumer indifference to specific, genuine, real needs. If true needs are a first step toward faith and prayer, false needs are the opposite.[13]

Interpreting ministry in the New Testament from a marketing perspective. In reviewing the ministry of Jesus there are certain aspects with which marketers can identify. Jesus was acutely aware of people's felt needs: feeding the hungry, healing the sick, delivering the demon possessed. He ate with social outcasts and delivered his disciples from shipwreck by calming the storm. He was accessible to the crowds as well as to individuals who came across his path, and he spoke a language that everyone could understand. Ordinary people marveled at his teaching, gathered in crowds to hear his stories and followed him from place to place.

Yet in the final analysis, it was not the demands of the crowds or the disciples or the religious authorities that determined Jesus' agenda. He came to do the will of his heavenly Father, and he restricted himself to what he saw the Father doing. He did not attempt to heal every sick person, deliver everyone who was demon possessed and feed every hungry individual. He did not restore to life everyone who had died and left grieving relatives. His actions were primarily signs of the kingdom and not universal panaceas.

Also, in the ministry of Jesus we see that our Lord not only ministered to meet those needs that people confessed to him, but he went on to uncover needs of which they were not aware or that they tried to conceal. Central to the gospel is the news that God has graciously provided something that humanity didn't even know it needed (Mt 9:1-8; Jn 4:1-42; 6:60-66). The example of the rich young ruler who came to Jesus is a case in point. He had to face the fact that his riches had become an obstacle in his life, and refusing to do so, he went away sorrowful (Mt 19:16-30). The considerable assets of the individual became his liability.

Church marketers insist that the "marketing approach requires that the congregation systematically study needs, wants, perceptions, preferences, and satisfaction of its members and others whom it is trying to reach," and then that "the planners must act on this information to meet those needs more effectively." The authors of

Marketing for Congregations: Choosing to Serve People More Effectively ask whether this is in fact what God called the church to do and whether this is what Jesus sent his disciples out to proclaim.[14] Church marketers have not in any convincing fashion demonstrated that Scripture warrants their practices.[15]

These criticisms should not be interpreted as a denial of the legitimacy or value of marketing insights.[16] If marketers are prepared to go to considerable lengths to determine what people are looking for in designing their products, if they are prepared to spend astronomical sums of money to launch campaigns to make their product known, if they make such efforts to establish outlets to make the product readily available, then the church should be making even more concerted efforts to make known the gospel of Jesus Christ. In many places, commercial marketing initiatives are a challenge to the church's inertia.

The underlying issue is that all marketing insights must be viewed with caution and discernment. They can be used for wrong ends and can be misused in a manipulative manner. Further, the final determination as to what is to be done should be made on theological, not pragmatic, grounds. For the means adopted must always be consistent with the aims to be achieved. The church is prepared to learn from every discipline because all truth belongs to God. At the same time it recognizes that sinful distortions and deceptions permeate the whole of life. Therefore, Christians need to exercise spiritual discernment and vigilance at all times.

The Christian church must not be subverted by a modern mentality into thinking that there is a technological solution to every problem. In communicating the gospel our confidence is not in the effectiveness of our techniques but in the inherent power of the message. The agricultural analogy employed in the New Testament for the dissemination of the word is more accurate than a mechanistic analogy. Paul puts things into perspective when he writes, "So neither the one who plants nor the one who waters is anything, but only God who gives the growth" (1 Cor 3:7). Without that miracle of germination, which only God can perform, we labor in vain.

Turning to the building analogy, Paul is concerned that we build only with fireproof materials that alone will be able to pass the test of time. Churches built on marketing strategies are particularly vulnerable in the midst of adversity because customers are notoriously fickle. Shopping around, visiting one store after another, is a way of life for them.

Churches that adopt a market-driven approach to ministry also jeopardize their own integrity. It should not be the customer who determines the agenda of the church but the Lord, whom the church is called to worship and obey. We are to become all things to all people not to satisfy as many people as possible but in order to save some (1 Cor 9:22). In pursuing that aim Paul was prepared to go to any lengths, employing all means that were consistent with the end in view.

Fulfillment is a gift, not a goal. The notion that God's purpose for humans is their happiness, realized through having their every need met, is a modern notion that has only partial biblical support.[17] The gospel is more concerned with people's holiness than their happiness. The goal of salvation is not just that we will be forgiven but that we will grow in spiritual stature to become more and more like Jesus, and we should be available to God for him to continue his purposes in the world, working through us by his Spirit. Pritchard strikes a right balance, recognizing that "there is substantial biblical teaching that emphasizes that the life of faith is often one of wholesome satisfaction." Yet he goes on to point out, "We find in Scripture vast evidence that Christianity is often not 'fulfilling.' Jesus promises his disciples that 'in this world you will have trouble' (Jn 16:33; cf. 2 Cor 1:8; 2 Tim 3:12; Heb 11:35-39)."[18]

We are frustrated in our efforts to achieve fulfillment in this life precisely because we cannot escape having to live with the tension of the "now" and the "not yet" of the reign of God. Christians, along with everyone one else, will continue to suffer in this sinful world. Personal fulfillment will only be realized as we see Christ at his second coming when we will be "changed . . . in the twinkling of an eye," when mortality will put on immortality (1 Cor 15:51-57). Prior to that momentous event we must be prepared for continuing frustration caused by personal limitations and physical deterioration through sickness and old age. "Fulfillment theology has an inadequate understanding of the biblical truth about the fallenness of the world and the role of suffering in the Christian's life."[19]

The exchange basis of marketing. Kenneson and Street expose an underlying problem in the marketing mentality that is incompatible with the very nature of the gospel—its exchange basis. "Marketing seeks to bring about a transaction for the benefit of both parties in the exchange. Marketers ask, 'Does making the exchange process central to the way we tell and embody our story allow us to tell it faithfully?' We don't think so. In fact, we think placing exchange at the heart of our story distorts the church and its narrative in several ways."[20] Kenneson and Street then apply this assertion specifically to worship, redemption, the Holy Spirit and love for others, none of which can be "bought."

God deals with us on the basis of his grace as undeserving and impoverished sinners who are not in a position to "buy" his services. Salvation does not signify an exchange, value for value, or even at a bargain price, but rather the costly renunciation of anything that gets in the way of our being able to receive (Is 55:1-7; Mt 13:44). The recipient receives gratefully, knowing that there is nothing he or she could do to earn or purchase the gift of salvation. It is not only beyond the resources of an individual but of all the world's resources combined! The only way we can come is empty-handed. And we are not drawn to the cross by self-interest but by an overwhelming love of the one "who loved me e'er I knew him."

A further aspect of the exchange basis of marketing that Kenneson and Street examine is its reciprocal basis. They write, "The reciprocity embodied in self-interested exchange is not the same as the reciprocity embodied in gift giving. . . . Gift giving establishes and sustains relationships by acknowledging indebtedness. . . . But this is precisely the kind of indebtedness that self-interested market exchanges seek to avoid."[21] In the marketing scenario once you have paid the price and received the goods, you are free to walk away. You only return if you have a complaint because the product failed to perform satisfactorily within the terms of the warranty.

In contrast, the gospel is not a product to be marketed but a life-long relationship to be established and developed. If converts are attracted on the basis of satisfying self-interest, it will be difficult to change this into the daily cross-carrying that is a characteristic of authentic discipleship. People are likely to continue on the basis on which they first came.

God's Call to Mission
Before the church can begin to address its mission challenge, it must also search its own soul, for the church does not exist in isolation from culture. While the church is enriched by contextualization, because God celebrates luxuriant variety as is evidenced throughout creation, it is also contaminated and compromised by the unhealthy aspects of culture.

How the church became marginalized and compromised. Rodney Clapp describes how the church has become irrelevant in the American cultural context. Some congregations have turned themselves into private clubs to which people are invited to have their needs met. Rather than bringing about social change, they help individuals adjust to the status quo. Other congregations have identified the church with the "manifest destiny" of the nation, so that Christianity becomes subsumed under the umbrella of a vague, deistic civil religion manipulated for political ends.[22] George R. Hunsberger, who drafted the chapter entitled "Missional Vocation: Called and Sent to Represent the Reign of God" in *The Missional Church,* describes the situation in the following terms, "The religious loyalties that churches seem to claim and the social functions that they actually perform are at odds with each other. Discipleship has been absorbed into citizenship."[23] Clapp appeals for the church to be the church, practicing the politics of Jesus, by which he means working out the implications of our faith in every area of our lives. He observes, "It is perhaps only the most affluent, socially stable people who can ignore social, economic and political questions and concentrate on their abstracted inner well-being."[24]

The church in its chaplaincy role has been assimilated to a disturbing extent by traditionalist cultures. It became isolated as traditionalism gave way to modernism and found that it had to compete to gain access to a shrinking and diversified religious market. Now, under the impact of modernism, the church is facing the challenge to reenter a world that has changed drastically. It cannot hope to regain its previous central position. As we have already noted, the church will need to reenter as a missionary presence with an apostolic stance, living adventurously as a subversive movement, realizing afresh its total reliance on the Lord.

The choice facing the church is not between assimilation and isolation. It must see beyond that dilemma, moving toward a position of critical contextualization.[25] This complex task is further complicated by the fact that the church itself is immersed in the culture. This means that it is both the subject examining the situation and the object of that examination. The missional church recognizes the dynamic interplay of church, gospel and society. We can no longer naively hold to the view that the church is above culture and so is able to stand aloof in its judgment on the ills of society. We are coming to recognize increasingly that the church is itself a culture, or a subculture within its larger culture.[26]

What is a "missional church"? The term *missional,* which we are using in relation to churches in North America and other parts of the Western world, draws attention to the essential nature and vocation of the church as God's called and sent people. It sees the church primarily as the instrument of God's mission. Following Lesslie Newbigin and others, a church that is missional understands that God's mission calls and sends the church of Jesus Christ to be a missionary church in its own society and in the cultures in which it finds itself. Mission is the result of God's initiative, rooted in God's purposes to restore and heal creation. *Mission* means "sending," and it is the central biblical theme describing the purpose of God's action in human history.[27]

The Gospel and Our Culture Network provides the following twelve empirical indicators of a missional church: (1) It is a church that proclaims the gospel. (2) It is a community where all members are involved in learning to become disciples of Jesus. (3) The Bible is normative in the life of the church. (4) The church understands itself as different from the world because of its participation in the life, death and resurrection of its Lord. (5) The church seeks to discern God's specific missional vocation for the entire community and for all its members. (6) Christians behave Christianly toward one another. (7) The church is a community that practices reconciliation. (8) People within the community hold themselves accountable to one another in love. (9) The church practices hospitality. (10) Worship is the central act by which the community celebrates with joy and thanksgiving both God's presence and God's promised future. (11) The church is a community that has a vital public witness. (12) There is a recognition that the church itself is an incomplete expression of the reign of God.[28]

When faced with the daunting challenge of this list, we readily recognize that this represents a process of becoming and not simply a state of being. It is a goal to strive for, if seldom fully realized. It forces us to recognize that the church here on earth is both imperfect and incomplete. In endeavoring to become increasingly a missional church, the congregation must soon recognize that its mission responsibilities are not confined to its immediate ministry context. The mission cannot be confined to our "Jerusalem" but must sooner rather than later move out into "Judea, Samaria and to the ends of the earth." The task is both local and global.

Rediscovering the missional nature of the church. The missional church will need to constantly examine the Scriptures, bringing different questions to the text in the light of changing circumstances and new insights that arise out of engaging with the culture. It must also recognize that it brings to the text its own biases and limited range of vision. Therefore, the local church will always need the witness of the wider church to point out those aspects that are being overlooked, whether deliberately or unintentionally. The wider church brings the richness of its own understanding and experience of the gospel into the cultural setting of the local church.

The missional church must be attentive to the voice of the world, even when the tone is strident and the message is hostile. We need to acknowledge that God may have something very important to say to the church through its strongest critics. To the degree that the church itself is learning a greater faithfulness to the gospel within its culture, it will be empowered to address the world. The church-in-mission is always evolving as it responds to the challenge of the Word of God both to its own internal life and to its engagement in an ever-changing world.

The church knows to expect a life full of ambiguities because it is shaped by its context even as the gospel reshapes that context. Such a calling never leaves the church in a finished, settled or permanent incarnation. The church's vocation to live faithfully to the gospel in a fully contextual manner means that it can sometimes find itself either unfaithful or uncontextual. In addition, the human context that shapes the church continues to change. Therefore, the questions of the church's faithfulness are always fresh ones. The gospel of God is never fully and finally discerned so that no further transformation can be expected. The interaction between the gospel and all human cultures is a dynamic one, and it always lies at the heart of what it means to be the church.[29]

A second and equally important realization that must dawn upon the church is that mission is not a one-way movement but one that entails the willingness to receive as well as the desire to go. Churches throughout the Western world are becoming increasingly aware of their need to learn from churches in the Majority World. These mission churches that have learned to witness effectively in situations that are both pluralistic and hostile to Christianity, and where local congregations have few material resources and yet are rich in faith and powerful in their testimony, have much to teach us. Are we ready to learn from them?

The church in North America is listening with increasing attentive-

ness to Lesslie Newbigin's clarion call that the Western world constitutes one of the greatest missionary challenges to the church today.
Many sociologists in the 1960s predicted that Western societies would
become increasingly secularized and that religious issues would
become increasingly irrelevant and the churches marginalized. These
predictions have not been realized, as the sociologists themselves are
forced to admit. Religious interest remains as strong, if not stronger,
then ever. But more people are seriously examining alternatives to
Christianity or for sources to supplement their religious diet. From a
missiological standpoint Lesslie Newbigin wrote in 1986 that Western
societies have become "far more resistant to the gospel than the pre-
Christian paganism with which crosscultural missions have been familiar. Here, surely, is the most challenging missionary frontier of our
time."[30] Church leaders are in urgent need of retraining to face this new
reality. This has profound implications for seminary education and ministerial training, as we will explore in chapter four.

Motivation to Mission
We can define evangelical churches as those that have been committed to certain theological nonnegotiables including the personhood
of God revealed as three in oneness in the Trinity. Evangelicals
believe in the uniqueness of Jesus Christ as the Son of God, who is
fully divine, yet who became fully human through his incarnation.
They uphold the belief that God has chosen to reveal himself to
humankind through his mighty acts and spoken word faithfully
recorded in Scripture and supremely in the person of Christ. They
insist on the universal need of salvation and of the uniqueness of
Christ's saving work to bring about forgiveness, deliverance, regeneration, adoption and sanctification. They are upheld by the certain
hope of the personal return of Christ, and they affirm that all people
will stand before God in the final judgment. It is these unshakable
convictions that provide the basis for their commitment to world
evangelization.

However, the motivational drives that have characterized the commitment of evangelical churches to world evangelization now need to be reaffirmed and applied to the domestic missional challenge.

Obedience to the Great Commission. The importance of Christ's command to his followers to go into all the world to proclaim the gospel and make disciples is evidenced by the fact that this command occurs in all four Gospels (Mt 28:18-20; Mk 16:15-18; Lk 24:45-49; Jn 17:18; 20:21). Each version contributes a different emphasis,[31] but each underlines the same objective of sending the church out into the world bearing the good news.

Roland Allen, Hendrick Kraemer and Donald McGavran all stress the need for the church to remain obedient to this command, with an unrestricted worldwide focus. Their challenge is equally pertinent to the evangelical community because it calls every church to fulfill the Great Commission in its immediate context. For there are many churches describing themselves as "evangelical" that are not evangelistic. They display little concern for, and make little effort to reach out to, those who are not yet Christians. And then there are those churches that claim they are committed to evangelism but conceive of evangelism only in terms of inviting nonattenders to swell their ranks. In so doing they have reversed the command of the Great Commission, replacing "going into all the world," with "inviting all the world to come to us." We need to recognize afresh that the Great Commission represents a vast and unrelenting search and find operation, as Donald McGavran proclaimed to his dying day.[32]

The Great Commission represents both a necessity and a limitation. It is necessary in that it represents the bottom line, a nonnegotiable, to which one can resort when all else fails. We may ask the Lord, "Why do *I* have to engage in witness, and why does *the church* have to become involved in global mission?" "Because I have told you to," the Lord replies. The Great Commission cannot be reduced to a voluntary activity engaged in by a few enthusiasts. On the other hand, a command also brings limitations. It can be used to induce a guilt trip, but guilt is a poor motivator and is subject to the law of diminishing returns. Guilt that is too legalistic and exhortations that dwell on our failure to obey the Great Commission can become a ploy used by Christian leaders to express their personal frustrations and project their own sense of failure and guilt. The obligation has to be *felt* if it is to be willingly and consistently obeyed. As the old adage goes, "One volunteer is worth ten individuals pressed into service."

Contagious experience of discipleship. Jesus' disciples were commanded to share what they themselves had learned through experience, command and commentary. They were to teach in the same way that they themselves had been taught—by the apprenticeship method. In other words, they were to draw others into the orbit of their own experience (1 Jn 1:1-3). The early Christians did not become ensnared by a self-centered caricature of true discipleship (1 Cor 9:23). They realized that an essential ingredient of discipleship is the making of other disciples. The call to reproduce is not something that can be postponed until one has achieved a high level of maturity as a follower of Christ but is part of the ongoing process of discipleship. "Follow me and I will make you fish for people," was the challenge Jesus gave the Galileean fishermen. *Following* and *fishing* are inseparably linked.

Discipleship is associated with the fruit-bearing analogy of a transmitted life, which results in fruit that can be transplanted (Jn 15:1-2, 8). Samuel Shoemaker writes in *How to Become a Christian*, "The test of a man's conversion is whether he has enough Christianity to get it over to other people. If he hasn't there is something wrong in it." Staleness always undercuts urgency. If we are bored with our experience of the Christian life, let's face it honestly.

Throughout North America in the decades of the 1960s through the 1990s there has been a stress on the need to be both a disciple and a discipler either one-on-one or through small groups. But the evangelistic element seems to have been muted. Discipleship becomes a private and individual matter, and few groups have included the outward journey along with the inward journey. They have failed to reach out to their neighbors and friends and have not allowed their groups to spawn new groups to welcome and disciple

new Christians. Granted, there are many exceptions to these generalizations, but they still remain exceptions rather than the rule.

Christ's continuing presence in his disciples. The mission of our
Lord is an unchanging mission that he transmits to his disciples. "As
you have sent me into the world, so I have sent them into the world"
(Jn 17:18). "'As the Father has sent me, so I send you.' When he had
said this, he breathed on them" (Jn 20:21-22).

Following the example of the first apostles, we will have to place
our faith in the two assurances that the Lord gave them at their com-
missioning to make disciples of all nations. The first was, "All authority in heaven and on earth has been given to me" (Mt 28:18). Nothing
and nobody is outside the sphere of Christ's ultimate control. And second, "I am with you always, to the end of the age" (28:20). If the first
promise guaranteed his magisterial presence, the second assured them
of his intimate presence. The apostles of the New Testament had to
believe those promises as though their lives depended on it, and so do
their successors in the twenty-first century.

This commission is all the more powerful when we consider that
the gospel is addressed primarily to Jewish believers, who at the
time of writing were strongly tempted to become introverted as they
battled with the issue of self-identity. Now that the temple had been
destroyed, they found themselves as aliens in a strange land facing
the growing antagonism of the Pharisaic party within Judaism.[33]

During his earthly ministry Jesus had established the closest association between his own ministry and that of his disciples. For
instance, he reassured them that, "Whoever listens to you listens to
me, and whoever rejects you rejects me, and whoever rejects me
rejects the one who sent me" (Lk 10:16). The resources available to
them after his death would be undiminished. The Lord's departure
would not disadvantage the disciples. By virtue of his victory on the
cross and his ascension into the heaven, they would be empowered
to perform even greater works (Jn 14:12). As the early witnesses
were filled with his Spirit, they were emboldened to proclaim the
message of a life-transforming gospel.

The apostle Paul was driven by a two-pronged motivation. He was urged on by a reverential "fear of the Lord" (2 Cor 5:11) as he anticipated the day when he would stand before the judgment seat of Christ to given an account of his ministry. He was also constrained by the "love of Christ" (v. 14), which drove him forward like a raft tossed about on the tumbling white waters of a cascading river.

For the church in North America this means a profound renewal of our personal and corporate spiritual lives through our worship and our practice of the spiritual disciplines. If evangelism means those who know Christ introducing him to those who don't, then those who are seeking to make him known must themselves reflect an intimate relationship with the Lord. Otherwise the introductions are likely to prove abortive. We cannot convincingly introduce people to someone we knew a long time ago or to someone we simply read about.

Concern for the greater glory of God through the extension of his kingdom. To bring glory to his heavenly Father was the consuming passion of Christ's life. Just prior to his crucifixion he informed his disciples, "The hour has come for the Son of Man to be *glorified"* (Jn 12:23, emphasis added). He likened his death to a grain of wheat falling into the ground and dying in order to produce many grains. His soul was greatly troubled at the prospect. " 'What should I say— "Father, save me from this hour?" No, it is for this reason that I have come to this hour. Father, *glorify* your name.' Then a voice came from heaven; 'I have *glorified* it, and I will *glorify* it again' " (Jn 12:27-28, emphasis added). Then later, "I *glorified* you on the earth by finishing the work that you gave me to do. So now, Father, *glorify* me in your own presence with the *glory* that I had in your presence before the world existed" (Jn 17:4-5, emphasis added).

This is a concern that his followers are expected to share in every age. We are to let our light shine that people may see our good works and *give glory* to our Father in heaven (Mt 5:16). Jesus said that his Father would be *glorified* as we bear much fruit (Jn 15:8). We are to be holy and without blame before him in love, to the praise of his glorious grace (Eph 1:4-6). We who first set our hope in Christ might live for the praise of his glory (Eph 1:11-12). In Athens Paul was concerned that God's glory should not be shared with other gods (Acts 17:16, 29-31). The ultimate goal of Christ's mission is that "every tongue should confess that Jesus Christ is Lord, to the glory of God the Father" (Phil 2:11).

Johannes Verkuyl describes this as the *doxological motif* of mission. "God's glory summarizes all of his features—his holy love, his grace, his mercy and justice. . . . The doxological motive implies that people who know the true and living God discover that he is such a delight that they want others to get acquainted with and live in fellowship with him as well."[34] Here is another consideration that is so applicable to our situation in that it provides a much-needed correction to our concern for results and for achievement. We need to be reminded that the results are for God's glory and not for the enhancement of our image.

The universal character of human need. The New Testament makes it clear that all of humankind stands under the judgment of God and that it is found guilty of breaking the law of God (Rom 3:10-12, 23). The present world order is described as under the rule of the evil one (Jn 7:7; Gal 1:4; 1 Jn 5:19). Not only is the world in darkness, but false spirits that deny Christ delude people (1 Jn 4:1-6), whose rejection may be either passive or active. There are those who scoff outright, living to satisfy their own lusts and denying the fact that they will one day be held accountable at the return of Christ (2 Pet 3:3-7). In our witness to a lost world we must display both theologically informed zeal and Spirit-inspired love.

When the strength of the evangelical movement is found in the suburbs and among the people who are socially upwardly mobile, there is a tendency to think that the gospel is primarily for the achievers in society. It is a message either to those who have become casualties in the rat race or to help the ambitious reach the heights to which they aspire. While the upwardly mobile must not be neglected, because they need the gospel as much as any other segment of society, the church must not ignore those who are at the bottom of the pile. It is good news just as much for the marginalized who aren't going anywhere because they have nowhere to go.

Sometimes we need to be reminded that the gospel is the power of God for salvation to *everyone* who has faith (Rom 1:16). The gospel is not so much a supercharge to boost achievers but a depth probe to rescue those who have gone under. Paul's ministry to both Jews and barbarians and to every level of society provides an inspiring example.

Loving concern for the plight of the lost. There is no doubt about the intensity and extent of the Father's concern so eloquently and succinctly expressed in John's Gospel (3:16). Note also Jesus' expression of that concern. He wept over an unresponsive Jerusalem (Mt 23:37). Notice the intensity of concern that characterized Paul's ministry in Ephesus (Acts 20:31). He also felt just as intensely about his own people (Rom 9:1-5). Contrast Paul's passion with Jonah's disregard for the citizens of Nineveh as he sat on a vantage point overlooking the city in a sulking attitude of judgmental detachment (Jn 4:1-3). Dwight L. Moody expressed his own mission in the dramatic terms of a sea rescue. "I look upon this world as a wrecked vessel. Its ruin is getting nearer and nearer. God said to me, 'Moody, here is the lifeboat—rescue as many as you can before the crash comes!' "

An older generation of evangelicals spoke of "a passion for souls." Due to the shallowness of our spirituality and the nervousness that we feel in the face of a secularized and pluralistic world, this passion seems to have largely evaporated. It is one of the most disturbing characteristics of the contemporary evangelical church. The questions raised in the verse of an old hymn need to be faced:

> Shall we whose souls are lighted
> With wisdom from on high,
> Shall we to men benighted,
> The lamp of life deny?

Does our fellowship, teaching and training in churches and seminaries intensify that passion or evaporate it?

The completion of the church. Jesus challenged his followers with the fact that he had other sheep that were not of this fold (Jn 10:16). The concept of the "fullness of the Gentiles" and the completion of the body (Lk 21:24; Rom 11:25) indicates a definite number, known only to God, to be gathered into the fold, and the Lord will not return until that number has been reached. This concept may have one of two effects: a paralyzing effect, as is demonstrated by William Carey's opponents,[35] or a great incentive. Augustine found it to be an incentive, arguing that, because we do not know who belongs to the number of the predestined or does not belong, our desire ought to be that all may be saved. Hence, every person we meet we should desire to be with us as a partaker of peace. Count von Zinzendorf cannot be understood without this attitude. The Student Volunteer Movement was driven by a like passion.

Today we need a fresh emphasis on the completion of the church to correct the myopia that we demonstrate when we are only concerned for the welfare of our own movement, denomination or tradition. A concern for the completion of the church means longing that its many branches be renewed and restored to apostolic faithfulness. It means concern that the church's growth occur in every place where the Lord intends his people to be witnessing in the power of the Spirit.

The judgment of Christ and the reality of hell. The topic of hell is one of the great unmentionables in most Protestant churches; this is an overreaction to hell-fire preaching. Many deny the existence of hell, regarding it inconceivable in the face of a God of love. Hell is penal, not disciplinary (Jude 15; Rev 14:11). It is not that God sends anyone arbitrarily to hell; anyone choosing wickedness rather than righteousness thereby chooses condemnation, because God will by no means clear the guilty (Ex 34:7). Much of what we sing and pray is largely eyewash—when the concern is not genuine.

Hell was a prominent theme among nineteenth century missionaries. Amy Carmichael had a vision of Christians sleeping near a cliff while multitudes continued to fall over the edge. Hudson Taylor, founder of the China Inland Mission, had a similar picture. C. T.

Studd, the pioneer missionary to Africa and founder of the World-wide Evangelistic Crusade, wrote the following couplet,

> Some would live within the sound of chapel or church bell.
> I would rather run a rescue shop within a yard of hell.

In contemporary America there is an understandable reaction to the scare tactics adopted by a previous generation of evangelists, coupled with a desire to distance ourselves from the doomsday sandwich board characters so gleefully drawn by cartoonists. Yet the somber message remains that God will hold us all accountable for our moral choices and especially for the way we have treated Christ in our lifetime. Have we tried to ignore him, been outwardly rebellious or selectively obedient? One day, sooner or later, the truth will be revealed, and we will have to face the consequences. Ours is a generation in which we must shoulder our responsibilities and make ourselves accountable. We are so busy claiming and defending our rights that we neglect our obligations. And we can blame everything and everyone but ourselves—"It's my upbringing!" "It's my genes!" "It's my environment and associates!" And the ultimate cop-out, "The devil made me do it!"

The shortness of the time until Christ's coming. The motive of the kingdom plays an important role in the Gospels. The second petition of the Lord's Prayer, "Thy kingdom come," expresses this central motive succinctly. The second coming of Christ is dependent on the prior preaching of the gospel to all peoples (Mt 24:14). The principal activity that is to span the two comings of Christ is outlined in Acts 1:6-8. The repentance of Israel must come first.

Paul continually warns his readers to make the most of their time since the days are evil (Gal 6:10; Eph 5:16-17; Col 4:5). Karl Barth could cite sluggishness as one of the major sins of the church today. This sluggishness can take so many forms: theoretical analyzing that fails to put ideas into practice, inertia, indecision, lack of vision and inventiveness, passing up opportunities, and planning without implementation. We must be alert to what the New Testament calls the "times and seasons."

Even among the people of God there will be deviations from the truth of the gospel and the requirement to live a holy life (Mt 7:15-20). Trees that do not bear good fruit will be cut down. False prophets will bring in destructive heresies, denying the Lord, to satisfy their own greed (2 Pet 2:1-3). Even as his opponents were dogging his heels, Paul said that things would not improve after his departure. He foretold a time when wolves would pounce on the flock of God from outside, and from within the church's ranks there would rise up those who speak perverse things (Acts 20:29-30). Therefore, the gospel must continue to be proclaimed not only to the world but also to God's people to reinforce the truth they already know (cf. Rom 1:12-13).

In one sense the motive of the shortness of the time remaining before the Lord's return was easier to proclaim in the first century when Christians believed that the Lord would return at any moment. Nearly two thousand years later some feel that if so much time has passed since Christ's ascension, there may be as many more years ahead of us. Yet as we teetered on the edge of the new millennium, there were more and more predictions of the Lord's return, each of which became discredited as soon as the declared date passed.

Nevertheless, what is beyond dispute is that change is coming at us at an escalating pace, and the world is becoming an increasingly polluted and dangerous place. The planet does appear to be fitted with a time clock. But whenever the Lord returns, sooner or later, each generation of Christians is responsible to make the gospel known as widely as possible to our own generation. And another thing is certain—every one of us will come face to face with the Lord at the moment of death if not during our lifetime.

Mission can never be reduced to marketing. Otherwise its motivational drive will be subverted by promotional considerations. The church's outreach may be informed by marketing insights but must never become market-driven, because mission proceeds from the heart of God.

The missionary operating in the complexities of the Western

world must learn the skills and ask for the appropriate spiritual gifts to equip him or her for the task, just like a missionary working overseas in a crosscultural situation. It will require spending much time listening and questioning. It will require a humble and discerning spirit. It will entail developing listening skills used carefully and prayerfully to catch what God may want to say through the other person. That word, spoken by the seeker, may be one of valid criticism of the institutional church as a whole or, even more painfully, may be a critique addressed to believers themselves, questioning their consistency, authenticity and credibility. At times the criticisms may seem unfair and uninformed. The questions raised may seem irrelevant, diversionary or even incomprehensible. It will require a great deal of patience to listen long enough to hear.

Implementation
To understand "missional" as the church *being* in the world as a transforming presence:

1. Identify those attitudes and values prevalent in the church through the permeation of secular culture that are a contradiction of the values inherent in the gospel. Due to our being so immersed in our cultures, we frequently need the insight and frank comment of persons from outside of our congregation, race and church tradition to unmask those issues.

2. Imagine that your church leadership has just arrived in the area and that you want to establish a credible witness, communicate the gospel and establish a new church in the community. How would you go about this? On completing this first part of the exercise, relate your findings to your existing church. What changes do you need to make? What important things are you failing to do? What programs need to be redirected or dropped altogether?

3. Partner with a new missions outreach or new church plant in a situation like your own, located elsewhere in the country or overseas. Become prayer partners and arrange exchange visits, as partners assisting one another and holding one another accountable.

three

From Bureaucratic Hierarchies
to Apostolic Networks

I n the opening chapter we noted that the transition from modernity to postmodernity has contributed to the collapse of an integrated and self-contained worldview. Now we are faced with a
fragmented society characterized by confrontation as each piece
strives to secure its own survival and extend its power base. It is also
a society of discontinuous change, which has rendered long-term
strategic planning all but impossible. Targets move after you have
fired the arrow, new targets pop up in unexpected places, and we are
trying to take aim from a lurching platform! This cultural chaos has
affected all institutions, including churches. We then critiqued the
marketing response to the missionary challenge that the church
encounters in seeking to communicate its message across cultures
and to incarnate its life in new settings.

In the next three chapters we will examine the implications of
these challenges for church leadership. In this chapter we will
explore how the cultural transition from modernity to postmodernity
impacts the ecclesiastical structures linking congregations. In chap-

ter four we will address the urgent issue of equipping leaders for this changing environment, and in chapter five we will address the need for spiritual foundations in leaders who model the character and leadership style of Jesus himself.

Problems Facing Mainline Denominations

Mainline denominations are facing an avalanche of problems that place question marks over their future. Some of these problems are so pressing that they may even threaten the denominations' survival. Some mainline denominations lack the necessary finances to maintain their bureaucratic structures and specialist personnel, their congregations are aging, and their numbers are shrinking. Denominational leaders and local church pastors can no longer take their members for granted or count on their loyalty to the institution.[1]

Many institutions are battling for survival. But, as this book seeks to point out, a defensive stance will not suffice. It is not simply a case of battening down the hatches until the storm has passed. What we are experiencing is not a short-lived turbulence but the dawn of a new era—or the creeping shadow heralding a new Dark Age, depending on your perspective.

We will now look at some of these challenges in greater detail. In so doing we will suggest ways in which traditional denominational churches might move from a hierarchical mentality to a networking mindset. Our approach is based on the premise that God hasn't given up on denominations, for in the overall scheme of things, it is the denominational churches that make up by far the greatest segment of world Christianity. It is hard to imagine that they are all destined for the scrap heap.

While it is sometimes said that it is easier to have babies than to raise the dead, it might just be that God has the greater miracle in mind. This is not to suggest that denominations can emerge intact. Far from it! For the present cultural upheaval from modernity to postmodernity, however the latter term is defined, will necessitate not merely the structural reengineering of denominations but their death and resurrection. In this assessment I am in agreement with Mike Regele, who speaks of the death of the church in terms not of its final demise but of the essential precondition for resurrection. It is those churches that refuse to bury their nostalgia and dismantle their defenses that will fail to survive.

Increasing diversity. In a postmodern world, diversity is celebrated. This should not come as a threat to biblically informed Christians because creativity and variety are characteristics of the world that God created and that he saw was very good. The world is a riot of colors, forms, shapes and textures. The church, described as "the body of Christ," is an organic miracle of diversity expressed in a unity of purpose. Denominations that are monochrome in ethos and cookie-cutter in their approach to organizing existing churches and establishing new ones emaciate the gospel. Even within the most monolithic of church structures there is more variety than would appear from official pronouncements or from the ill-informed outsider's perspective. Either this diversity must be celebrated or churches will simply go their own way.

When one compares the growing congregations across traditions, it becomes apparent that they have more in common with one another than they do with stagnant churches within their own denominations. This means that denominations of the future will be less cohesive and less controlled from the center. Tony Campolo addresses the challenge that many denominations face at the present time:

> Mainline denominations need to be groupings of churches with shared traditions, theological convictions, social values, worship styles, and overall missions. Now, within any given denomination there are many churches so vastly different from one another that one might fairly wonder if they are truly part of the same religion.[2]

If denominational structures are in place primarily as instruments of control, then the identity problem is probably insurmountable. But if these vertical structures can be dismantled to provide financial and personnel resources by which local churches can be effectively serviced, their diversity celebrated and a variety of models assessed, then structures can play an important role. In our diverse and fragmented world, church leaders can all too easily develop a microvision restricted to their own pieces of the social mosaic. They can jump to the conclusion that one model of church that is proving effective in one segment of society is the definitive model of renewal for our times in every other segment of society. Just as a local church can become introverted, so can new church movements. Due to their lack of experience of the wider church, they come to believe that they are the exclusive recipients of God's blessings.

Distrust of institutional authority. Widespread distrust of social institutions, including government, military, business and the church, became evident in North America in the aftermath of the Vietnam debacle. Wade Clark Roof records the results of a 1985 Gallup poll concerning boomer attitudes that "alienation and estrangement born out of the period continue to express themselves as generalized distrust of government, or major institutions, and of leaders."[3]

Coupled with this distrust for authority structures, boomers have developed a compensating belief in themselves. Thus the "me generation" emerged, with high expectations and a determination to achieve at all costs. The price is often highest when it comes to personal relationships. Other people are regarded as the means for personal gratification or advancement. Thus relationships have become self-serving and manipulative. Yet high aspirations for achievement have been translated into reality for only a minority of boomers. The majority of baby boomers have become disillusioned as their hopes failed to materialize.

In the years since the 1985 boomer survey members of the younger generation have become even more distrusting than their parents. Educational costs have soared and high-paying jobs have become inaccessible to the underqualified. At the same time the overqualified find that they cannot obtain entry-level positions in their chosen specialties.

The profound sense of distrust toward institutions held by boomers and Gen Xers has clear implications for the church. Its authority base must be less positional and far more relational than in previous generations. In other words, authority is not invested by virtue of the office bestowed but by the trust and respect that are earned. This shift is particularly hard to digest for older and more traditional pastors who were told during their seminary years not to make their friends in the parish!

Financial concerns. We have already noted that tens of thousands of churches with small, aging and dwindling congregations are finding themselves in a financially precarious position. Many only manage to keep their doors open because they can draw upon endowments or outside subsidies. Leith Anderson draws attention to the plight of denominational churches, where denominational loyalty is in decline. Church members resent their dwindling resources being siphoned off to shore up bureaucracies they no longer trust. Benefactors and donors in the twenty-first century will not be interested in shoring up failing causes; they will require "a bang for their buck."[4]

Increasing pastoral load. Especially burdensome for old-line churches are the large "external constituencies" consisting of inactive members who suddenly become "active" when they face a family crisis, when they are in need of a service from the church or when church leaders propose unwelcome changes. In an age when the family structure is under so much pressure, pastoral loads have increased. There are many dysfunctional families, young families without the support of the extended family, single parents and an aging population.

The therapeutic ministry model in which many pastors were trained has led them to become embroiled in counseling more people than they can handle. Without the professional safeguards of a client relationship, the pastor is stuck with the difficult cases and demanding individuals for the duration of his or her ministry. Whereas a high degree of specialization is appropriate for larger churches served by a team, it becomes diversionary in churches that are led by pastors who focus on what they like doing and lose sight of the bigger picture.

In order to respond to so many pastoral demands, leaders must establish relational networks to provide the support everyone needs, so that eighty percent of the pastoral needs are met by small groups. The group leaders will themselves require training to ensure that the groups are not put under intolerable strain by individuals who are overdemanding and destructive. People who are the most emotionally draining and time consuming are precisely the ones who are avoided by group members; they then rebound to the clergy for care.

Control issues. "Do denominational leaders disempower others?" This important question is raised by Professor Donald Miller, who cites Chuck Smith, the founding pastor of Calvary Chapel, maintaining that denominational leaders sometimes protect and consolidate their position by creating rules that strip subordinate churches of their independence.[5] Church leaders must learn that people need to be released to use their God-given gifts in response to a God-given calling. The task of the leader is to serve in a mentoring relationship of mutual accountability so that discernment may be exercised to identify the true motivation of the person being mentored while providing wise counsel and spiritual support. But people must be free to make their decisions and to carry the responsibility for the course of action to which they commit themselves.

Leaders operating within a hierarchical structure see their role as one of delegating and granting permission. People who function within a network empower and grant resources to those around them without trying to exert control. Controllers bring a mentality of suspicion and inhibit individuals from exercising initiative. They thereby deprive others of the opportunity to grow and mature through learning, through having their faith stretched as they reach for the unlikely and the seemingly impossible. Many valuable lessons can be learned only from failed attempts.

William Easum describes controllers as people who are set

against change. One of their key strategies is to favor consensus building "because they know consensus can never be reached on most innovating ministries." He helpfully distinguishes between control and accountability. "Control is deciding what people can and can't do. Accountability is rendering an account of what a person has or has not already done. Control is more of a power issue. Accountability is more of an integrity issue."[6]

The Changing Shape of Western Protestantism

Turning now to the issue of church structures, we have already noted that those traditions that are centrally organized with a hierarchical structure have suffered the most damage, finding it increasingly difficult to maintain institutional integrity and to continue to recruit quality leadership. Their organizational fabric is tearing apart at the seams, requiring urgent repairs and patching in an effort to keep the garment intact. While the older churches flounder and dwindle, many of the new, freewheeling independent congregations seem to thrive in the present cultural climate.

A North American historical perspective. This is not the first time in the history of the United States that religious organizations have been forced to come to terms with the fact that they need to undergo significant changes in order to survive. In the nineteenth century the consequences of failing to respond to population expansion and migration were evident in the loss of prime places occupied by Episcopalians, Presbyterians and Congregationalists to the Baptists and Methodists with the great treks westward.

At present the plight of mainline denominations is also evident in those parts of the United States, such as the West Coast, that have no dominant denominational tradition. The more cosmopolitan and mobile the population, the more precarious becomes the position of denominations that fail to shed their European parochial mentality. Their long-established mindset is to regard evangelism in terms of opening the doors and offering a range of services to those who call upon them. They regard as their primary evangelistic target group their inactive members. When there is no "external constituency" whose loyalty church leaders can appeal to, they find themselves at a loss to know what to do next.

Fortunately, the scene is not all gloom and doom. For at the same time that we see the demise of one section of the church, we see the flowering of another. Lyle Schaller considers this to be a "new reformation," which he identifies by twenty-one highly visible signs. His list includes the following: contemporary, creative worship; new resources from a wide range of agencies; market-driven planning; lay-empowered ministry; the emergence of approximately four thousand Protestant megachurches; an emphasis on prayer and spiritual formation; staff teams replacing the superstar preacher; the flattening of hierarchical ecclesiastical structures; the rapid increase in independent churches, numbering twenty thousand churches with 15 million adherents; and lay-led Bible study groups.[7] In the years since 1995, when Schaller provided this list, the signs are shining even more brightly.

This "new reformation" is not confined to independent churches, for within a postmodern culture denominational churches can neither be neatly catalogued nor confined. Within old-line traditions there are exciting examples of churches that have shed the shackles of their traditionalism without forfeiting the enrichment of their heritage. They too are demonstrating youthful vitality and growth. For it is those who wait upon the Lord who will renew their strength and mount up with wings like eagles, irrespective of age. They are prepared for the long haul, believing that "they shall run and not be weary, they shall walk and not faint" (Is 40:31). The pace is less important than the need for perseverance.

How should denominations respond? Should concerned Christians focus on reforming the contemporary denominational expressions of American Protestantism from within? Should the old wineskins be repaired? Or should the top priority be to invest in new wineskins to carry the gospel to new generations, both U.S.-born and foreign-born? Lyle Schaller responds, "The question is not whether these mainline Protestant denominations can be turned around. The turnaround already has begun. We are in the midst of a new reformation in American Protestantism."[8]

Bureaucracies can no longer depend on the loyalty of congregations to maintain them. Positions in the hierarchy will no longer simply be a prestigious reward for loyal, if sometimes undistinguished, service. Rather, bureaucracies will have to justify their existence by being cost-effective, proving that they can provide the needed resources to support the front-line mission of local congregations. Leadership will have to be apostolic, not bureaucratic.

The psalmist holds out the promise: "The righteous flourish like the palm tree, and grow like a cedar in Lebanon. . . . In old age they still produce fruit" (Ps 92:12-14). If God has not given up on the righteous, I personally find it hard to believe that he has given up on tens of thousands of churches that can still produce fruit in their old age. Fruit represents the superabundance of life produced by the tree. Fruitfulness signifies both character replication and numerical reproduction; in other words, growth in quality and quantity. Old churches must not simply stand as monuments to the past but as spiritual grandparents that have invested in the future by passing on their life to others and releasing their offspring to form new congregations. Church planting needs to be given high priority by old-line denominations.

The megachurch phenomenon. According to current estimates over 100,000 churches are struggling to keep their doors open in the face of rising insurance costs and the price of securing the services of a seminary-trained pastor. Some of these struggling churches are further weakened by megachurches that siphon off their younger members.

In his book *Do Mainline Churches Have a Future?* which primarily addresses his own American Baptist denomination, Tony Campolo maintains that leaders must "now face the fact that the average, ordinary local church that has typified mainline denominations throughout the twentieth century is increasingly unable to meet the desires of the people we need to reach in the twenty-first century. . . . The so-called superchurches have made the average local church outdated and noncompetitive in America's religious marketplace."[9] He is convinced that "traditional mainline churches will decline in size and importance in the face of this competition."[10]

Megachurches therefore carry an enormous responsibility for the future of Christianity in North America because of the rapidly increasing percentage of churchgoers being attracted to a small number of megachurches. Most of these churches are entrepreneurial, first-generation churches. Great skill will be needed to successfully make the transition to a second-generation pastor. In addition, with the likelihood of many small, old-line churches closing their doors, the megachurches that replace them will have to give high priority to planting new churches. Alternatively, denominational megachurches could have a significant ministry in the rejuvenation of dying congregations in their area. For example, England provides a number of examples of renewed Anglican churches that are breathing new life into churches facing closure and reoccupying empty churches that had been declared redundant.

The emergence of "new apostolic networks." C. Peter Wagner has had the insight to identify a new emerging-church paradigm and the foresight to appreciate the potential significance of "new apostolic networks." He has also become a central figure in bringing together formerly independent networks to help bolster their self-awareness and identify their common characteristics. This task is far from straightforward because the groups he features in his most recent book are exceedingly diverse both theologically and ecclesiastically.[11]

Wagner identifies the following characteristics that make up the "new apostolic church" profile. First, they are increasingly adopting the new name that Wagner has given to the movement. His first attempt at assigning a name to these emerging churches was to refer to them as "postdenominational," but this was abandoned because a number of the churches he identified as fitting the profile were within traditional denominations. Also, this initial term might have set up a negative reaction if it were interpreted to imply that denominations had had their day. However, with regard to the second objection his preferred title is no less controversial, as will be apparent in our discussion of the second characteristic of apostolic churches.

A second characteristic is that these churches have a new authority structure. Of nine features Wagner enumerates, this one, in his view, is the most radical. He describes the main difference between apostolic churches and traditional ones in the following terms. "We are seeing a transition from bureaucratic authority to personal authority, from legal structure to relational structure, from control to coordination and from rational leadership to charismatic leadership."[12]

At one level this new authority model reflects postmodern trends in that it is highly relational. There is a sense in which authority is invested in the leaders of apostolic networks by the followers in recognition of a spiritual anointing and leadership charisma. Yet it also depends on the level of trust that has been built up and the continuing credibility of a leader in being able to deliver on what is promised. At another level the claim to having an apostolic anointing is open to abuse because it can degenerate into manipulative authoritarianism. Ego trips that go unchecked lead to an eventual downfall due to the absence of accountability structures. An apostle can attract a coterie of people around him who dare not question any of his decisions for fear of incurring divine displeasure for opposing or even questioning "the Lord's anointed."

In recent decades there has been a welcome, renewed emphasis on the apostolic calling of the church. Within the new apostolic movement identified by C. Peter Wagner, David Cannistraci is emerging as a leading exponent. He describes apostolic ministry in terms of the restoration of the first century role of apostle:

☐ restoring the New Testament office of the apostle

☐ imparting Christ's apostolic anointing to equip, mature and activate the people of God

☐ a dramatic revival of supernatural signs, wonders and miracles of the kinds that followed the first century apostles

□ a worldwide deployment of thousands of apostles; their development will transcend groups, denominational boards and agencies, and will not be the work of any one organization

Cannistraci believes that "thousands will take their places in the final thrust of world evangelization through this life-changing *apostolic positioning*. Each apostle will be unique but will walk in the patterns of the early church apostles: traveling, strategically ministering and building the kingdom of God."[13] Cannistraci's position is based on the belief that the Lord will soon return, and in preparation for that momentous event the office of apostle, as represented by the foundational apostles of the New Testament, will be restored and authenticated by the same miraculous gifts and authority over churches.

There are, however, a number of problems with this understanding of the apostolate and its application to the new apostolic movement. The first problem is theological, in that the term *apostle* is imprecise in the New Testament. John R. W. Stott distinguishes between the various ways in which the term *apostle* is used in the New Testament. He begins by noting that, broadly speaking, all Christians are apostles in that they are sent out into the world to share in Christ's apostolic mission (see Jn 13:16, where "messengers" translates the Greek term *apostolos*). He goes on to note that the word is also used to describe the "messengers of the churches" (2 Cor 8:23; Phil 2:25) whose task is to serve as representatives from one church to another. The third use of the term is in reference to the twelve disciples together with two or three others, including Paul, who were eyewitnesses of the historic Jesus and to whom the risen Lord appeared.[14]

Cannastraci seems to interpret *apostle* in this third sense, on the basis of the special anointing present-day apostles receive directly from the Lord. But clearly contemporary claimants to the office of apostle cannot be regarded as equivalent to the first-century apostles of Christ. Notwithstanding their miracle-working credentials or effectiveness in church planting, you cannot have apostles building fresh foundations on top of existing foundations after almost two thousand years! Furthermore, the growth of new apostolic movements seems to have come about as much through franchising among existing churches as through planting new churches. Apostles cannot be self-appointed. Nor can they qualify for the office by acclaim from their followers among local church leaders who have placed themselves under the "covering" of an apostle. Present-day apostles do not have recognition in the universal church; rather, they each develop their own fiefdoms.

Apostolic leadership, as experienced in the first century of the church, cannot be replicated in the vastly different scenario of the twenty-first century. For the first century represented a pioneering phase of missionary expansion, with brand-new communities of believers being birthed in pagan contexts. New churches were being led by recent converts who were dependent on oral teaching that came to them with an apostolic guarantee of authenticity. We cannot at this point in time set aside nearly two thousand years of church history.

Today there are countless local churches that benefit from the leadership of biblically literate and spiritually mature pastors and laypersons. But the church is far too fragmented and multilayered for apostolic authority to assume leadership of a geographical region. Consequently, what is emerging is a "network" led by an apostle. This leadership may be exercised over a number of churches that choose to associate with the network and place themselves under the "covering" of a particular apostolic leader. Or the congregations may be part of a network by having been planted by the mother church of an apostolic fellowship of churches. The function is no less vital today, but it will be expressed in varying ways and modified by changing circumstances.

New church movements in Europe. In many European countries it is more difficult than in the United States for new movements to flourish alongside long-established churches. This is because the church scene is far less fragmented, and national identity may be closely associated with a particular ecclesiastical heritage. Established churches have enjoyed a privileged position, receiving government support and legal privileges. Most of Scandinavia is solidly Lutheran. Germany is either Lutheran or Catholic, according to region. The Church of England is the established church in England, with the reigning monarch as the defender of the faith.[15]

This state of affairs contributes to widespread nominalism, with a large percentage of the population claiming the rights of belonging without accepting the responsibilities of membership or any requirement to believe in the basic tenets of Christianity as expressed in the historic creeds.[16] For instance, in Norway, Denmark and Sweden, over 90 percent of the population is baptized in the Lutheran Church, and a high percentage of teenagers are later confirmed as members, while church attendance is seldom more than 5 percent—and as low as 2 percent in Denmark. The Church of England and the Church of Scotland hold less of a monopolistic position, but they only attract about 3 percent of the population to church on a given Sunday! Also, churches that enjoy special legal status and are nicely endowed have been prone to pretensions of grandeur.

One of the most encouraging signs has been a growing realization by many mainline congregations of their need to become missionary churches in their own contexts. When there is so much crumbling institutional fabric to be maintained, this is no small achievement. This realization has been heightened with growing economic woes, the burden of maintaining historic buildings and keeping open churches in urban areas that have become increasingly multicultural. One positive aspect of the parochial system is that it has anchored the church in the more socially deprived areas and put a break on the church's flight to the suburbs.

Alongside the "established churches" there has been a free church movement throughout Europe; some of them are several centuries old. For a period of time Congregational chapels flourished along with Baptist and Methodist congregations. But all have stalled and most experienced decline in the decades following both the First and Second World Wars.

Evangelicals in Europe have tended to remain within the denominational tradition in which they were reared rather than leaving to form independent congregations and establish new denominations. They have networked with one another through the Evangelical Alliance and parachurch organizations, and with periodic citywide evangelistic outreaches. During the 1960s a further significant development was the emergence of the charismatic movement, which brought renewed spiritual vitality to many mainline congregations. Throughout Northern Europe at present, the great majority of growing congregations are those influenced by the charismatic movement.

The house church movement has also brought a radical challenge to the established churches. Initially this movement consisted mostly of disaffected members of existing churches who abandoned their congregations to meet in private homes. Some groups became introverted and eventually disbanded; others used the home as a base for outreach into their neighborhoods. Homes made "church" more accessible to people who found the old church buildings uninviting, their worship lifeless and their ministry irrelevant. As a result of their popularity, house churches could no longer accommodate the numbers attending their meetings and so had to move into rented premises. Eventually the name "house churches" was changed into "new churches," and the congregations were characterized by a more expressive, exuberant and participatory form of worship and an apprenticeship model of leadership training.

These newly planted churches have in turn provided impetus to existing churches within traditional denominations that have a vision for church planting. As they initiated this ministry, they found that they were inhibited by the parochial structures. New churches being established in the geographical area that they regarded as their ministry domain angered other clergy. Bishops and area superintendents were caught on the horns of a dilemma, wanting to impose organizational restraints, while at the same time rejoicing in the appearance of new life. This is a local version of what Donald McGavran writes about at the national level, with mission boards

meeting to divide territory in order to avoid competition and dupli-
cation. He calls this "dog in a manger" courtesy, applying Aesop's
fable about a dog who doesn't eat straw barking at a cow to prevent
it from getting to the straw, with the result that both animals die.
Mission courtesy can lead to churches that have no heart for evangelism preventing other churches from undertaking the task that they
are neglecting.[17]

New groups should be welcomed to work alongside existing
churches, pooling their resources to meet the ministry needs of area
that are beyond the resources of any one group. Whereas the presence of new churches has undoubtedly contributed to this end in a
growing number of local contexts, the overall picture is of a shrinking churchgoing population. The new groups have contributed to
further fragmentation, with increased bureaucratic overhead.[18]

Wherever we look throughout the Western world, there is no evidence to date that current renewal movements, including charismatic
churches, megachurches, new paradigm/apostolic networks and new
churches have been sufficiently influential to turn the tide in national
churchgoing trends. As small mainline churches close due to escalating operational costs, they are being replaced in part by the newer
churches. Many of the newer churches are also small, but they do
not have the same overhead as the churches they replace. They meet
in rented facilities or in more economical modern premises and are
serviced by bivocational pastors or nonsalaried leadership teams.

The key question remains to be answered: Does the presence of
new churches represent new growth or simply a significant reconfiguration? New groups entering an area where churches have had a
long and faithful presence must come as learners and be prepared to
be held accountable for the consequences of their presence in the
community in relation to the overall progress of the gospel.

Dynamic Churches in the Majority World
In many countries in Africa, Asia and Latin America mainline Protestant denominations continue growing alongside both Roman Cath-

olic and independent churches. This growth cannot simply be explained in terms of the spiritual responsiveness of the people among whom they work. The reality is that pastors who are themselves first-generation Christians lead many of these churches, composed largely of first-generation converts. Even when the pastors are from Christian homes, their training has been by the apprenticeship method that has kept them in close contact with the non-Christian people to whom they are reaching out in Christ's name. Furthermore, these churches are not preoccupied with maintenance needs but demonstrate the characteristics of "missional" churches. They are in the apostolic mold.

Leaders are emerging from the grassroots, while others have broken off from the older denominations out of frustration with bureaucracy or the domination of an older generation of leaders. These dynamic personalities are gathering large crowds and mentoring leaders who are then sent out to plant new churches. In addition, they are mobilizing new missionary movements consisting of non-Western missionaries who are able to take the gospel to areas of the world where Westerners are barred from entry.

Whether the movements consist of megachurches with satellite congregations and cell groups as in South Korea, Singapore and many countries in Latin America, or of independent house churches as in the People's Republic of China, their organizational structure is of a networking nature. Leadership emerges in such structures on the basis of mutual recognition and by the building and maintaining of strong relationships.

The Age of Networks

In the first chapter we briefly described the era of discontinuous and chaotic change that characterizes much of the Western world today. Whereas hierarchies can operate in societies that are homogeneous and centralized, they begin to fall apart when societies become pluralistic and each segment develops its own agenda. In reaction to such diversification, repressive regimes might be superimposed, which will bring a semblance of social order for a time, but they are doomed to crumble in the long run. We have seen this demonstrated in the fall of Marxist regimes in Eastern Europe at the end of the 1980s. The more oppressive these regimes were, the more traumatic the transition to stability is proving to be.

The widespread impact of the cultural shift. William Easum has argued that because established Protestantism was born into the Industrial Age, characterized by slow, incremental change, it finds it especially difficult to cope with the current climate of change, which is of an entirely different order. Change today is so distinctive that Easum gives our times a distinctive name, the Quantum Age, in which "the relationships between the parts consist of invisible fields that fill all of space and are observable to us only through their effects." This is the world of cyberspace. While in the Newtonian world inertia was the norm of the universe until some object struck another object, in the quantum world "change is the norm of the universe. No constants exist."[19]

In the business world the dawn of the information age has demonstrated that hierarchical structures are too cumbersome and its leaders too remote from the grassroots to respond quickly enough. Consequently, many businesses have created semi-independent units within the conglomerate. In a culture of discontinuous change, long-range planning is no longer an appropriate management strategy. It is replaced by a plan-do, rapid-response mode of operation.

Among today's churches we can compare the cumbersome decision-making process of denominational churches with the rapid-response approach of the new apostolic churches. Here key individuals gather the necessary data, confer together, make their decisions and take prompt action. Church leaders and members trust them with the responsibility and are ready to implement the decisions they make. Some of these networks represent consensus style decision making, in which information is shared widely and opinion canvassed. Others rely upon revelations given to the apostolic leadership with prophetic confirmation. Some of these new movements seem to represent a last hurrah of modernity in the guise of end-time restorationism (i.e., the restoration of all the spiritual gifts, offices and apostolic leadership to the church, in preparation for the Lord's return). Others most closely represent a postmodern, decentralized, relational paradigm. The effective networker is constantly asking two question, "Who knows?" and, "Who needs to know?"

Flattening of organizational structures. The network-based movement should not be regarded as a place where everyone is free to do his or her own thing. This would simply result in a network becoming a tangle and ripping itself apart. Rather it represents a significant change in the decision-making process. Whereas in the hierarchical pyramid, decision-makers are removed from the scene of action and delegate their decisions to the people responsible for their implementation, in the network, decision-makers are available when needed to ratify a decision. At the same time they resist the temptation for decisions to float to the top of an organization, emphasizing that each key decision must be taken and acted upon at the appropriate level. Most decisions are *operational* rather than *policy-based* and therefore must be made as close to the operation in progress as possible by those individuals most directly involved. On the other hand, decisions are often not made in isolation but are communicated to the network for input by anyone who can make a worthwhile contribution.

The cyberspace revolution that got under way in the decade of the 1990s has changed for all time how information is disseminated. Tom Beaudoin, writing from a Gen X perspective, spells out the radical implications of this revolution for religious hierarchies:

> The environment of cyberspace provides resources that are ripe for upsetting hierarchies. Access to e-mail is fairly widespread, and one does not need to be part of the cultural elite to set up a Web page. The most socially unacceptable topics can become the subjects of discussion groups. Fugitives from orthodoxies of all sorts become the kings or queens of their own hills (or home pages) in cyberspace and expect that many will read what they have to say. It is new, experimental, and imaginative space in American culture, as yet largely

unregulated, and certainly beyond the control of religious institutions. . . .

Cyberspace also threatens the stability of religious institutions because it is a radically pluralistic space. Cyberspace unsteadies many religious dichotomies: private/public, holy/unholy, sacred/profane, Jewish/Gentile, Christian/pagan. The divisions that set one religious institution off from another are not immune to this leveling effect.[20]

Church leaders are slow to realize the significance of the cyberspace revolution because the vast majority are still from the silent generation, which preceded the boomers, or are older boomers who struggle to make the transition to a high-tech society.

Relational dynamic. In networking organizations, authority is based on relationships, not on status or position. Individuals who can build strong relationships and expand networks of people are those who relate well to one another and who exercise incredible influence within networks. Also, networks are capable of rapid expansion because they are often woven around a person with charisma and a clearly articulated vision.

Consistent with the definition of charismatic leadership, new-paradigm pastors tend to be authoritative and even autocratic. Thus in spite of espousing a decentralized form of social organization, the pastors hold ultimate veto power over individual programs, and they set the vision that defines the institutional culture of the church. This power could erupt in a hundred destructive ways—and occasionally it does—but it is moderated by the pastors' firm belief in accountability, not only for the laity, but for themselves.[21]

Leadership in a network is precarious because the authority of the leaders can be challenged at any time. Individuals and groups are free to sever their links and to start independent networks. Whenever possible, leaders of existing networks celebrate the creation of new networks because it honors their own leadership in developing a new generation of entrepreneurs. This results in greater overall growth and further opportunities for creative innovation.

When network leaders overextend their authority or lose credibility, they are likely to find themselves increasingly isolated. Knowing this, they tend to work with supportive teams around them. These teams function not simply as a workforce but as a mutually supportive group of people who affirm one another and relate informally. The senior pastor serves as their friend and mentor and is accessible to the whole team. William Easum describes the team dynamic in the following terms:

> Relationships and the flow of information are the two most valuable assets of the permission-giving network. . . . The sum of an organization is the sum of its parts plus the relationships between the parts. . . . Relationships are based on the person and his or her skills instead of the role the person has in the organization.[22]

Team members relate together not to establish their position in a hierarchy or to defend their professional "turf" but to get a job done efficiently and effectively, and to enjoy themselves and each other's company in the process. Unlike in hierarchical organizations, a department does not grumble about unrealistic expectations or limited resources. Rather, it will develop creative responses by forming another team to look at the problem with fresh eyes. Networks do not work within set boundaries but step outside of existing parameters. The people who work best in networks are those who like to color outside of the lines, in contrast to hierarchical people who paint by numbers. "If a problem emerges for which there appears to be more than one solution, the network organization forms a team for each solution and encourages each team to work on the same issue. Turf issues are a primary obstacle to networking a congregation."[23] Networking partnerships are here to stay. Over the next twenty-five years I foresee that churches and denominations will form alliances and networks across denominational lines.

Permission giving. To move from a delegating to a permission-giving leadership and management style requires significant adjustments. Controllers operate from a premise of distrust and suspicion. They build dependency networks around themselves, which bolster their egos and ensure their position by making them indispensable. Items requiring decisions are pushed up the layers of management.

Leaders responsible for areas of ministry find that they are given responsibilities without commensurate authority. Controllers tend to be insecure people who surround themselves with "clones" or individuals of lesser ability who will pose no threat.

Permission givers, on the other hand, are secure individuals who trust their team members and acknowledge their expertise in their particular area of ministry. They work closely with each team member in a mentoring relationship. Organization is fluid, not represented in a hierarchical and departmentalized way typical of organizational charts. Rather, the leadership team reconfigures according to the issue being addressed, and outside resource persons are invited to join to bring their expertise and insights. Permission givers are ambitious for the people working around them and are not intimidated by people more able than themselves. Permission givers are in the business of growing people, not of "cloning" people. Therefore, they celebrate diversity and creativity. They are prepared to give unlikely ideas a try and allow individuals to take responsibility for their implementation.

The permission-giving organization only works if there is a clear unifying vision, if the team leader maintains close contact with the leadership team, and if the team members understand the boundaries in which they need to operate. William Easum declares that such boundaries cannot come from rulebooks or procedures but must flow from the basic values of the congregation.[24] Permission givers walk around a great deal, talking with all and sundry to check out what is happening through the organization and the communities it seeks to serve and impact. This style of leadership is problematic for pastors trained in a classical academic model because they like to preserve their privacy and are prone to be office bound.

Equipping. Networking organizations train people on the job. The best models ensure that theory and application go hand in hand. Theory informs practice, but equally important, practice develops new theories. These theories can then be tested rigorously in order to ascertain their broader validity. Knowledge and wisdom must be kept in tandem, for when our knowledge outstrips our wisdom, we are likely to become an embarrassment or a menace. Discernment is the combining of knowledge and wisdom. People are equipped to the extent that they develop competencies in areas of ministry through this interactive process.

Churches committed to developing their own leadership must also recognize the limitations of the "in-house" apprenticeship training approach. This can result in a narrow vision and in producing leaders who only know how to do what is already being done. What's more, ministry competencies do not consist simply in technical expertise. For a church to operate as a transformational missional presence in any society, be it traditional, modern or postmodern, leaders require theological and missiological preparation as well as the development of ministry skills.

Indeed, to focus simply on ministry skills, without those foundations, will increases a church's vulnerability to cultural subversion. Without these training foundations, leaders will function without the benefit of a broader frame of reference beyond the norms and demands of their cultural context. They will lack the sensitivities developed through training in the biblical and missiological disciplines. They will not have the benefit of the lessons of church history. They will not be aware of how the Christian movement advanced in the face of the many challenges it faced in centuries past. They will not be aware of the periods when the church faltered in its advance because of failure to consolidate its gains, when it retreated because internal matters were neglected or, conversely, when domestic issues became the overriding preoccupation and consumed far too much energy.

The emergence of "new paradigm" or "new apostolic" networks presents an exciting challenge for seminaries, which can partner with networks in preparing a new generation of leaders with the necessary insights and skills for a new day. In the following chapter we will explore some of the implications in greater detail.

Empowerment. Church leaders are prone to disempower the people of God in two areas. They may disempower them in the church through the exercise of restrictive controls that exclude the laity from ministry and from taking initiative. With even more devastating consequences they may fail to recognize the calling of laypersons in the world as their primary area of ministry. Robert Slocum draws attention to the need for churches to consider ministry in a new light. He rightly maintains that the issue is not "how to get the laity involved in the ministry of the church," but "how to get the church involved in the ministry of the laity!"[25] The people of God are disenfranchized when their primary ministry is ignored and when the preaching and teaching in the church ignores the questions and challenges of the workplace. Slocum identifies the serious problems that arise from this split between the sacred and the secular.

> First and foremost, it is a nonbiblical view; it simply is not at all what God had in mind. The second problem is that it tends to cut God out of the three "secular" arenas (work, family and government) and to allow the power of sin unrestrained freedom to devastate and wreck lives. A third problem is the tendency to isolate the church from the rest of human life. This isolation can transform the church from a source of strength and renewal into a theater of irrelevant ritual.[26]

According to Slocum's analysis, church professionals represent 2 percent of church membership, and a further 18 percent consists of the "church laity," who are needed to assist in running the church's ministries. If this is so, then what about the remaining 80 percent "worldly laity"? Slocum argues that the task of the 20 percent should be to provide resources for the 80 percent for their ministry in the world.

As hierarchical organizations become increasingly dysfunctional, leaders must deal with the frequent flare-ups arising out of frustration and anxiety, and must shore up crumbling structures. In networking organizations that hierarchy is dismantled, and the focus is placed on supporting people to function beyond their church commitments. This entails leaders being in touch with the situations in which people live and work, and restructuring the church so that its fellowship and support are available at the point of need. For William Easum it means encouraging ministry "to be delivered any time, any place, by anyone, no matter what. . . . The shorter the time lag between discovering a spiritual need and putting it into an actual ministry, the more effective the church will be in the Quantum Age."[27]

Diversification. Hierarchies are by their very nature monolithic. They were developed in the Industrial Age to produce a range of standard products with speed, efficiency and quality maintenance. They have proven too sluggish and unimaginative in the high-tech information age, or Quantum Age. Today most of the innovative technologies are developed in new start-up companies, or in teams granted a great deal of autonomy and freedom to experiment within old conglomerates. Similarly, within a fragmented and variegated postmodern society the church will need to diversify its ministries and release its financial and human resources to develop ministries appropriate for each population segment.

Networking churches consist of a range of self-organizing ministry teams. The range will be in constant flux as some teams disband when the need for them is no longer present, while others are formed around people who have identified a fresh need they feel called to meet. Teams are not elected, representative bodies. Instead they are formed by invitation or by calling for volunteers with specific skills and experience. Before one can be a team member, a firm commitment has to be made. Each team has its own social dynamic, a "chemistry" that not only makes it work but creates a fulfilling and joyful experience for the participants. Teams are formed with great care to ensure that the leaders are in wholehearted agreement with the defining vision of the church and can relate their particular ministry interest within that vision. In addition, each member not only must be competent but also must be a team player. Each team recognizes itself as one team among many and that together the teams make up the church, with the whole being greater than the sum of the parts.

Decentralization. Donald Miller argues that the pyramidal structures inherited from the past need to be replaced by a much more democratized structure with a high degree of decentralization and empowerment in the present cultural context.[28] In order to achieve decentralization without experiencing the chaos of fragmentation, the church will need leaders with a strong commitment to vision and values. It will also require a board or steering committee that is in close touch with the team leaders. Board members may be assigned to particular teams with which they feel a particular affinity, not to control but to provide support for the leadership and to foster a broader church perspective. Teams should be required to give a regular report to the senior pastor and the board, with a progress report and expenditure update.

If the challenges are great in forming a network from scratch, they are even greater for a church seeking to move from a centralized, programmatic mindset to becoming a networking entity. Easum cautions that the transition will need to be made slowly, with two operational modes operating side by side during the transition period. But the same individuals cannot be committed to both modes. Some leaders will not be able to make the transition and will need to be given the opportunity to gracefully step aside when the time comes.

Accountability. One downside in the network organization is that relationships can become loose and self-serving. And leaders may emerge who, through force of personality, through misuse of their God-given charisma, or because of their sheer creative genius, end up assuming too prominent a position. They become increasingly dictatorial and arrogant, and their demise can unravel the entire network. Leith Anderson acknowledges this potential problem, noting that "as long as the network meets our needs, we continue the association, knowing that we are free to leave at any time. . . . Networks tend to be loose in organization, simple in structure, highly flexible, and comparatively temporary.[29] At all points in a network there needs to be mutual accountability, not only for the safety of the network but for the spiritual well-being of the participants.

Exponential growth potential of networks. By definition a network is an open-ended system. The larger the network the greater its potential for growth, because growth very often occurs through initiatives taken at the periphery rather than through directives issued from the center. The periphery does not represent distance from power. Rather, it is where the bulk of the significant action takes place. To change the analogy from a network to a cellular structure, every cell has within it the genetic code for its continuing reproduction.

In addition, networks gain added strength and influence through partnerships with yet other networks as they form relationships that work to their mutual advantage. Healthy networks are concerned not with control but with empowerment; this means that they are able to work cooperatively and not in competition with other networks.[30]

Implementation

1. If you already have a vision statement, find what percentage of the congregation—especially small group leaders and those responsible for the various ministry departments—can state it. Assess to what extent the vision statement serves as a motivating force behind the various initiatives of your church.

2. Review the structures of your church and then work toward a single supervisory board whose task it to ensure that the church remains true to its vision. Its primary concerns are to ensure integration, continuity and accountability. Allow each area of ministry that reports to this board to be led by a task force, with members appointed (not elected) according to vision, passion, giftedness, experience and spiritual maturity.

3. Set up a "listening group" that will (1) take the initiative in talking to groups and individuals about ministry needs and opportunities and (2) enable people with ideas to check out their ideas with this group. As a general rule the person who sees the need is the one who should take a leading role in establishing a new ministry to meet that need.

four

From Schooling Professionals
to Mentoring Leaders

S*o far we have looked at the extent and significance of the cul-*
tural changes taking place and the fact that the church now
finds itself increasingly marginalized from society. We have
considered the precarious position in which many churches now find
themselves, causing them to wonder how much longer they will be
able to maintain business as usual. We then looked at the need for
the church in the West to become a mission church within an
increasingly pluralistic environment. Collectively these issues hold
enormous implications for the process of leadership selection as
well as the equipping of the next generation of pastors, which we
will be considering in this chapter.

There are many debates about the future of theological education
around the Western world, especially in North America, addressing
such issues as its relevance and accessibility. There is a serious
decline in the number of students taking the Master of Divinity
degree, which has long been regarded in academic circles and
denominational hierarchies as the professional degree for ordained

ministry. The reality is that the majority of pastors serving churches in the United States do not have a Master of Divinity degree. It is not required by some of the largest denominations. Nor do independent churches, megachurches that increasingly train their own staff members, and the fast-growing "new apostolic" movements require it.

Seminaries and the Mission of the Church

The task of the seminary is to work alongside churches to assist in resourcing them for their manifold ministries in diverse missionary situations in a rapidly changing world. While establishing a symbiotic relationship, each must also maintain its distinctive contribution to the training process, providing a challenge to the other. The church calls for relevance, while the seminary emphasizes the need for theological integrity and critical evaluation. When they covenant to work closely together, they are able to sharpen one another and hold each other accountable.

Recruitment pressures. The increasing cost of providing quality education in a traditional setting means that seminaries will need to be further subsidized, either through grants to the students or through legacies and donations to the institutions or through both. An alternative approach is for the seminary to operate a two-tier program, the basic level consisting of a certificate qualification made available with low-cost courses. These certificate courses can be offered for mature students in ministry who want to improve their knowledge in order to minister more effectively. Many potential students are not interested in receiving academic credit. They simply want to extend their knowledge and enhance their ministry skills.

If a seminary is simply interested in enrolling as many preservice students as possible with the minimum amount of screening and without local church endorsement, then standards will inevitably decline. In addition, more students will find themselves in courses beyond their academic ability and of minimal benefit for their future ministries.

There is a growing concern regarding the ability of seminaries to attract the most promising students. Local churches need to play a far more active part in recruiting and mentoring individuals they deem suitable for receiving further training. Lyle Schaller shares this concern.

> From the perspective of the year 2018, perhaps the most far reaching bad news is the inability of today's theological seminaries to attract adequate numbers of highly competent, exceptionally gifted, deeply committed, and clearly extroverted adults born after 1965 who possess a compelling call to the parish ministry. . . . The time has arrived for a new system for enlisting, training, screening, and credentialing the next generation of parish pastors.[1]

Donald Miller makes a similar point, arguing that both traditional churches and seminaries are often demotivating to persons with exceptional leadership skills. He believes that the newer models of leadership development and ministry training being offered by the new paradigm churches need to be studied carefully.[2] This is an appropriate time—perhaps even a "strategic inflection point"— when new models need to be developed and tested as pilot projects. Some of these new church networks now have sufficient experience to recognize both the strengths and limitations in what they are able to offer for the training of their leaders, and some of their leaders are being encouraged to enroll in seminary classes. Rather than simply fitting this new category of student into existing programs, leaders of seminaries and new paradigm churches need to sit down together to redesign curricula and course formats so that they will more adequately meet current needs.

Cost and value. By what criteria is the value of theological education to be measured? One way is to consider it in terms of access to the potential job market. A Master of Divinity or a professionally equivalent degree from a prestigious seminary can open doors of opportunity. Yet this educational advantage is far less true in today's job market, in which churches are looking for experience, character, competence and agreement on key doctrinal issues. A more fruitful measure of value in education is to assess its adequacy in training leaders to face the issues and pressures encountered in ministry in the world today. In this regard the level of concern begins to rise because many recent graduates confess that they do not feel equipped for the challenges they face.

Another indicator that there are serious problems with the current method of selection and training is the high drop-out rate in the first ten years of ministry. In the case of individuals who leave the ministry in the first decade, whatever the price they paid for their seminary education was too high because it proved to be of little value to them in the long run. The price tag for theological education includes more than dollars paid. It includes also dollars owed, time wasted and the frustration that ensued.

The high cost of theological education also means that many smaller congregations can no longer afford to pay the salary required by a seminary-trained, younger pastor with heavy financial commitments to repay loans as well as support a family. As many midsized congregations with multiple staff people encounter increasing financial pressures in maintaining their programs, there are fewer openings for pastors trained with specialist concentrations in particular areas of ministry.

The impact of modernity on the seminary and the church. Seminaries find themselves straddling two worlds, the world of the academy and the world of the church. It is extremely difficult for any one professor to do justice to both because each is so demanding. Alan Roxburgh observes that:

> Seminaries are classified as professional schools, like those of law, business, and medicine. Thus the business of the seminary, especially on university campuses, is to train professionals. The seminary has assumed a social function within the canons of modernity. . . . The symbols of the pedagogue and the professional belong to a period when the pastor did function at the cultural center.[3]

In addition, some professors are primarily called to become experts in a narrow field of academia in which they can make a sig-

nificant contribution. They have neither the calling nor the experience to apply their learning to a variety of church contexts,
developing the implications of their field of study to the tasks of
ministry and mission. In order to perform more adequately in both
the academy and the church, a seminary will have to be large
enough to allow for narrow specialization among its faculty. It will
need to recognize and affirm faculty members in their distinctive
disciplines and callings. For some faculty members, their primary
identification will be with the church, parachurch or secular agency
rather than with the academic guild.

What are the primary influences shaping the seminary student? A
seminary offers much more than an academic course of study. It is a
community with a faculty which molds the institution's values,
expectations and reward system. Additionally, it is a community of
students that exerts powerful peer group influences. The combined
impact of these pressures can draw the student away from the church
at the very time when he or she is being trained for a lifetime of service in the church.

The situation is made somewhat better by the fact that increasing
numbers of students commute to the campus and pursue their studies while they continue in secular employment or work in a church-
related ministry. Of course, this option is only open to those students
who live within driving distance of a seminary.

Reengineering theological education. Pastors involved in ministry to the congregation and mission to the community in the post-
Christian and neopagan world will find that they are in leadership
vocations that have less and less social acceptance and professional
affirmation. Tomorrow's leaders are unlikely to be the respected figures in their communities that yesterday's clergy were. Richard Kew
and Roger White state in *Toward 2015* that "it will be increasingly
inappropriate for them to identify themselves with other professionals like physicians, lawyers, or academics, and they must be prepared to make significant personal sacrifices in ministry."[4]

Those assuming leadership must not consider their calling primarily in terms of a professional career path but as a holy calling with minimal material rewards.[5] They must be able to operate with few resources, think creatively and live the life of day-to-day trust in the Lord's provision and guidance. "As seminaries come up against the post-modern reality, risk-taking must become part of their way of life, or they are likely to go the way of the dinosaur."[6] Mike Regele invites us to

> take a simple tour of mainline seminaries. Where are the strong visionary leaders? Where are those in training who are moved by a passion for the kingdom of God? In which classroom do we tell theological students that the church of the twenty-first century needs visionary leadership able to think big and bold? Where do we instill in them the level of courage necessary to face a world that is antagonistic to the church? We have taken Jesus' model of servant leadership and reduced it to insipid peonage.[7]

If this assessment seems overly harsh, at least it should make every seminary student stop to ponder the questions: "Do I regard my education as providing prestige and security in the future? Or do I consider it as essential preparation for a high-risk mission?" During our preparation for ministry, as well as in the performance of ministry, we need to reflect on the price paid by our Lord and by those who came after him. There are many passages in Scripture that state frankly and sometimes in graphic detail the sufferings and privations that the leaders in the early church endured.

More and more students may well find themselves in a position, either during or at the end of their training, where there is no job open to them in an existing church. Rather, they will have to be ready to plant a new church, not as an isolated church planter but as a member of an entrepreneurial team of "dreamers" with a God-given vision. Church planting will become an increasing priority due to the closure of many small churches that are no longer viable and are unable to adapt to a new challenge. It will also be significant because many of today's churches are unlikely to be able to win for Christ and disciple the under-thirty-five-year-olds.

Some Practical Suggestions for Revamping Theological Education to Provide More Adequate Ministerial Training

Reengineering theological education and leadership training is not a task for seminaries to undertake in isolation. Rather, it must be a cooperative venture that includes church and parachurch leaders and mature Christian laypeople whose primary calling is to minister in their secular vocations. In approaching this daunting task those involved must share responsibility for the failures of the past, because all have contributed to the problems that must now be addressed.

Bring churches and seminaries together into a partnership of life-long learning and equipping. Given the seismic shifts taking place in Western culture, it is evident that the next generation of church leaders will need to retool both academically and in terms of ministry insights and skills to face challenges that are life-threatening for many local congregations stuck in old paradigms. Furthermore, just as car manufacturing companies need a periodic recall of particular models and vintages of vehicles because of manufacturing defects, so we need a "recall" of pastors who find that they are increasingly unable to function and survive in their ministry. And like the computers we work with, regular program updates are necessary to enhance performance and to perform new tasks.

Leith Anderson observes, "Traditional seminary education is designed to train research theologians who are to become parish practitioners. Probably they are adequately equipped for neither."[8] He sees a switch from Master of Divinity degrees to various Master of Arts degrees (which is evident in many seminaries, certainly at Fuller where I serve) as the beginning of a long-term trend. In response, he insists that institutions must change, for few schools have the resources to offer both. In his opinion, "We will need comparatively few graduate schools of theology and comparatively more professional schools of ministry."[9]

There is danger of a chasm being created between academic theology and training in ministry competencies. This would simply reposition the already existing chasm from its present location between the church and the seminary, to create a fault line within the institutions themselves—with fatal consequences. The challenges presented by both modernity and postmodernity require greater theologically informed discernment, not less. The issue is not whether theology per se is important but *what kind* of theology. It must be theological training that provides the skills to apply the biblical texts to contemporary situations. It must be rewritten in the course of cultural engagement rather than limited to formulas determined by yesterday's battles. At the same time, some ancient battlegrounds have to be repeatedly fought over.

Church-based schools for training in ministry. One of the most significant developments in the area of training for ministry is the initiative that several large and influential churches have taken in establishing their own schools for ministry. These schools train their own emerging leaders and also make their programs available to other churches. In part they represent the frustration churches feel with seminaries that are more closely identified with the academy and scholarly pursuits than with the churches and their pressing needs.

While these initiatives are commendable in many ways, they are in danger of being so competency-based that they fail to provide theological and missiological foundations and critiques to ensure that the growth they seek to enhance is authentic and substantive in terms of kingdom values. We must be mindful of the fact that we reproduce after our own kind and our blind spots and false trails are likely to be perpetuated if there is not an adequate, broad-based critique. In addition the curricula of these schools should not simply be shaped by the ministry needs of the local church but by the church's engagement with the wider culture and the whole counsel of God, informed at every point by the Scriptures.

A more fruitful approach is to bring church and seminary resources together in a collaborative working relationship, recognizing that neither one has the necessary insights and research resources by itself. Each needs the other. Churches leaders draw the attention of the scholarly community to the theological, philosophical and ministry-skill related issues that they face. The scholarly communities act as consultants who provide the churches with an independent critique to grant correction and guidance.

Restructure the scholarly community. In the seminary there will be faculty members whose primary call is to pursue their scholarly discipline within the academy. The contributions made by evangelical scholars during the past four decades in their academic guilds must be affirmed. The dialogue that the academy provides with scholars representing other schools of thought should be maintained for the enrichment of all. Evangelical scholarship will itself be further refined, expanded and strengthened by this wider engagement. In order to facilitate their contribution faculty members should not be expected to engage constantly with ministry-driven agendas. Yet their scholarship needs to be made available to a wider constituency and its ministry implications explored.

Alongside scholars pursuing the traditional theological, biblical, philosophical and historical disciplines will be scholars who have a ministry focus, much as you would have pure and applied sciences in a secular university. Another model suggested is that of schools of business and management. Here faculty members are in constant dialogue with the business community, which provides their case studies and consultation opportunities. In the seminary there needs to be increased interaction and integration to work on projects that require interdisciplinary expertise, including both theologians and ethicists alongside professors of practical theology. Many of these issues will be tackled in collaboration with pastors of local churches.

Teach those who are called and who show potential in their ministries. The point is frequently made that many people who could most benefit from formal theological education are not in a position to avail themselves of the opportunities, whereas some of the people studying in seminaries should not be there. The absence of the former is due to the fact that they are already engaged in fruitful ministries that they either do not want to or are unable to leave. They may also have a mortgage to pay and a family to support. The strength of church-based training is that it is accessible and builds the competencies such people need for effective ministry.

The presence in seminaries of those who ought not to be there is due to their having fulfilled the academic entry requirements but without any assessment of their sense of call to ministry, their suitability or their individual gifting. They are trained entirely on the basis of their future potential rather than to enhance ministry gifts that they already exercise.

By making courses available through extension programs, intensive courses and interactive, individualized distance learning via the Internet, seminaries could have a much wider impact. The present educational ladder that gets narrower the higher you climb could be turned into a wide staircase accessible to a much larger constituency. As an added benefit, developing a much larger educational market would help bring down the cost of tuition. Donald Miller also affirms the need for seminaries to take the initiative in bridging the gap between themselves and the churches.

> I also think that seminaries need to be radically restructured, allowing more theological education to be done in the local churches. Let clergy who want a graduate education go to a major university and study philosophy, church history, or theology. Seminaries, in contrast, should be professional schools where people are mentored and taught while they serve within a local congregation. Learning disconnected from day-to-day practice may be appropriate for those pursuing a Ph.D. and doing graduate-level research, but I am not certain that it is appropriate for those responding to a pastoral calling. Indeed, I would favor downsizing the physical plant of most seminaries and instead creating "lay institutes" on the campuses of the larger mainline churches.[10]

The ideal of education through a full-time, residential community of students and teachers becomes today more and more of a myth than a reality, given the fact that an increasing number of students are older, in ministry and commuting to seminary. They are on campus simply to take the courses they need and to have access to the library. They look to their churches and fellowship groups for community support and have little time to sit around with students and faculty.

Seminaries need to respond in a more creative and proactive manner to this reality. Students can be grouped into cohorts with a supervisor supplied by a local church. They can further interact with the professor and fellow students through intensive courses and Internet discussion groups. If students take responsibility for their own learning by pre-reading lecture notes and assigned books prior to coming to class, then the classroom experience can be used to process what they have learned, to stimulate further discussion, and to provide additional input from the professor.

Learn on a need-to-know basis. Just like the pastor in the local church, the professor also suffers from the imposition of unrealistic expectations. There is simply not enough time to address all the areas that need to be covered to prepare an individual for the thousand and one demands of ministry today. Students vary so much in their experience, gifting and abilities. The ministry situations for which they are being prepared vary enormously, from rural to small town to suburban and urban to specialized paraparochial ministries.

Some students will leave seminary to assume sole charge of small churches, while others will go to larger churches as a junior member of a full-time staff. A further factor needs to be taken into consideration. Younger students may lack the experience to appreciate the value of what is being taught; or they are not motivated to listen because the issues do not seem relevant as they sit in the classroom, unconnected to the church and its mission. Adults learn best on a need-to-know basis.

Bearing in mind the rapid expansion of knowledge, increased specialization and new challenges presented by society's transition from modernity to postmodernity, theological education will need to come in line with other types of professional training in providing lifelong learning opportunities. Some denominations are already requiring annual in-service training through seminars and intensive courses for their pastors to retain their credentials.

The Challenge Facing Pastoral Leadership

At several points in the preceding chapters we have drawn attention to the challenges that face many pastors in surviving the increasing stresses and strains of ministry. These challenges take different forms, depending on the location and size of the church, as well as the personality, skills and "fit" of the pastor. George Barna draws attention to the growing uncertainty regarding the role of pastors in society and to the increasingly unrealistic expectations placed on them. He believes that being a pastor these days may be the single most thankless task in America.[11]

In society at large social support systems are collapsing, both in terms of the fragmentation of the extended family and the inability of both government and voluntary agencies to mobilize the resources to meet the demand. Consequently the church finds that pastoral demands are increasing. People turn to the church for emotional support, counseling and therapy, financial resources and recovery programs. The garbage cans lined up each week outside every home and the dumpsters located by every office and business are a reminder of the spiritual, emotional and social "dumping" that the churches must handle each week. The question both for the city and for the churches is the same, "What do we do with it all?"

Prone to self-absorption. The therapy model of ministry in which so many clergy have been trained during their seminary years has resulted in many becoming overwhelmed by their pastoral load. They do not have sufficient energy in reserve to meet the demands of providing strategic leadership. That role demands time to pray, to plan and to mentor others in contributing their gifts while developing their spiritual well-being. Given the individualistic nature of contemporary Western society, people tend to be self-absorbed and demanding. Pastors themselves are not immune from this tendency.

To have the idea that we can supply answers for all the problems brought to us is to place ourselves in the position of playing God. Failure is inevitable!

We must not labor under the misapprehension that our counseling skills in themselves are adequate to mend people's broken lives and to heal their hurts. Nor must we think that our leadership and management skills will be sufficient to grow the church. Only the gospel and the regenerative, healing and sanctifying work of the Holy Spirit will bring about significant and permanent change in the lives of the people. Only God can grow a church. Our task is to collaborate with God in his work. Episcopalian authors Richard Kew and Roger White argue that we need to move from a self-absorbed to a self-emptying approach to ministry, which means setting aside considerations of status and professional expertise:

> The self-emptying ministry and service of our Lord should be the pattern for the ministry of each person who claims to be one of his followers. While the self-absorption of our culture will constantly try to tempt us away from rootedness in God, if we give in to these enticements we will eventually find ourselves powerless in the presence of God.[12]

The issue of self-understanding has profound implications both for ministry emergence and training. On what basis are people recognized as called to ministerial leadership? What should be the selection criteria? How is the person to be trained for ministry? How does that training relate to one's personal spiritual development, spousal and family relationships, and the need to find finances to fund educational preparation for ministry? To what extent does removing individuals from their ministry setting in order to train them for ministry contribute to a pattern of self-absorption? Are unacceptable levels of strain and stress introduced as a consequence of the disruption caused by uprooting people, creating financial pressures and then intimidating them with seemingly insurmountable academic hurdles?

From the Industrial Age to the Quantum Age. To what extent are the leaders of today and tomorrow being prepared for the cultural transition from the Newtonian world to the quantum world? William Easum contrasts these two very different worlds. In terms of thought processes, there is a shift between these two worlds from linear thinking to interconnectedness. All of this raises questions about the highly departmentalized structures of theological education. To what extent do they inhibit the work that needs to be done across disciplines in relation to the missionary task?

The Newtonian world is a world of order and predictability, whereas the quantum world is characterized by chaos, which has resulted in new studies in the area of chaos theory, through which complex patterns can be discerned. How do systems function, including church structures, in the midst of unpredictable and discontinuous change? The quantum world is not the straightforward world of cause-and-effect relationships but of unanticipated consequences and previously unidentified potential and resources. Preparation for ministry in such a climate of uncertainty and surprise cannot best be accomplished in a highly structured environment or with predictable routines. Rather, the student must be faced with the unexpected and the need for rapid response.

Leadership Challenges
In the second half of this chapter we will address the key issues of leadership in the church. As we noted in chapter one, when an institution finds itself at a "strategic inflection point," there is a growing dissonance between what the leaders think or pretend is happening and what is actually occurring on the ground. Leaders are heard saying one thing while doing another, resulting in loss of confidence and respect among leaders, the pastor and the congregation. All these symptoms destabilize leadership so that leaders become increasingly defensive or abdicate their responsibilities.

Perhaps the emphasis on "servant leadership" espoused by some

pastors has more to do with their insecurity than their humility. In
order to unmask any pretense in this regard John Ortberg, an associate pastor at Willow Creek Community Church, has suggested
that we speak in terms of "leading servants," insisting that leaders
must lead. Servanthood describes a distinctive style and function
of ministry. It is leadership alongside, rather than *from above.*
Leadership is exercised for the benefit of the people we lead, not to
enhance our own reputation or to help get *our own* job done more
effectively. Leaders in the Christian movement are God's
appointed agents to bring about transformation, to set direction
and to monitor the pace.

   Leadership training. Leadership training entails a number of
vital elements. The first concerns the leader's self-identity, not primarily in terms of one's role as leader but in relation to one's
standing before God. Our Lord himself faced this issue in the wilderness when he confronted Satan. Each of three temptations
attacked his very identity as the Son of God. The first temptation
was directed at Christ to presume upon his sonship. "If you are the
Son of God, command this stone to become a loaf of bread." In the
second temptation, following the order in Luke's Gospel, the devil
tempted Jesus to abandon his sonship by promising him all the
kingdoms of the world if he would fall down and worship him; this
was meant to be an outright denial of Jesus' sonship by transfer-
ring his allegiance from his heavenly Father to Satan. The third
temptation was to prove his sonship. The devil, taking Jesus to the
pinnacle of the Jerusalem temple, taunted him by saying, "If you
are the Son of God, throw yourself down" (Lk 4:1-13).[13] Anyone
called to minister in Christ's name is liable to face the same temptations. The devil not only undermines our sense of call, he directs
his attack at our very identity.

   A second important element in leadership training is to identify and develop the leader's gifts. This presents a particular
problem when leadership training is conducted in isolation from
the leader's ministry context. People are not simply born to lead,

as some have claimed; rather, leadership is in large part situational.[14] It is a case of the right person being in the right place at the right time. In one situation, one person will emerge as the leader, while in another, a different and sometimes surprising individual will assume leadership initiative and provide motivation for others. For this reason, leadership training in military and business contexts includes problem solving and performance evaluation in real situations. Those in training are observed dealing with situations both as individuals and in relation to the others involved in the exercise, and their performance is monitored. In relation to the classic theological disciplines, role playing would include situations that test to what extent students can apply their theological, historical and ministerial training to problem solving, planning for a church or ministering outside the context of a local church.

In a poll conducted by the Barna Research Group in 1997 with a sample of 601 pastors, only 5 percent considered their primary gift to be that of leadership. Several questions can be asked: Is this low percentage due to modesty or because respondents have been frustrated in trying to exercise leadership in the past? Is it due to a selection procedure that weeded out people with leadership initiative? Do leadership types not consider ordination? Or does the low percentage reflect a misguided emphasis in their training? It is impossible to say for sure where the problem lies. But without doubt a serious problem does exist in the area of leadership emergence and development that needs to be addressed.

Team building. Lyle Schaller has drawn attention to the shortage of gifted, cohesive and productive staff teams in local churches.[15] This is partly because the vast majority of churches are small and are served by a lone pastor. A lone pastor all too easily becomes a lonely pastor. This is because the way pastors are trained reinforces an independent and individualistic mindset. Schaller comments that "public education places a premium on individualism, self-reliance, and individual performance."[16] This is the model that has been adopted in seminaries until now. Thus the church leaders of tomorrow have been trained in a competitive environment where private study is at the heart of the learning experience—a habit that is hard to break.

Where does the individual student learn to work with a team of peers in addressing issues, dividing tasks and achieving group consensus? These skills are not developed by sitting in straight rows in a classroom environment and working at a carrel in the library. "Theological seminaries are designed to welcome persons who have excelled in an academic environment that rewards individualism and trains these students to go out and function as individuals, not as members of teams."[17]

Another consideration that bears upon this important issue is the increase in the average age of seminary students. This means that students bring into the classroom not only questions but experience and insight often beyond that of the professor in particular areas. This pool of wisdom needs to be recognized as a valuable learning resource for the whole class.

The classroom becomes a conference room in which we work with the material we have read and relate it to experiences from life. This allows for far more interaction both with the professor and with fellow students. The class time can be treated with great flexibility. At appropriate points the class will divide into groups to go over a point. In some instances the group might consist of people from the same area or country of the world, speaking their own language together to get to the heart of the matter. At other times the groups might consist of people from a wide variety of ministry contexts or different parts of the world, so that there can be an exchange with contributions from very different contexts.

Large-sized classes make it harder to achieve satisfactory levels of participation. They also make small-group interaction difficult due to the noise level and the need for group supervision. Teaching assistants can gain valuable experience through interacting with groups and meeting with other teaching assistants and the professor to process the groups' interactions. Another idea is for students, at the beginning of each academic year, to form cohort groups—or study groups—consisting of several students who elect to study together in the same classes. Such partnerships allow students to apply what they are learning to their ministry situations with the benefit of gaining input from their cohorts. These groups are also of great value for students who study by extension. In this case, students interact in a local group, which provides each of them with peer mentoring.

An ability to wear different hats. Pastors are called upon to fulfill a wide variety of roles in leading the local church. In addition to caring for the members at every stage of life and in the many crises that come along, they are also expected to be preacher, teacher and evangelist. They are expected to be managers of the institutions and leaders of the total enterprise. Only in large churches, where there is a pastoral team with each individual contributing particular specialist skills, can each staff member focus on one particular area of ministry. But because most churches are small, the great majority of pastors must function as generalists. The distinctive nature of the call to be a senior pastor entails taking responsibility under God for the spiritual well-being of an entire congregation of believers as well as for leading the community into effective ministry in the world.

Yet many pastors face a problem in relation to their role in the congregation, for, as Philip Kenneson and James Street note in *Selling Out the Church,* "Gone are the days when people respected pastors primarily for their theological insight and learning."[18] The decline in the appeal of the Doctor of Ministry degree is partly because of a desire for a narrower focus and an increase in specialization. "Within a secularized culture of experts, the professional pastor must seek out a realm of expertise that is considered relevant by his or her consumers."[19] Pastors must resist the pressure to fill the role of the expert to satisfy a misplaced consumer mentality. No matter how multitalented pastors might be, they cannot hope to master the wide range of skills required to meet the high number of expectations generated and imposed by the people in the church.

The role of pastors is not to staff the complaints department for the Almighty or to be a general contractor, able to fix anything and everything. The cry for an "expert" to meet needs and resolve difficulties simply reflects an abdication of responsibility by individuals or groups to work together in solving problems, providing support and enlisting commitment. Sometimes it is also used as a strategy to find someone else to blame for one's own failings and foolhardiness.

Making music. Traditional theological education may encourage the pastor to pose as the expert on the basis of the training he or she has received. The purpose of such training, however, is not to make the pastor indispensable in every situation but to develop the necessary skills to facilitate group learning and acceptance of responsibility. Herein lies an inherent weakness, in that the basis of theological education is on absorbing content rather than on developing competencies.

In our understanding of the role of pastoral leadership we have evolved from the "one-man band" (the gender exclusive language here is intentional!) to the conductor of the orchestra. The weakness of the conductor model is that it is still a controlling model of leadership. Within networking organizations the role of the leader is not to be the conductor of an orchestra but to be the leader of a jazz band, to use Max De Pree's apt analogy:

> Jazz-band leaders must choose the music, find the right musicians, and perform—in public. But the effect of the performance depends on so many things—the environment, the volunteers playing in the band, the need for everybody to perform as individuals and as a group, the absolute dependence of the leader on the members of the band, the need of the leader for the followers to play well. What a summary of an organization!
>
> A jazz band is an expression of servant leadership. The leader of a jazz band has the beautiful opportunity to draw the best out of the other musicians. We have much to learn from jazz-band leaders, for jazz, like leadership, combines the unpredictability of the future with the gifts of individuals.[20]

As we have already emphasized, today's culture is characterized by discontinuous change. It is a plan-do environment. Such a context requires an ability to improvise. But this can so easily degenerate into chaos when leaders do not know how to build teams around them. Team building constitutes a whole new area that urgently needs to be addressed in training centers for the church leaders of today and tomorrow. The jazz-band leader, unlike the orchestra conductor, does not have a score in front of him that he can follow. The skill of the conductor is in the area of creative interpretation, while that of the jazz-band leader is in facilitating creative improvisation by every member of the group. Each performance is different, creating a serendipitous experience as each performer makes a free-spirited contribution, while at the same time being at one with the others in the group. Jazz bands cannot simply be assembled on the spot as a group of strangers able to perform together. Time is required for each player to understand the others' personalities and "style."

One predicament of ministry is that it cannot be managed in the sense of being controlled and scheduled to ensure predetermined outcomes. Management, particularly in the realm of the Spirit, is not so much a hard science but a discerned art. Kenneson and Street provide a salutary reminder that "the church may be in no greater danger than when it is led to believe that these risks are under control."[21] They make the valid point that in Scripture there are many examples demonstrating that the church does not always need to know where God is leading or how to get there.[22] This was true both for Abram's venture into Canaan and for Paul's missionary journeys. Apostolic leaders must have a profound understanding of the nature of their mission and be concerned to pursue that mission using all their God-given faculties. Yet at the same time they must remain open to the leading of the Holy Spirit, responding to course corrections and to unexpected, seemingly insurmountable obstacles—which are not always sent by Satan to frustrate progress but may be part of God's overall scheme, the complexity of which we humans cannot hope to fully understand, much less resolve.

Dealing with conflict. One cannot have community without conflict. This is as true in the church as in any other area of life. In some respects the potential for conflict is even greater in the church than elsewhere. This is due to the diversity of constituencies that make up many congregations, the fact that the church is not selective but welcomes all comers, and the fact that the matters of faith and life with which the church deals represent deeply held convictions. Throughout this book we have been discussing ministry in a culture of comprehensive, far-reaching and discontinuous change. In the face of such momentous challenges, people predictably become anxious and self-protective. Kenneson and Street make the following observation:

> We know of many pastors who have been trained in forms of "conflict management" and who thereby assume that conflicts in the church can and should be managed (which usually means suppressed or even defused before they arise). But the church does not (or at least should not) fear conflict the way the world does. For example, a church that grasps the pervasiveness of sin, God's bountiful grace, and its own character as both forgiving and forgiven will approach conflict in a quite different spirit.[23]

You can no more manage conflict than you can manage a wave when surfing. The wave is a given. It is a product of a whole weather system over which surfers have no control. The surfer's delight is to ride the wave without becoming overwhelmed by it. The skill of the pastor in relation to handling conflict is to identify the root cause of the conflict, which might be quite different from the immediate issue. Some conflicts are the result of unfair criticism. Other conflicts arise through mutual misunderstandings that need to be cleared up in calm, respectful dialogue. Leaders themselves might be the cause of conflict by allowing themselves to become involved in triangulation or by becoming abusive. Conflicts can only be resolved as the people involved talk *to* one another and not *about* one another.

Many conflicts are necessary growing pains in the life of a community. If people avoid them or take the opportunity to walk away, they deny themselves an opportunity for growth. Tensions need not be destructive but can prove extremely beneficial as we work patiently through different perceptions and agendas to try to achieve a common mind. Furthermore, leaders must not think that they have to achieve agreement with everybody. In a community where love and trust prevail, we can sometimes agree to disagree.

Leaders have to learn to value the "loyal opposition," and those who find themselves outvoted need the grace to occupy the important role of being just such a one who has been outvoted. Within seminary life at every level—among faculty, administrators and students—valuable lessons need to be learned in how to handle conflict in a Christian manner. Unfortunately the confrontational, litigious tendency of our society has even impacted Christian campuses, sometimes undermining the determination to resolve issues through reconciliation. How can we then hope to take a message of reconciliation to a warring world?

Leadership in the Christian Community

Within a networking environment, leadership does not consist in persons being appointed to positions either by their being proposed or elected through a political ballot. Leadership emerges through demonstrated competence in specific areas. It also entails an ability to work alongside others in such a way that relationships deepen and ideas are generated that give rise to further ideas.

Networking leaders are not jealous of one another's positions. Instead they recognize the gifts of those around them. They do not feel threatened and "upstaged" by persons with greater expertise in areas vital to the success of a project. They are ambitious for the people around them. They encourage new teams to spin off to develop alternative approaches to the same problems or to tackle new issues. Networking leaders see structures in terms of organic interconnectedness and not as an inflexible, mechanistic framework. Organizational charts hide more than they reveal and inhibit more than facilitate the functioning of a community in a culture that is in a state of flux.

In order to prepare students to function in such an environment, seminary courses need to contain surprise elements. For in the course of ministry in local churches, pastors are confronted with issues without warning, with the ringing of the phone or a knock at the door or a question posed across a restaurant table. Students will need to be challenged to share what they know without prior notice. In the midst of learning about biblical, systematic and historical theology, students need to be presented with contemporary problems to test their ability to contextualize and apply what they are learning. These challenges should not be presented in an individualized, competitive manner, but through the formation of ad hoc groups to address the issues, thereby pooling knowledge and insights.

Leadership defined. George Barna provides a definition of leadership that is compatible with the considerations that have been outlined above. "A Christian leader is someone who is called by God to lead and possess virtuous character and effectively motivates, mobilizes resources, and directs people toward the fulfillment of a jointly embraced vision from God."[24] In an uncertain and rapidly changing environment, it is even more important that leaders demonstrate courage and dependability. Also, as values are being questioned and renegotiated, character is as important as charisma and competencies. Before people are prepared to follow someone, they want to know that the person is one they can trust.

When leaders find that they are marching past the edge of the map into uncharted territory, they must be prepared to learn as they go. They also need to develop the skills to consolidate without halting their advance, because once momentum is lost, it requires much more energy to regain it. Also there is a high risk entailed when embarking on any new enterprise. Just as there is a high failure rate among start-up businesses, so there is a high failure rate among new ministries and churches.

Yet it is groups that venture into new territory that demonstrate growth and spiritual vitality. Frustration and failure are essential and valuable ingredients in the learning process. Bearing in mind the vulnerability of any community of witness that seeks to extend ministry into new segments of society, leaders need to be highly supportive of their ministry teams. They share in the disappointment of defeats as well as in the celebration of victories.

Richard Farson strikes a wise balance in placing leaders and managers alongside one another, not as agents of control but as facilitators and empowerers who provide a catalytic presence to one another.

> In my experience, effective leaders and managers do not regard control as the main concern. Instead, they approach situations sometimes as learners, sometimes as teachers, sometimes as both. They turn confusion into understanding. They see a bigger picture. They trust the wisdom of the group. Their strength is not in control alone, but in other qualities—position, sensitivity, tenacity, patience, courage, firmness, enthusiasm, wonder.[25]

Leaders, teachers and managers. Just as it takes a disciple to make a disciple, so it takes a leader to mentor leaders. Herein lies a problem that we have already alluded to, namely that pastors and potential leaders in the various ministries of the church are not, as a rule, mentored by individuals with leadership gifts. Professors may be leaders in the world of ideas, but they do not have experience in leading a high-risk enterprise, which requires attracting talented and committed people and raising the necessary capital for the enterprise to function. Many seminaries have no department of Christian leadership, which means that those students who later emerge as leaders do so because they gain their leadership abilities elsewhere.

It is important for pastors to learn good study habits because teaching is an important part of their leadership role. They influence through teaching, and pastoral surveys indicate that the majority of pastors consider teaching to be one of their primary gifts, which incidentally is the gift most affirmed in seminary. A good student relishes an intellectual challenge and is more comfortable in the study than in either the office or the marketplace. Teachers love an audience but struggle to know how their teaching can move people into action. Preaching and teaching can all too easily become ends in themselves.[26]

The classroom is, on one hand, too intimidating an environment to encourage leadership. Yet on the other hand, it is too safe an environment for the academically inclined. For a number of years I taught a class in personal evangelism. Such were the timetable pressures that most of the students lived with—between studies, work, family responsibilities, church commitments and commuting, little could be done outside of class. Trying to teach evangelism under such constraints seemed as futile as teaching people to ski down the corridor!

Richard John Neuhaus underscores the need for theological training to embrace the students' spiritual formation rather than focusing almost exclusively on their religious education:

> What is needed is not the training of religious technicians but the formation of spiritual leaders. It is important for seminaries to impart skills and competencies; it is more important to ignite conviction and courage to lead. The language of facilitation is cool and low risk. The language of priesthood and prophecy and the pursuit of holiness is impassioned and perilous. . . . The pursuit of holiness is not the quest for the Holy Grail. . . . It is rather a question of actualizing the gift that is already ours.[27]

The other entrapment that undermines pastors' ability to lead is the pressure to spend the bulk of their time in managing the minutiae of daily church life. In churches where there is only one paid staff member, the lay leadership may try to abdicate their responsibilities, taking the attitude that they pay the pastor to run the church. When leaders become swamped by details, they soon lose any awareness of a unified vision and withdraw into survival mode.

The formation of spiritual leaders. It is worthwhile to compare and contrast the typical leaders emerging from seminaries to those emerging among the "new paradigm" churches. In one sense it is unfair to generalize because there are many individuals among traditional churches and new paradigm churches who bear the characteristics of the other. However, while admitting a degree of overlap, there is a distinctive new paradigm type of leader. These leaders tend to be at the younger end of the boomer bracket, and increasingly they are drawn from Generation X. This is to be expected from a younger movement. The average age of their congregations is probably two decades younger than that of traditional churches. These new paradigm church leaders tend to be initiative takers who are prepared to accept the risks involved in innovative ministries. They are internally motivated, creative and sometimes even gregarious, and they surround themselves with people who share many of these same characteristics. They are the prime influence for recruiting and mentoring more leaders to maintain further momentum in the movement.[28] Donald Miller, who makes these observations, then asks:

> But why are the mainline denominations not creating leaders with the same qualities? One possibility is that their selection and acculturation process weeds out people with innate leadership ability. Successive levels of higher education may domesticate leadership, rewarding those who think and write well but are not risk takers and entrepreneurial innovators. Conversely, it is possible that the young leaders of new paradigm churches—in part because of their lack of education—do not realize the odds against them in building a megachurch. Still another possibility is that the leaders of the megachurches simply happened to be in the right place at the right time and rose to the occasion.[29]

Making leadership training available. We have already mentioned the need for training to be made more widely available on a multilevel basis. The problem with the present system is that the bottom rungs of the ladder are missing, and the ladder itself is far too narrow. Once students have been accepted into seminary, their learning program needs to be designed on a customized basis that bears in mind their previous experience, gifts and calling. At the same time, the training may need to cover a core curriculum to ensure that all students have a firm foundation on which to build the more specialized aspects of their training. Students must accept responsibility for themselves in shaping their own programs and in ensuring that they learn in such a way that they will continue to benefit from what they have learned.

In the new paradigm church setting the focus of ministry specialization is not as much to equip students to serve on multiple-staff teams in large churches or in parachurch agencies as it is to equip them for apostolic ministry in pioneer situations. The training is designed to produce the church planters of tomorrow—those people who will be comfortable and competent ministering outside the structures of the local church as witnesses and team builders in pieces that make up the mosaic of urban, industrialized and high-tech societies.

Surviving an unpredictable future. How can any educational or training institute equip church leaders with the necessary tools to deal with the range of situations they are likely to encounter in the years of ministry that lie ahead of them? Any "tool kit" approach will soon prove deficient because we do not know what lies ahead. As we have already noted, these are not the times for long-range planning in any endeavor. "Planning is built upon the flawed idea that it is possible to predict the future. Yet the future almost always takes us by surprise. Since there is simply no good way to predict future events, there is no sure way to plan for them."[30]

At the heart of training must lie a thorough knowledge of Scripture, coupled with the exegetical skills to apply the Word of God to contemporary situations, many of which will have no direct correspondence with the situations addressed in the biblical text. A reliance on proof texts as a sure-fire way of settling issues will prove woefully inadequate. There must be a much stronger emphasis on spiritual formation to ensure survival in a high-stress and culturally hostile environment. In a postmodern culture the pastor is likely to receive far fewer "strokes" than in bygone generations. Also, training must offer healthy leadership models. It should provide a mentoring experience that will be so valued by students that they will seek other mentors in the future to help them pursue lifelong learning. Finally, learning opportunities must be provided throughout a person's years of ministry to address Christian responses to new situations, current events and the vital topics of the day.

Implementation

1. Establish a liaison group between the seminary and a consortium of churches to evaluate current programs and identify future needs.

2. Identify a core curriculum of traditional theological disciplines, which are team taught with a facilitator to explore the ministry implications of selected topics.

3. Team-teach ministry courses, with a local pastor providing the case studies.

4. Establish a more flexible structure, encouraging new configurations of scholars and practitioners working on multidisciplinary projects and serving particular constituencies.

5. Make the resources of the seminary much more widely available through extension sites and Web-based courses.

6. Increase the range of programs on a mix-and-match course basis.

7. Recognize the importance of mentoring in the educational and training process. Employ mutual mentoring with professors, with peers, with spiritual advisors and with apprentices sharing life lessons and providing encouragement. Having to teach others is one of the best ways of reinforcing what one is learning.

five

From Following Celebrities
to Encountering Saints

I n the previous chapter we considered the implications of the major cultural shifts and their impact on the church in relation to the training of the next generation of pastors. We now turn our attention to the leader as a model of Christian spirituality. We will focus on two main concerns. First, we will consider the nature of the relationship between the leader and those who follow. Second, we will look at the character, integrity and spirituality of the leader. The basic question is not how they perform but how well they know God and whether the way in which they live and serve the church reflects that intimacy.

Over forty years ago A. W. Tozer made the comment that it was increasingly difficult to get Christians to meetings where God was the chief attraction. Since that time the celebrity focus of evangelical Christianity has been further enhanced by television shows, the video market and the emergence of media-wise megachurches eager to build up and promote the image of their pastor. Much of the Christian publishing world is also driven by the need for celebrity authors who generate big sales. Being an evangelical superstar places the individual on a precarious pedestal of fickle popularity; it also undermines authentic spirituality by emphasizing publicity hype and image at the expense of substance.

Fortunately, many good Christian leaders are honest enough not to believe their own publicity. They are humble people who are embarrassed about the superlatives that surround their every performance. Yet they find themselves trapped by the culture of modernity that has permeated the evangelical world, especially in the United States, where there is more marketing in religious matters. Os Guinness asserts that evangelicalism and fundamentalistism have become the most worldly traditions in the church.[1]

I believe that we are beginning to see a welcome course correction. There is a new demand for honesty and accountability in the wake of the highly publicized scandals surrounding some well-known televangelists and unscrupulous pastors. And their exposure and demise is but the tip of the iceberg. The increasing tensions experienced by Christian leaders at all levels of the church and within many paraparochial organizations as the church finds itself stretched on the rack between the pulls of modernity and postmodernity has proved unbearable to many. Casualties abound, consisting both of those who have deserted the ranks and those who have surrendered to addictive behavior patterns as their way of escape, only to find that they lead them into even graver entrapment. Many Christian workers are in rehabilitation programs in an effort to put back their broken lives and deal with their self-destructive habits.

In today's world one's sense of well-being and security cannot be found in one's professional position as a church leader. Pastors are increasingly aware that they cannot find the answers to effectiveness or survival in either their training or their ministry skills and experience. As never before they are seeking to be renewed spiritually and to discover and strengthen their identity in Christ as forgiven sinners and adopted sons and daughters. The overemphasis on the Holy Spirit to the neglect of the Father and the Son, which was character-

istic of so many churches in some branches of the charismatic movement from the 1960s to the 1980s, is being corrected by a more
balanced appreciation of the three Persons of the Trinity.[2] There is a
welcome fresh appreciation of the distinctive, complementary and
mutually dependent roles of the three Persons as they function as
community in unity.

The answers to pastoral effectiveness depend not on one's ability
to develop the charisma, communication skills and management
acumen of pastors leading superchurches but on one's authenticity
as a follower of Christ. Most of us do not have an extraordinary
combination of gifts and are not in locations where we can expand
our facilities to attract large crowds. Yet we can still play a significant role as part of a network of Christian communities, developing
reproducible units that will facilitate the church's continuing expansion.

Once relieved of the pressure to emulate celebrities, pastors are
freed not only to be themselves but to become the authentic person
that the gospel frees them to realize. As we move from modernity to
postmodernity, the church must focus on saints, not celebrities.
Poets and prophets must replace the pulpiteers. The spiritual superficiality that has characterized so much church leadership in recent
decades has resulted in spiritually shallow churches. Congregational
members seldom rise above the level of their leaders.

Confusion in the Search for Authentic Spirituality

While it is true that a significant number of boomers returned to
church in the 1980s, an even larger percentage did not return. For an
increasing percentage of the American population, the chasm
between church and society has been widened by the arrival and
growing influence of the children of the boomers. To a much greater
extent than previous generations, Gen Xers have not been exposed
to Bible teaching and worship experiences through Sunday school
attendance.

Syncretistic spirituality divorced from institutional religion. If boomers have customized the Christian faith, then their offspring have created their own religious beliefs. They have celebrated the diversity present in a pluralistic society that affirms toleration of other faiths and alternative lifestyles. The predominant mindset is, "If your beliefs work for you, that's just fine!" George Barna's research corroborates this viewpoint. He states, "For the most part, Americans consider the major faith groups interchangeable. . . . Indeed, given people's underlying assumption that religious faith exists for the personal benefit of the individual, it is only natural for them to assume that defining, organizing, and practicing spirituality in ways that satisfy their personal needs is completely legitimate."[3]

Like their boomer parents, Gen Xers are deeply suspicious of religious institutions, from which they are a step further removed. Unlike their parents, the majority of Gen Xers did not attend Sunday school, so they are ignorant of the basic stories, personalities and teachings of the Bible. Many have no personal memory of the church but see it through the eyes of disillusioned parents and cynical media idols. Wade Clarke Roof writes in regard to the boomers, who have been influential in shaping the attitudes of their children, "As has always been the case, the normative faiths of Americans are amazingly fluid and flexible. But especially today a dynamic, democratic religious culture is evolving, its many elements are recombining, mixing and matching with one another to create new syncretisms."[4] Tom Beaudoin explains how the trend begun by the boomers has been radicalized by Gen Xers.

> Xers did not invent this interest in paganism and mysticism; they learned it from their baby boomer elders. Generation Xers, however, are much more immersed now than boomers in experimentation, alienation, and pop-cultured religiousness, because we were steeped in popular culture, and on our own, at an earlier age.[5]

As I will argue in the next chapter, seeker-sensitive worship held in an auditorium devoid of religious symbols and led by polished, professional performers who are removed from the tattered and tawdry world of daily experience holds little appeal for many Gen Xers.

They learn by being involved, not by passive observation. Their spiritual appetites are more likely to be whetted by life situations that leave the involved onlooker grappling with an unsolved problem because they know that life is not tidy or filled with predictable, happy endings. Their spiritual awareness is triggered by symbols and rituals both ancient and relevant. If the Christian church fails to rediscover its own rich heritage, created in *pre*literate societies, it will find it increasingly difficult to hold a generation shaped by a *post*literate culture.

Irreverent irony. Gen Xers delight in shocking religious traditionalists, to the extent that their more irreverent statements are all too readily interpreted as verging on blasphemy. Tom Beaudoin cautions against interpreting their irreverence in this way because by so doing we miss an important challenge that the church needs to hear from Generation X. His explanation of their confrontational attitude is particularly insightful.

Gen X's culture of virtuality, of both reality and its imitation, uses irony to communicate religious ideas. Irony is often misunderstood, especially when Xers use it, as a purely negative attitude toward the world. Irony mocks, to be sure, but it does not just poke fun. Irony undoes the supposedly self-evident meaning of a statement, idea or image, and empties that image of what it was previously thought to contain. Irony on the part of Xers is a way of marking distance from what is received as religious in order to collapse that religiousness playfully, to iron(ize) it flat. Then through pop culture, Xers suggest something else in its place, however vague that replacement may be. To operate ironically, as Gen X pop culture does, is not merely to take a negative, dismissive tone. It is to engage for the sake of reclamation—but only after the devastation of an engagement that destroys. Irony sucks the air out of its object, only to reinflate it later.[6]

If Beaudoin is accurate in his interpretation, then Christians need to avoid going on the defensive. Instead need to learn to decode the gospel message. If the Jesus the Gen Xers are ridiculing is not the authentic Jesus as presented in the biblical witness but rather a pastiche, a commercialized and sentimentalized Jesus, then they are making an important point. A blanket denunciation is not an adequate response; rather, the church needs to engage with Gen Xers so that together, in a biblically informed dialogue, they may come to a more comprehensive understanding of the person of Jesus. Gen Xers will also challenge us to turn our orthodoxy into *orthopraxis* (a term that signifies living out what we say we believe).

Eclectic sources. Wade Clark Roof identifies how the religious landscape has been transformed among boomers. It was among them that we saw the reemergence of spirituality beginning in the mid-1960s. Yet this movement was diverse and eclectic, drawing upon Eastern, nativistic and pre-Christian spiritual beliefs and experiences. The boomers passed on their multilayered belief and practice to the next generation, which in turn has radicalized it still further. Their emphasis was not so much on developing an integrated and comprehensive belief system as on discovering and developing techniques to bring about the transformation of selves.[7] In their spiritual quest baby boomers explored Eastern religions, evangelical and fundamentalist teaching, mysticism and New Age movements, goddess worship and other ancient religious rituals, and twelve-step recovery programs.

With their suspicion of institutional religion, their rebellion against being told what they must believe, and their strong commitment to freedom of choice, Gen Xers are eclectic in their approach to religion. Theirs is a pick-and-choose spirituality, cobbled together from an amazing variety of sources. Seeming contradictions between the sources are simply overlooked or held in paradox. "They move freely in and out, across religious boundaries; many combine elements from various traditions to create their own personal tailor-made meaning systems. Choice, so much a part of life for this generation, now expresses itself in dynamic and fluid religious styles."[8]

If the boomers plotted the course, then Gen Xers have set the sail and have been blown much further in the direction of radical pluralism. They are able to juxtapose Christian and pagan sym-

bols, the worship of Mother Earth, and Satanism. The result is
not a coherent syncretistic pluralism but rather the holding
together of a ragbag of disjointed elements. However, this lack of
focus should not be interpreted as indicating superficiality
because the search for significance through transcendence is genuine and deeply felt. It is the product of a mindset shaped by a
postmodern worldview.

*The relationship between right teaching and authentic experi-
ence.* Previous generations of evangelicals, and some leading theologians among their ranks today, place a great emphasis on divinely
revealed propositional truth. For Gen Xers what is true is what is
true for you and is verified by your own experience. This goes one
step further than the pragmatism of boomers; it is based not simply
on pragmatic outcomes but on deep-rooted significance, contributing to one's self-identity.

From an evangelical standpoint, God speaks decisively through
Scripture, and God's judgments and promises are valid for his people in every age. Yet the people's understanding of God, in both the
Old and the New Testament, came as a result of encountering the
presence of God in the midst of a great variety of situations. Propositions were not simply parachuted from heaven but were forged on
the anvil of life's hard knocks. Such contextualizing of revelation
provides a helpful approach with Gen Xers. Leith Anderson underlines the significance of the new paradigm presented by Gen Xers,
whose thinking has been shaped by postmodernism:

> The old paradigm taught that if you had the right teaching you will
> experience God. The new paradigm says that if you experience God,
> you will have the right teaching. This may be disturbing for many
> who assume that propositional truth must always precede and dictate
> religious experience. That mind-set is the product of systematic the-
> ology and has much to contribute. . . . However, biblical theology
> looks to the Bible for a pattern of experience followed by proposi-
> tion. The experience of the Exodus from Egypt preceded the record-
> ing of the Exodus in the Bible. The experience of the crucifixion, the
> resurrection and Pentecost all predated the propositional declaration

of those events in the New Testament. It is not so much that one is right and the other is wrong; it is more a matter of the perspective one takes on God's touch and God's truth.[9]

It is not for us to dictate how God will make himself known to a new generation. It may be through experiences that will trigger a soul search, drawing them to God revealed in Jesus Christ. Only as they encounter in the Scriptures the truth they seek will they recognize it as the "pearl of great price" for which they are prepared to sell all that they have. In Wesleyan terminology, we are speaking here of "prevenient grace" leading to a convergence of God's touch with God's truth.

Replacing word with image. Even more than their boomer parents, Gen Xers are influenced by television. Theirs is a postliterary culture for which sound and image have largely replaced the printed word. Wade Clarke Roof underlines the significance of television in relation to communication. "Perhaps the most important impact of TV was that it replaced the word with the image: Henceforth the dominant medium would be the fleeting, discontinuous flow of electromagnetic pictures. Instancy and intimacy would be the distinguishing features of this new medium; seeing, not reading, would become the basis for believing—a major transformation in mode of communication."[10] Their thought process is lateral rather than linear, making random connections, or no connections at all. Tom Beaudoin describes their culture as "a culture of moments," a dizzying mania of montage. Transience and disposability characterize their world.

Symbols of the sacred. In the decades from the 1940s to the 1980s, the culture of modernity was at its peak. Secularism was unassailable, and worship in churches was cluttered with an alien traditionalism characterized by archaic language, liturgical actions and sensory images that became obstacles instead of channels of communication. Partly in response and partly in reaction to that state of affairs, new nondenominational community churches emerged with a clearly focused mission to reach out to the dechurched population. In order to do this effectively, the most appropriate worship style was informal and contemporary, and the worship sanctuary was devoid of Christian symbols and ecclesiastical trappings. Church buildings more closely resembled the color-coordinated decor of a Nordstrom store than a traditional house of worship. The sanctuary became an auditorium where you could hear and see the proceedings from the comfort of your theater-style seat.

That state of affairs is now changing rapidly as we usher in the new millennium. As Gen Xers look forward in apprehension, they look back for a lost sense of security. As we noted in the previous chapter, nostalgia is in. Furthermore, this generation is one that responds to a multisensory message. Some of the churches reaching out to Gen Xers resemble the seeker-sensitive churches of the 1980s in some respects but even go beyond them in informality, a relational style of communication and an updated contemporary style of worship. In other respects they are very different. They combine ancient forms of worship with the modern, ranging in style from Gregorian chants to Hip Hop, and using icons, candles and incense as aids to worship, plus strobe lights and knee-high clouds!

There are regional and cultural variations to these trends in worship style. The new trends are less evident in churches reaching out to the older Gen Xers and in areas such as California where historical amnesia is prevalent. I believe this is reflected in Donald Miller's research into the Calvary Chapel, the Vineyard and Hope Chapel in southern California. In regard to what he describes as "symbols of the sacred," he argues,

> The church architecture, stained glass, statues, frescoes, incense, candles, and all the liturgical activities may play an important role in guiding the shift from everyday to religious consciousness. But for many baby boomers and Generation Xers, these conventional triggers to religious consciousness no longer work because they are associated with images of false or dead establishment religion.
>
> Reformist religion has the choice of scrapping the old symbols or

trying to resuscitate them. New paradigm churches have taken the former approach, by and large.[11]

While this may remain true for people who have many memories of boring worship experiences, it is not true for increasing numbers of young people who have been raised with little or no reference to the church. Some have become fascinated by the worship styles and meditation techniques of non-Christian religions and come with an open attitude and a desire to experiment. The approach to God that they encounter in the Christian church must be equally holistic. Whatever the worship style, Miller addresses the heart of the matter when he describes worship in the three movements of new-paradigm churches he studied as "a form of sacred lovemaking, transcending the routinized rituals that so often structure the human-divine communication."[12]

The goal of the worship experience is not to bring about an altered state of consciousness as a way for the devotees to detach themselves from the mundane experiences of daily life. It is not an escapist activity but an empowering one—the whole of life is infused with a sense of God's presence. Donald Miller found no evidence that the people who have these experiences are psychologically unhealthy or dysfunctional. To the contrary, he maintains that people who experience altered states of consciousness may be psychologically *healthier* than those who remain confined in the limited perspective of the rational, empirical world. He relates their experiences to instances in both the Old and New Testaments, and, we might add, to the mystical tradition within the church throughout history. He challenges the dismissive attitudes of reductionalistic rationalists. "Rather than dismiss these experiences a priori, perhaps we should acknowledge that religious people of all times, of all ages, and, very likely, of all traditions have had mysterious encounters with the sacred that the rational mind, and more particularly, Enlightenment science, simply cannot comprehend."[13]

Communicating among Gen Xers. The spiritual search of Generation X does not consist primarily in an intellectual quest. This is not a generation seeking answers to the philosophical questions that have preoccupied Christian apologists, such as arguments for the existence of God, the origin of the universe, the believability of miracles or even the deity of Christ. They are not interested in listening to people who presume to have all of the answers. Rather, they want to meet people who have a transforming relationship with God.

As people who have created their own reality out of many disparate elements, they are careful not to judge the faith choices of others. They want a place where they can relate and contribute. Otherwise they will drop out.[14] They are drawn to Christian communities that are prepared to operate from the margins, in an attitude of humble witness. Polished performances and impeccable images turn them off. Barna reminds us that they are suspicious of bigness, of advertising and ego trips. They want something: churches that are down-to-earth and unpretentious."[15]

Gen Xers want to see individuals who demonstrate God-inspired service to their fellow human beings. They are attracted to people who are prepared to speak the truth whatever the personal cost. They respect honest people who are prepared to admit that there are things they don't understand as well as to own up to their own shortcomings. And as we move into a new millennium, they want people who have hope for the future. The source of that hope is not confidence in human abilities to solve the intractable problems of war and peace, epidemics and environmental damage. The hope arises not from an apocalyptic vision in which the universe is dissolved in blinding light or searing heat but from a vision in which there will be a transformative divine intervention. Theirs is a faith prepared to live with ambiguity. Gen Xers don't mind question marks. It's the prospect of an unfinished sentence marking the moment of oblivion that is so scary.

Jesus, during his earthly ministry, was moved with compassion at the sight of the crowds who were like sheep without a shepherd. We need to be reminded that there was no shortage of religious professionals in his day. The problem was that the rabbis were not in touch with the majority of the people and dismissed them as lawbreakers. In contrast, Jesus was just as at ease talking to people on the roadside and the hillside as in the synagogue or temple courtyard, perhaps even more so. Regarding today's generation, which is wandering in a spiritual wilderness, or more appropriately, getting lost in a spiritual jungle, Tom Beaudoin, speaking from within the Gen X cultural context, alerts the church to the fact that

> here is a generation that stays away from most churches in droves but loves songs about God and Jesus, a generation that would score very low on any standard piety scale but at times seems almost obsessed with saints, visions, and icons in all shapes and sizes. These are the young people who, Styrofoam cups of cappuccino in hand, crowd around the shelves of New Age spirituality titles in the local book market and post thousands of religious and quasi-religious notes on the bulletin boards in cyberspace. And remember, it was this puzzling and allegedly secular generation that turned out a million of its representatives to welcome Pope John Paul II to that most secular of cities, Paris, France, in the waning weeks of summer 1997. No wonder the classifiers simply throw up their hands in defeat. Like the God envisioned by the mystics of the via negativa, it seems that whatever one says about Generation X, one must immediately say just the opposite in the next breath.[16]

The diversity represented by Generation X and even more by the next generation, who are variously called the "Mosaics" and the "Millennials," means that no single approach is going to be appropriate for all. The one-size-fits-all approach that characterized evangelical outreach to the returning boomers was successful in reaching only a segment of that generation, as Wade Clark Roof's research reveals. In responding to the challenges presented by the generations that follow them, church leaders must resist the strong temptation to simply reproduce a single model that seems to be making an impact. Instead we must recognize that there may be a wide variety of models that are equally effective alternatives for reaching different subgroups. In addition to surveying the contemporary scene, there may also be valuable and long-neglected insights from the past that need to be rediscovered and reinterpreted.

Resources to Be Mined

Just as we have much to learn from the New Testament about a closer walk with God, so also we can tap into the experiences of those who have earnestly sought a more intimate relationship with him over nearly two millennia of Christian history. Many of these rich streams have been overlooked or deliberately avoided because of doctrinal suspicions and abuses through going to extremes in the practice of spiritual disciplines. We have also tended to compare the best of our own tradition with the worst aspects in other traditions, rather than examine with honesty the spiritual impoverishment of much of contemporary evangelicalism. But the growing recognition of the nominality within our ranks and the disturbing amount of evidence of spiritual superficiality has led many to reexamine other traditions.

Yet our suspicion of other traditions is not the only explanation for our spiritual impoverishment. We have also neglected the deep wells within our own tradition—the wells of our Puritan and Holiness heritage. Our superficiality is a product of our secularization, which has caused us to look to our shallow and contaminated human resources, only to discover that our cisterns are cracked and empty (Jer 2:13).

A further obstacle to our appreciating the benefits of Catholic, Orthodox and Celtic spirituality is their association with monasticism. We may admire from afar the dedication of monks and nuns to their daily routine, with time allocated throughout the day and night for times of prayer. We may even benefit from visiting a house of prayer for a retreat lasting a few days. But how can their disciplines be made accessible to people who earn their living and meet their pressing family responsibilities in the workaday world?

As a starting point, the insight of Diogenes Allen is pertinent. He says the main purpose of the contemplative life is "to perceive all things in relation to God and to know God's continuous presence in and through them."[17] It is this integration that is sadly lacking within contemporary Western Christianity. Many laypersons find that the church is disconnected from the issues that concern them through the remainder of the week.[18]

Catholic and Orthodox spirituality. As soon as we mention Catholic spirituality, a number of names leap to mind of individuals who have gained the attention of the evangelical world. We think of Mother Teresa's example of humble, self-denying service, of one who saw the castoffs from society with the eyes of Christ and heard Christ's appeal to her through them. We think of Henri Nouwen's depth of spiritual understanding, which was not only the fruit of his scholarly life but which flowered through his immersion in the L'Arche Community and his bonding with the mentally challenged, whose needs he served and from whom he derived profound spiritual insights. We think of Thomas Merton and the many thousands he has introduced to a deeper life of prayer through the retreats he has led and his many books.

From the Orthodox tradition, leaders like Archbishop Anthony Bloom and Kalistos Ware have helped Western Christians to discover the spiritual depth and appreciate the God-directed focus of worship. A healthy change is underway as more and more evangelicals are coming to recognize that they have more to learn from saints than from celebrities.

"Lectio divina." Traditionally, evangelicals have placed great emphasis on the importance of sustaining a daily "quiet time" as an essential discipline in maintaining one's walk with God and of growing in the Christian life. Many individuals could not maintain the daily discipline, while others reacted against a perceived legalism and opted to read the Bible as and when the Spirit moved them. One would hope that they would have read it with greater, not less, frequency than prevailed when they were driven by "legalism."

People were demotivated by a number of factors. The problem for some people was the lucky-dip approach they had adopted, consisting of a random opening of the Bible for inspiration. Others fell away because they set themselves too rigorous a schedule and became discouraged when they dropped hopelessly behind. Yet others were overly cerebral in their study of the Scriptures, with their mind disconnected from their heart and will. Then there were those who gave up because they failed to understand the text, either because they couldn't make sense of the ancient version they were using or because they became preoccupied with obscure and difficult passages.

Some people who had given up on Bible reading, or who had been grinding on in a mechanical way, have come to appreciate afresh the rich spiritual treasure of Scripture by learning to meditate on the text. It is a simple exercise but one capable of jump starting a dead spiritual battery by cultivating the art of meditation—lost due to the noise, rush, distractions and soul-neglect of modern living. The first step is to center upon God by relaxing your body, breathing deeply and placing yourself in the presence of God. The second is to read a passage from the Bible of between ten and twenty verses out loud, not once but twice, pausing to let the meaning sink in. Then turn it over in your mind, asking God by his Spirit within you to draw your attention to what is important and to what you might easily miss either because it is too familiar or too unwelcome. Express the thoughts that come to mind as brief, specific prayers. Finally, rest silently in God's presence.[19]

Biblically inspired meditation carries over into contemplation, which, drawing upon accumulated spiritual insight, opens up into a wider field of vision. Thomas Merton reminds us that there is no fruitful contemplation without imagination.

Imagination is the creative task of making symbols, joining things together in such a way that they throw new light on each other and on everything around them. The imagination is a discovering faculty, a faculty for seeing relationships, for seeing meanings that are special and even quite new. The imagination is something which enables us to discover unique present meaning in a given moment of our lives.

Without imagination the contemplative life can be extremely dull and fruitless.[20]

The practice of *lectio divina* (literally, "divine reading," signifying meditation on Scripture) is especially appropriate for boomers and Gen Xers who have already experimented with various non-Christian meditation techniques for looking inward to find divine light. *Lectio divina* provides them with a more dependable biblical alternative.[21]

Respiratory prayer. What I mean by "respiratory prayer" is the kind of regular, habitual praying that is the spiritual equivalent of breathing to sustain life. This has been popularized within the Orthodox tradition by the nineteenth century account *The Way of the Pilgrim,* by an anonymous Russian layperson, which has been translated and is available in a number of versions. The Jesus prayer is a simple prayer consisting of a longer version, "Lord Jesus Christ, Son of God, have mercy upon me, a sinner," or more simply, "Jesus, have mercy on me," which is said over and over again.

Our immediate response to such a way of praying may be to dismiss it as vain repetition, and certainly there is danger of such a practice degenerating into a *mantra.* However, correctly used, it is a way of overcoming distractions or obsessive anxieties by disciplining the mind to focus on Jesus. It is a form of knocking at heaven's door until we are calm and centered enough for that door to be opened. Diogenes Allen explains it well in stating, "The Jesus prayer is simply another way to lead us from discursive thought and prayer ('indirect' knowledge of God) to nondiscursive thought and prayer—('direct' knowledge of God), or silent contemplation (in Greek, *hesychia)*."[22] It is a form of prayer that one can maintain throughout the normal activities of the day. It develops the attitude to life expressed in George Herbert's famous lines

Teach me, my God and King,
In all things thee to see,
And what I do in anything,
To do it as for thee.

Or in the words attributed to Bernard of Clairvaux:

> Jesus, the very thought of Thee
> With sweetness fills my breast;
> But sweeter far Thy face to see,
> And in Thy presence rest.
>
> Jesus, our only joy be Thou,
> As Thou our prize wilt be;
> Jesus, be Thou our glory now,
> And through eternity.

For the many people who have been introduced to yoga and New Age meditation techniques, the Jesus prayer provides a Christian alternative to a seemingly meaningless mantra that may turn out to become a vortex leading into demonic bondage.

The influence of the Taizé community. Taizé is a village in Burgundy, in eastern France, which has become world-renowned through the ecumenical community located there. The community was founded by Swiss-born Brother Roger, and since the 1950s it has attracted thousands of young people each year from all over Europe and beyond. They go to be part of the daily rhythm of the community, which involves private prayer, eating together, joining in small groups and gathering for prayer each morning, midday and evening. The distinctive style of worship practiced at Taizé involves the repetitive singing of simple chants, which woo the worshiper into the presence of God, followed by extended periods of silence.

The Taizé experience has caught the attention of many mainline churches—Episcopal, Presbyterian and Methodist—among which it has been particularly appealing to the younger boomers and the Gen Xers. Although of a very different style from the worship currently prevailing in the new paradigm churches of southern California researched by Donald Miller, it could be described, equally appropriately, as "spiritual lovemaking." Some of those churches that were also impacted by the charismatic movement find the Taizé style of worship even more popular than the more boisterous prayer and praise services. The singing is reflective, as Brother Roger explains it, concerned with going down deep rather than with being upbeat. It is another sign of a new day dawning, and the long-standing appeal of Taizé indicates that the change in style is more than a passing fad.

Celtic spirituality. There is also a growing fascination with Celtic Christianity as one of the earliest traditions in the Christian church. Its identity is distinct from the Western Roman tradition and has a closer affinity to the Orthodoxy of the desert fathers and of Byzantium. It is found in Ireland, Scotland, Wales, the Isle of Man and Brittany. The exploding interest in Celtic culture and spirituality is evident in the popularity of Celtic poetry, Irish dance and university-based Celtic studies programs. Within evangelicalism in the United Kingdom, Celtic rhythms and instrumental accompaniments have surpassed soft rock tempos in popularity. What insights can we draw from this ancient Christian tradition that might resonate with faith for the new millennium? For the insights that follow in this section, I am indebted to the work of Esther de Waal.[23]

The first emphasis of Celtic Christians is on life as a journey. The outward journey is taken in response to an inner prompting and signifies "a passionate conviction that they must undertake what was essentially an inner journey. Ready to go wherever the Spirit might take them, seeing themselves as *hospites mundi,* 'guests of the world,' what they are seeking is the place of their resurrection, the resurrected self, the true self in Christ, which is for all of us our true home."[24]

Emphasis is placed on the *going* rather than on *arriving* at one's destination at some holy place, believing that "I shall not find Christ at the end of the journey unless he accompanies me along the way."[25] This emphasis on venturing and process is appealing to Gen Xers. We must bear in mind that the persons to whom we are witnessing have already embarked on their spiritual journey, so we need to discover where they are at the present time.

As in the repetition of the Jesus prayer, Celtic spirituality nurtures a life of prayer in which God is acknowledged in all of life's mundane activities. In this ancient tradition there is a rich variety of brief prayers associated with the banking of the fire, the making of beds, the spinning, sewing, weaving, farming, cooking and so on. The simple prayers see in all of these activities a parable of the spiritual life. It is almost as though each action takes on sacramental significance.

The songs and poems of a rural people have close affinity with the Psalms, which also occupied a central place in the prayer life of the people. Each psalm was given a prayer heading so that it could be prayed more readily. The God of the Israelites was intimately involved in the whole of creation. Yet there is no pantheism here. Another great characteristic of Celtic prayer is its constant references to the Persons of the Trinity. In contrast to the Roman tradition, the Persons of the Triune God are regarded not in abstract philosophical terms but, in their distinctive but interrelated aspects, in terms of their engagement with people. The Trinity steps right out of the creed into the real world.

The Celtic peasant's awareness of the divine presence was inspired by the poets of the monastic life to which they felt so closely connected, who dedicated themselves to a lifetime of listening to God.[26] The pattern of each day was punctuated by the call to prayer, by a sense of rhythm today's world seems to be losing, by a holistic way of life, day and night, with the ebb and flow of seasons.

> Monastic life of whatever culture or tradition knows about aware-ness, mindfulness, a total listening to God, living in the present, being alive to the world around, finding in that world [of] the visible a reflection of the invisible. This is, of course, also true of the way in which the poet sees the world, so when the two come together in one person it is hardly surprising to find that we have such extraordinary poetry.[27]

The most famous Celtic prayer, attributed to St. Patrick, reflects an intense awareness of the presence of God even during the most perilous of times. Tradition dates it to the year 433, and the occasion was when Patrick defied high king Laeghaire, who had commanded that all fires be extinguished before he lit his fire, as a ritual proclamation that he alone provided his people with light and fire.[28] In challenging the king by lighting a fire to represent the brighter light of Christ, Patrick took his life into his own hands and uttered his prayer, which has been handed down to us as *Patrick's Breast-plate.*

> This day I call to me; God's strength to direct me, God's power to sustain me.
>
> God's wisdom to guide me, God's vision to light me, God's ear to my hearing, God's word to my speaking, God's hand to uphold me, God's pathway before me, God's shield to protect me, God's legions to save me: from snares of the demons, from evil enticements, from failings of nature, from one man or many that seek to destroy me, anear or afar.
>
> Be Christ this day my strong protector. . . . Christ beside me, Christ before me; Christ behind me, Christ within me; Christ beneath me, Christ above me; Christ to right of me, Christ to left of me; Christ in my lying, my sitting, my rising; Christ in heart of all who know me, Christ on tongue of all who meet me, Christ in eye of all who see me, Christ in ear of all who hear me.
>
> For my shield this day I call: a mighty power: the Holy Trinity! Affirming threeness, confessing oneness in the making of all— through love.

Such praying is permeated with a profound sense of the presence of God—alongside, behind, before, above, below. This is what I have already referred to as "respiratory prayer," in which the transcendent God becomes incarnated as companion, guest, fellow traveler, friend and fellow worker. This kind of intimate relationship prayer is not a formal exercise but a state of mind.

Celtic spirituality both affirms and challenges. It calls us to the solitary life with the question, "Unless we learn to live with ourselves, how can we live with others?"[29] It resonates with the feeling of *anomie* that permeates contemporary society. In the totality of that encounter there is dark as well as light, harshness and severity as well as beauty and tranquility. Solitude is not idealized but recognized as a place or state of mind in which the individual is likely to

encounter and be particularly vulnerable to dark forces and destructive invitations, as Jesus himself experienced in the wilderness of
Judea immediately following his baptism. It is not the solitude of
escapism or self-preoccupation, but rather a solitude that "becomes
a means of empowering and refreshing their engagement with the
world."[30]

The cross, worn as a religious adornment by so many Gen Xers,
whether as jewelry or as a tattoo, identifies them with a stripped,
scarred and suffering Christ—a young person dying a violent death.
Such a Christ is not easily commercialized and hangs in stark contrast to the jogging athleticism of self-help Christianity. The cross is
also central in the Celtic tradition. Theirs are not the diminutive
crosses of costume jewelry and precious stones but the high-stand-
ing, rugged, quarried-stone crosses that tower over the land with
even greater significance than today's electricity pylons.

Esther de Waal describes these crosses as a focal point in the
countryside, claiming the land for Christ and boldly proclaiming
belief in the possibility of a transfigured universe.[31] They provide a
poignant challenge both to the secularist who seeks to marginalize
and privatize religious faith and to the postmodernist whose world
has exploded into fragments, just like Humpty Dumpty's world that
cannot be put together again, even by the horsemen of the apoca-
lypse.

Furthermore, the Celtic cross, with its intricate symbolism, is an
icon for spiritual contemplation. Esther De Waal writes, "In a Celtic
cross we see that great round O, the circle of the globe itself, held in
tension by the two arms of the cross—creation and redemption
together."[32] She explains that the decorative patterns and intricate
designs of spirals and interlacings "seem to speak of God's unity
and eternity, the interlocking forms suggest the order underlying the
complexity of creation."[33] She contrasts the two sides of the cross:
"On the right side we see the suffering Christ, with two figures, the
lance bearer (representing the church and the sacrament) and the
sponge bearer (representing the synagogue and the bitter gall of the

Jewish faith). While on the opposite side Christ is shown as the Lord of Hosts, at the Second Coming, on the Day of Judgment."[34] Especially among Gen Xers there is a strong emphasis on both suffering and foreboding.

One Episcopal church that is immersing itself in this culture in an effort to speak of Christ in a meaningful way has a poster of a classical oil painting of the crucifixion produced by the Episcopal New Church Center. Scratched across it is the invitation, "Of course people with pierced body parts are welcome in our church." The fact that their wounds are self-inflicted gives added poignancy, since these young people have sought to draw attention to their own "wounded" state. Yet the Celtic cross points *beyond* death to vindication and victory, or perhaps more accurately, *through* death to life. On account of the atoning sacrifice of Christ, there is now hope for humankind, consisting not only of life after death but of life before death. This is a powerful message to Gen Xers who have adopted the macabre death masks and black clothes of mourning as a defiant gesture and sardonic response to a reality they cannot face in any other way.

Last and of particular relevance to the title of this chapter is the distinctive Celtic understanding of "saints." In the Roman tradition the saints of the church are remote and become saints only after a lengthy legal process of canonization. In contrast, Celtic saints are native, approachable and close at hand. They are encountered each day and are emulated as adventurous individuals who are in touch with heavenly realities. "They have, from the beginning, been a natural part of life, associated above all with the place in which they lived out their vocations."[35] De Waal observes that "in Celtic countries the landscape itself has become virtually an *ikonastasis,* a living reminder of the presence of the saints."[36]

Over the centuries many stories and legends have grown up around these figures, enhancing their reputation as wonderworkers. How much truth is represented by these colorful narratives is open to question, but all of them are homespun tales of humble individuals, at one with the people and with nature, who continued their vocations as individuals in close contact with God and touching the needy people around them. They held no celebrity status. Likewise, in our day people are looking for individuals and communities who are in touch with God—a reality demonstrated in their personal and corporate living. This aspect we will explore at greater length in the following chapter.

Spirituality and Holiness

Spirituality is a term much in vogue, and through overuse its meaning has worn thin. For many, it is a permanent dreamlike quality—a mild anesthetic to carry you through the turmoil each day brings. For others, spirituality represents rare or spasmodic mystical experiences, which might be induced through mind-altering drugs. The problem here is that every "high" is followed by a "low," until eventually so much stimulus is needed to reach new heights that the subsequent lows become a crash-dive, and the search for spirituality becomes a perilous journey. Some forms of spirituality rely on meditation techniques to release the human potential buried in the subconscious. Other forms encourage individuals to open themselves to spiritual forces from highly questionable sources that have the nasty habit of taking control once they have gained entry.

Biblical spirituality, in contrast, is concerned with bringing our body and soul into an intimate relationship with the heart of God. It is concerned with holiness, which means that it relates to every aspect of life, as lived from day to day, rather than focusing attention on transient experiences. Its development rests on a disciplined life, without which we cannot live as disciples. It employs the classical spiritual disciplines of meditation, Scripture study, silence, solitude, frugality, fasting, contemplation (dwelling quietly in the loving presence of God), intercession, simplicity, submission, service, worship and celebration.[37]

In pursuing our spiritual journey, we need to be clear about the goal. The spiritual life does not consist in self-realization but in the vision of God. The path toward that goal includes an initial conversion—nothing short of a complete about-face made possible by the regenerative operation of the Holy Spirit within the individual, followed by regular course corrections. It entails developing virtues that are the fruit of the Spirit itemized in Galatians 5:22-23: love, joy, peace, patience, kindness, generosity, faithfulness, gentleness and self-control.

A genuine spiritual search is not characterized by self-preoccupation but must be lived out in community and in love for one's neighbor. It requires taking time to meditate upon the Scriptures, ponder life and appreciate nature. Then there is the hardest discipline of all in our hyperactive culture, which stresses doing at the expense of being: to be still and to focus on the presence of God.[38]

Protestant spirituality in the Puritan and Holiness traditions. In the evangelical tradition as well there are deep wells of spiritual wisdom from which we need to draw afresh. In eighteenth century England the church was spiritually impoverished and morally decadent. At that time God raised up a diverse group of people from within the Church of England and the independent churches who emphasized the need for the new birth, leading to holiness of life and a commitment to social justice.

Among the stellar leaders, who were contemporaries and knew one another, were the hymn writer Isaac Watts, George Whitefield, John and Charles Wesley, the countess of Huntingdon (Lady Selina), the high church Anglican William Law, prison reformer Hannah More, John Newton, and former-slaver-turned-preacher William Wilberforce. Wilberforce called the church out of its nominality into a clear and practical faith and pursued antislavery legislation through the English Parliament.[39] These individuals were, for the most part, the heirs of the Puritan tradition passed down from the previous century. It is through the hymns of Watts and Wesley that we most readily capture their devotional depths, even though their ponderous prose and flowery expressions tend to put off some modern readers.

In the nineteen century we see the emergence of the holiness tradition, rooted in Wesleyan Arminianism. As with the previous century, their style of writing is difficult for today's reader, so we must persevere to see beyond the style to the substance. Also, the call to personal holiness in the later Wesleyan tradition needs to be reconnected with the strong social concern of evangelical writers and activists of the previous century.

The response of new paradigm churches. One encouraging sign of renewal in contemporary evangelicalism is a growing desire for an authentic and rich experience of God, and for that experience to be related to a personal call to holiness and to service in the world. New paradigm churches are recapturing a sense of the transcendence of God encountered through his immanence. Donald Miller recognizes the need for truth to be rooted in experience:

> Our post-modern world is a fractured place of competing interest groups, discourses, and perspectives, and the desire for something that is unchanging, eternal, and divinely inspired is undoubtedly attractive, especially when one can experience it through joyful, culturally current worship forms.[40]

Whereas a great deal of rhetoric spills from churches of the liberal tradition, and their voices need to be heard by pietists, evangelicals are themselves more and more on the frontlines of social service and emergency relief. They are feeding the hungry; caring for the growing number of young people with AIDS; visiting the prisons; and providing famine, flood and earthquake relief. By doing so, they are reconnecting with the earlier traditions of evangelicalism that existed before the unfortunate split between the personal and social gospel took place.

Implementation

1. Attend a retreat to learn more about the disciplines of meditation on Scripture *(lectio divina)*, silence and contemplative prayer.

Read from the classical texts on spirituality. For example, Richard Foster and James Byran Smith have prepared a collection of such readings that spans the centuries and a wide range of traditions.[41]

2. As a church leader, set an example by forming a discipleship group that takes priority in your calendar planning.

3. Visit a church that identifies with one of the new apostolic networks and that has an impressive commitment to church planting. Learn from them and pray with them. Take along some of your church leaders.

s i x

From Dead Orthodoxy
to Living Faith

I*n our consideration of the responsibilities of Christian leader-*
ship within the local church, we move now from personal spirituality, which we discussed in the previous chapter, to the church's
corporate spirituality expressed in its worship. In true worship, God
is the audience, not the congregation, and those who lead worship
are not the center-stage performers but the off-stage prompters and
facilitators. While the basic question in the previous chapter was, "Is
there evidence of the presence of God in the life of this individual?"
Here we pose the question, "Is there an authentic divine encounter
as the people of God gather to worship?"

During the past fifteen years attention has been focused on the
seeker-sensitive, contemporary worship service as a key element in
reaching the unchurched of North America. This model has been
impressively demonstrated and effectively promoted by a small number
of churches that have achieved world renown such as Willow Creek
Community Church in Barrington, Illinois, and Saddleback Community
Church in Orange County, California. Both of these churches have

succeeded, with the dynamic leadership of their founding pastors, in attracting thousands of the unchurched to their weekend services. These events are characterized by carefully scripted worship services, smooth transitions and skits that relate biblical truths to incidents in everyday life.

As a result of the highly publicized success of the model, many churches, not only in the United States but also in Europe and Australia, have pinned their hopes on this particular approach. It remains to be seen to what extent the model is transferable or to what extent the principles they enshrine can be applied as effectively in very different contexts. The leaders of these "flagship" churches are extraordinarily gifted and entertaining communicators who can attract highly talented leadership teams. Also, their churches are located in the midst of expanding, affluent populations.

Their seeker-sensitive worship service approach is also part of a carefully thought-out strategy, and it is dependent upon a range of vital components that are essential to its success. Bill Hybels, the senior pastor of Willow Creek, has developed a seven-step process designed to walk irreligious men and women all the way from spiritual indifference to radical commitment to Christ.[1] He and other pastors who take this approach relate closely to the cultures that make up their target groups, are gifted communicators and have a passion to reach the unchurched. They are reaching their kind of people through a wide range of need-meeting ministries. They have attracted sufficient numbers of people who have great confidence in and enthusiasm for their church. Thus these churches motivate their members to invite the people within their network of relationships and contacts. Any marketer knows that personal commendation is the most effective form of advertising. But triggering that momentum is no easy matter.

How the Church Responds to Cultural Shifts

At the outset, a distinction needs to be made between "seeker sensitive" and "market driven" in our consideration of worship forms in modern and postmodern contexts. The former represents a serious attempt to engage with the cultural setting in which the local church is endeavoring to bear witness. The latter signifies a church that tailors its message and employs any gimmick in order to attract a crowd. Our focus in this chapter is on the church that operates with theological integrity, evangelistic passion and pastoral sensitivity. In any attempt to reach those who are not yet Christians or who have become disillusioned with institutionalized Christianity, every obstacle erected by people needs to be removed. The only "offense" that must remain is that of the cross of Christ, where all roads to the Father must eventually converge.

Any church leader applying the seeker-sensitive model must be driven by a concern to reach the lost rather than simply to fill the church. This ministry model is fundamentally a missionary—and not simply an ecclesiastical—model. The seeker-sensitive pastor and missionary are attempting to engage culture, to understand the perspectives, priorities and needs of the people around them so that they can communicate in a way that they will be heard. For this to occur both the medium used to carry the message and the way the message is expressed will have to be carefully chosen and skillfully employed. Those critics who attack their bold attempts need to ask whether they themselves are doing a more effective job.

In response to the seismic cultural changes taking place, many churches have become so unnerved that they have resorted to fright-flight, while others shout in moral outrage from a safe distance, and still others adopt the approach of sending raiding parties into enemy territory as their primary form of witness. At its best, the seeker-sensitive approach attempts an incarnational presence in the community it seeks to reach in the name of Christ.

Herein lies a problem in that although we are called to minister like Jesus, we are not Jesus. We are forgiven sinners who have been adopted into the family of God. We still have a lot of growing and maturing ahead of us before we become like him in character, discernment and empowerment. In our attempts to identify with the world, we all too readily become like the world through failing to admit our vulnerability, naiveté and corruptibility. Jesus was not hoodwinked by outward appearances. He was not deceived by hidden agendas. He did not succumb to the temptation to find an easier and less painful path or to use his ministry position as a pedestal for personal gain. All that he did was in obedience to the Father. His purpose was as unswerving as his judgment was unerring.

For those who follow in Jesus' steps, to engage in incarnational ministry requires the safeguards of discernment and accountability. Incarnation is not simply a matter of being available and approachable. Rather it is a disquieting presence generating a range of responses: bringing to the surface deep-seated attitudes, calling forth the cry of the needy and triggering spontaneous acts of devotion to God. Authentic incarnation leads to significant transformation in the lives of those drawn into the orbit of the divine presence evidenced in the one who witnesses in the name of the risen Lord.

Incarnation entails contextualization because God characteristically deals with us directly and specifically in ways that, at times, can be alarmingly revealing. The entire biblical narrative is the record of God engaging with a particular people in the nitty-gritty of their daily lives, meeting them in the context of their contemporary world of family tussles, societal disorder and injustices, and political machinations. What is true of God's dealings with his people throughout history also holds true for the way the gospel relates to culture. It is indeed "good news" in bad times. But this does not imply that it is a panacea, baptizing culture with a heaven-poured whitewash.

While the gospel supports some cultural affirmations and fulfills some unrealized cultural aspirations, it also addresses the demonic element present in every culture. Therefore, contextualization is from a critical, not a naive standpoint.

In relation to worship, this means the recognition that all worship takes place within a cultural context that provides a distinctive texture, whether it be the subculture of a particular closed-off, ecclesiastical tradition or a reflection of the broader cultural context. The challenge facing seeker-sensitive worship is to find enrichment by drawing from a particular culture without being subverted by its self-serving and demonic elements. While I point out this tension, it must not be assumed that the closed-off, ecclesiastical tradition has therefore secured immunity, for it is just as prone to succumb to its own versions of self-serving tendencies or demonic subversions.

The Search for Relevance and the Secularization of the Church
Western cultures are currently undergoing rapid transition with the collapse of the modern worldview that represented the precocious and precarious pinnacle of the Enlightenment paradigm. The liberal tradition within the church that became intoxicated by self-assured claims of modernity now finds itself in disarray. Its search for relevance led to the cul-de-sac of redundancy.

This experience in the United States should serve as a caution to evangelicals elsewhere who have opted to travel along a dangerously parallel road for the seeker-sensitive model of the 1980s, which arose in response to the many baby boomers returning to church. It was a generation disillusioned and distrusting of institutions in the wake of the Vietnam War and the Watergate conspiracy. The baby boomers were of a generation with a strong sense of personal freedom and individual rights. They held high expectations and shopped in a highly segmented, customized market. Many of them had been reared in church and then had wandered away until, having sowed their wild oats, they returned to rediscover the heart of what they had left behind—but without the trappings. Many had also experimented with drugs as a means to heightened spiritual awareness, and in the depressing aftermath of those drug-induced highs they came seeking a more substantial experience, no less hungry but all the more wary. By the mid-1980s they were married, raising families and seeking deeper roots and a stronger sense of purpose for their lives.

For the most part they returned to churches of traditions other than those in which they had been brought up. In the 1970s and 1980s the community churches flourished. They were either independent of denominations, or they disguised their denominational labels and jettisoned their worship traditions in favor of a generic, contemporary look and feel. Christian symbols, ecclesiastical furnishings and pipe organs were replaced by Plexiglass podiums, soft furnishings, stage lighting, stage sets, surround-sound audio systems, theater-style seating and music bands. The graystone and whitewash church was replaced by a color-coordinated worship center. The medieval stonemasons who built the great cathedrals to the glory of God were challenged by the engineers of modernity who build the metal, glass and concrete rival cathedrals of our own day.

However, churches that have experienced spectacular growth by developing a seeker-sensitive strategy must not simply rejoice in a full church and additional worship services to accommodate the crowds. They must also ask where the new people are coming from. Sally Morgenthaler, on the basis of statistics provided by George Barna, concludes that the success of these churches is largely at the expense of smaller and often more traditional churches. They represent an ecclesiastical version of musical chairs, or church-hopping growth.[2] Morgenthaler maintains that 80 percent of those coming through the doors of the seeker-sensitive megachurches have been drawn from either traditional Protestant denominations or Roman Catholic churches. Before long, churches that grow by transfer will have to do their own seeking, otherwise their growth will stall once they have drained the churches that have functioned as their feeder networks.

Assessing the Significance of the Seeker-Sensitive Approach

The importance of the church's ministry to returnees must not be underestimated. Research conducted by George Barna in the United States and by Peter Brierley in the United Kingdom indicates that a high percentage of youngsters reared as churchgoers are likely to turn away from the church at some point in their lives. In the United

States the average time a person is a lapsed churchgoer is eight years, whereas in England it is twelve years.[3] Once young people are ready to return, churches must be ready to receive them with open doors and a genuine welcome. They must be like the waiting father in the parable of the prodigal son. Sadly, in some cases their response more closely resembles the judgmental attitude of the jealous and resentful older brother.

The formerly churched will not return to business as before. In fact, they often come back initially with a lower commitment level, because, having left home once, they will find it easier to repeat the desertion. Returning boomers often have a casual relationship with the church. They attend worship services less frequently than other members, and church takes a lower priority. They like to keep their options open as to how they spend their leisure time. If the relationship moves beyond the casual level, it is most likely to be contractual. That is, they will make commitments but only on condition that they prove to be self-gratifying. And once they feel that the contract has not been lived up to or has been deliberately broken, they will renegotiate elsewhere.

This reluctance to make commitments is reflected in all relationships, not simply with the church's fellowship. Even marriage is increasingly regarded as a contractual affair, sometimes based on prenuptial legal agreements. The challenge facing the church is to move its members from a casual and contractual relationship to a covenant. A covenantal relationship entails a commitment to one another through thick and thin. In the language of the marriage service, it is "to have and to hold from this day forward, for better for worse, for richer for poorer, in sickness and in health, to love and to cherish, until we are parted by death. This is my solemn vow."

It is important to unpack that imprecise and overused term *unchurched* because it generally means something different in the European and Australian contexts. The United States has been an anomaly in the Western world, for the overwhelming majority of its population has been orthodox in its Christian beliefs and around

40 percent of the population claims to attend church weekly.

Therefore, when American churches claim that they are reaching the unchurched through the seeker-sensitive approach, this may simply mean that they are reaching the formerly churched rather than the never-churched. They are succeeding in attracting spiritually hungry returnees who are looking for an alternative church. This is a very different scenario from that which faces churches endeavoring to attract the never-churched, who are either hostile or indifferent to the Christian message. The never-churched are not attracted to the church as an institution because it is constantly lampooned in the press and on television, and its domestic scandals are sensationalized, while the ongoing positive witness of the church is consistently ignored or trashed in the media.

Martin Robinson, director of mission and theology at the Bible Society in England, provides a European perspective on the significance of the seeker-sensitive approach within the European context:

> Despite its innovative approach, the original "Willow Creek" model still feels very much like a church to those from a European context. The imitators of Willow Creek in Europe have departed significantly from the detail of the model and are often attempting to create models for exploring faith which are much more avowedly secular in their feel. The heart of all these attempts is not slick marketing so much as the encouraging of the Christian community to build genuine friendships with unchurched, secular people in the natural social settings where everyday life is lived.[4]

Robinson's comment may not be restricted to the European context. It may prove just as applicable in the more secularized regions of North America, where there is a growing cultural gulf between churched and unchurched segments of the population. Later in this chapter we will look at a range of radical experiments of new forms of church found in both the England and the United States that illustrate the point made by Robinson. Whereas the large seeker-sensitive churches provide one response to the complex missionary challenges facing the churches in the West at present, they are by no means the only approach. They may even pass the zenith of their influence early in the new millennium.

The success of the seeker-sensitive approach has been limited to a certain section of the Boomer generation, as Wade Clarke Roof has revealed in his book *Generation of Seekers.*[5] With so many churches in Europe, Canada, Australia and now the United States struggling to survive, there is a desperate search for answers. This can lead to an uncritical acceptance of any model that seems to offer hope. The valid achievements of those megachurches experiencing healthy growth must be seen both in context and in perspective. The church's much-vaunted search for relevance has made a greater impact on the already churched and the previously churched, who are already looking for any satisfying alternatives. However, it has made little impact on the never-churched, most of whom have little interest in Christian entertainment. A further disturbing fact is that there seems to be a growing isolation and widening chasm between the churchgoing community and those who choose to stay away.

There is growing evidence, both statistical and anecdotal, that a significant percentage of baby boomers who returned to churches in the 1980s are now leaving in disillusionment. The statistical evidence is provided in the Barna Report of 1994-1995, showing that over a three-year period boomer attendance dropped by 11 percent and that a third or more are now attending church less frequently.[6] Wade Clarke Roof, on the basis of his interviews with boomers, also speaks of widespread disillusionment resulting in conservatives leaving mainline congregations and going into inactivity or to a period of church-hopping, then finally dropping out altogether.[7]

To the extent that worship degenerates into spectatorism, boredom will eventually set in. The seeker-sensitive model requires a continuous flow of creativity in order for the entertainment factor to be sustained. Smaller, resource-strapped churches soon run out of ideas and their performance level is often embarrassingly amateurish and lacking in audience appeal. Within the family of churchgoers this may be acceptable, but it will not prove to be a major attraction for new people.

Even for the big-name churches the entertainment is difficult to sustain over the long haul. The clientele is prone to drift away to the next new show in town. Entertainment has its place in the context of worship but is serendipitous rather than staged. It surfaces when a congregation has established a strong rapport with the worship leaders and has reached a level of trusting vulnerability so that it can laugh at itself. People are not looking so much for worship that is relevant as they are for worship that is real.

I have questioned a number of boomers who have left conservative evangelical churches (Baptist, Pentecostal and independent charismatic) to attend liturgical churches and have asked them why they made the switch. They informed me that they had tired of celebrity-based religion, built around the personality and communication gifts of one pastor, and had gone in search of a church where God is the center of attention. For them the centrality of the table in place of the pulpit was of special significance. They also find Christian symbols and rituals deeply meaningful, providing refreshing and evocative means of communication. They react to the deadening and, in some traditions, deafening wordiness of much of contemporary evangelicalism.

Sally Morgenthaler laments the fact that "we are not producing worshippers in this country. Rather, we are producing a generation of spectators, religious onlookers lacking, in many cases, any memory of a true encounter with God, deprived of both the tangible sense of God's presence and the supernatural relationship their inmost spirits crave."[8] In true worship God is the audience, and the congregation are the participants.[9] Worship is the wellspring of our witness.

Be Still and Know That I Am God

At the heart of the worship crisis encountered in many evangelical churches is the fact that our tradition has been too activist to understand the true nature of worship. Many church leaders say the primary purpose of the church is evangelism and growth. Yet the evangelistic motivation cannot be sustained indefinitely without the heartbeat of worship. Here, according to Morgenthaler, lies the heart of the problem. She expresses the conviction that "it is difficult to witness convincingly about a God we do not know and love in our inmost being. And when it comes to a worship service, we have already seen that seekers are not the least bit interested in watching us go through the motions. They are hungry to see evidence of God at work in our hearts."[10]

Worship must not be used for other means that result in it becoming both subverted and diverted. Worship is not entertainment. It is not an expression of cultural elitism. It is not religious education. It is not emotional self-indulgence or a vehicle for evangelism. Worship does not produce a quick fix but flows out into the whole of life, and the whole of life is then drawn into worship. The Old Testament prophets railed against those who made pilgrimages and offered sacrifices as a cover-up for their disobedient lives (Amos 4:4-5; 5:21-24). Worship is designed not to make people feel good about themselves or to help them become better informed about theology and the Bible but to make them holy.

Worship takes place in a sanctuary, not in an auditorium or a lecture hall. In our secularized society there is a need for holy places that are not places of divine containment but places where spiritual power is concentrated. We need places sanctified by prayer to serve as spiritual powerhouses where the sovereign Lord attracts the sincere seeker after truth. The ultimate people movement to which Old Testament prophets Isaiah and Micah looked forward is the day when the peoples of the world will stream to the Lord's house (Is 2:2-4; Mic 4:1-2). I remember walking into the sanctuary of an Episcopal church with the rabbi of a Messianic congregation. He paused for a moment to look around and absorb the atmosphere before declaring, "This is a holy place."

Worship is trinitarian in focus. It responds to God, who has acted on our behalf: through the Father in planning our redemption; through the Son, who implemented the plan of his heavenly Father; and through the Holy Spirit, who applies the benefits of redemption to the individual believer and the believing community. The triune God invites and requires us to worship in spirit and in truth (Jn 4:23). It is the presence of the Holy Spirit within us that transforms prodigals into worshipers. It is the Spirit who keeps worship alive, fresh and creative.

As Jesus promised the Samaritan woman at the well, "The water that I will give will become in them a spring of water gushing up to eternal life" (Jn 4:14). To worship "in truth" means to worship authentically. We say what we mean. We worship in response to the truth that God has revealed about himself and us. There is always more about God than we can possibly comprehend, and there is much about ourselves that we find difficult to admit and come to terms with.

Worship that is in truth is *enthusiastic* in the true sense of the word, being *en theos* (in God), inspired by the awesome, purifying, energizing presence of the Lord. The divine presence among us may lead on some occasions to an awe-filled silence and at other times to laughter, loud shouting, clapping and dancing in the aisles and around the table of the Lord. Even in the liturgical Anglican tradition there is a place for exuberant and exhilarating celebration, as well as a time for solemn assembly.

Worship is a human response to the divine initiative and is shaped by the very nature of God, who has graciously revealed himself. Evelyn Underhill describes adoration as the recognition of God's "otherness though nearness."[11] She also cautions that there is a tendency in all worship to decline from adoration to demand.[12] Once God's majesty and holiness confront us, we cannot avoid realizing our own unworthiness. At this point God graciously invites us to enter into dialogue—a conversation in which it is more important to listen than to speak. The highest form of prayer is one in which we allow God to guide the conversation.

Inevitably, there will be varying levels of intensity in our worship, with ebbs and flows, for an emotional "high" cannot be sustained indefinitely. While on the mount of transfiguration, Peter, with characteristic impetuosity, wanted to perpetuate the experience by setting up camp, but the Lord rebuked him. While we are on this side of heaven we cannot prolong or reproduce a fleeting experience of divine revelation. However intense and uplifting our experiences in worship may be, we have to recognize the following, as Evelyn Underhill explains:

> It is true that worship when thus embodied, loses, or seems to lose— something of its purity; but only then can it take up and use man's various powers and capacities, turning the whole creature towards the Eternal, and thus entering the texture of his natural as well as his supernatural life. Certainly, it is here that we encounter the greatest of the dangers that accompany its long history; the danger that form will smother spirit, ritual action take the place of spontaneous prayer, the outward and visible sign obscure the inward grace.[13]

When Devotion Degenerates into Sentimentality

Contemporary worship services, for the most part, have done away with the classical hymns of the church in favor of worship choruses. These have the advantage of being more simple and repetitive so that visitors unfamiliar with the church's hymns can readily sing along. The words are made available to them either projected onto a screen or printed in a bulletin or on a song sheet. The downside with worship songs addressed to God rather than making statements about God is that it is difficult for uncommitted people to express emotions they do not feel and to claim a relationship that has not yet been forged. Furthermore, their spiritual jargon and biblical allusions can be as obscure as the doctrinal content of the hymns that they replace.

For believers themselves an unchanging diet of praise songs can cause adoration to degenerate into religious sentimentality and emotional self-indulgence, which is so self-absorbed that it alienates the visitor. There is need for a new genre of hymn that declares the great themes of Scripture in a way that makes them clear to a visitor who is not familiar with biblical themes, events and characters. The lyrics of Graham Kendrick have played a key role in this regard, making the great doctrines of salvation accessible to the unchurched, doing for our generation what the hymns of Charles Wesley did in eighteenth century England. The following example leads the worshiper to encounter the risen Lord:

Led like a lamb
To the slaughter
In silence and shame
There on your back
You carried a world
Of violence and pain
Bleeding, dying (repeat)

You're alive (repeat)
You have risen!
Alleluia
And the power
And the glory
Is given
Alleluia
Jesus to you

At the break of dawn
Poor Mary
Still weeping she came
When through her grief
She heard your voice
Now speaking her name
Mary, Master (repeat)

At the right hand
Of the Father
Now seated on high
You have begun
Your eternal reign
Of justice and joy
Glory, glory (repeat)

Christian worship must reflect a range of responses to God. At one time it will reflect the intimate experience of God's immanence. On other occasions it will express the worshipers' sense of unworthiness as they realize God's holiness and transcendence. Intimate worship that degenerates into a casual overfamiliarity is both presumptuous and embarrassing to those who see God from a transcendental perspective.

At this point it is appropriate to state that the sense of the divine presence does not depend on any one style, whether high liturgy or folksy spontaneity that can become as predictable and boring as rote liturgy—and more threadbare. Rather, it depends on the preparation of the worship leader's heart and the core of believers in the congregation. High liturgy can pulsate with spiritual vitality, allowing freedom and spontaneity within a safety net of the familiar and formal.

God graciously approaches humankind along a variety of paths to meet us in our varied cultural settings. Worship is always contextualized so that no one style should be regarded as normative or more spiritual than another. What turns on some people is likely to put off others. One interesting development among independent charismatic churches that did away with hymns in favor of worship songs is that increasing numbers are beginning to reinstate traditional hymns. They eventually realized that they were suffering spiritual impoverishment from neglecting the devotional treasury of the ages. But in reintroducing hymns they have made the beat more contemporary and have revised wording that was archaic, obscure or in some cases downright misleading.

Yearning for Mysterious Transcendence

Within the postmodern context the worship scene is more complex than an older generation of evangelicals is often aware. Those people nurtured in traditional churches from the 1950s to the 1970s, with their stiff formality, archaic language and obscure rituals, experienced a refreshing liberation through the impact of the charismatic movement. This freer worship style enabled them to express their feelings toward God, made worshipers aware of one another as they engaged in more eye contact and linked hands, and deepened relationships through meeting in small groups. It provided a means whereby the great Reformation doctrine of the priesthood of all believers could find expression through the emphasis on every member ministering through the exercise of spiritual gifts.

Worship became less predictable and more eventful as people made room for God to make his presence known and to minister among them. But in time even these new expressions of worship became predictable with the routinizing of charisma. This has led to the children of liberated, mainline churchgoers becoming just as bored with the new forms as their parents were with the old.

Consequently, the worship traffic today is not all streaming in one direction. There are still significant numbers of people from Roman Catholic and traditional Protestant denominations being attracted to the contemporary seeker-sensitive worship services. Yet at the same time there are many among the baby boomers, and especially the Generation Xers, who are attracted to liturgical worship, represented by Roman Catholic, Eastern Orthodox and Episcopal churches. This attraction is highlighted by the desire of young people to establish deeper roots to compensate for the transience and fragmentation of the world in which they grew up. It also responds to their more introspective and reflective disposition as distinct from the achiever mentality of their boomer parents.

In 1985 Robert Webber reported on a movement that gathered momentum at Wheaton College, which he describes in *Evangelicals on the Canterbury Trail*.[14] As another example, Peter Gillquist led a group of senior Campus Crusade workers into the Antiochean Orthodox Church, where they have spearheaded a significant evangelistic and church planting ministry.[15]

These influences have encouraged a mood for songs that are quiet and repetitive, with periods of silence interspersed with readings. Still other indicators of the move away from the "soft rock" music style, beloved by older baby boomers, is the amazing popularity of Gregorian chants and Celtic music and songs that have surfaced in the pop charts to the amazement of the performers.

A further significant trend is the extent to which churchgoers will draw from a variety of traditions with the mix-and-match mentality characteristic of postmodernism. They are just as at home attending a Saturday night folk mass in a Roman Catholic church that has experienced charismatic renewal as they are in the Sunday morning contemporary worship service. We have noted in the previous chapter that evangelicals are drawing from the Catholic tradition of spirituality. Thus it will not come as a surprise to discover that there is also crossover in regard to worship. Doctrinal differences take second place to experiential authenticity.

To my knowledge there is no reliable data indicating how widespread this worship eclecticism is. But the anecdotal evidence seems to indicate that examples are not isolated but represent wider trends. Writing in *Christianity Today,* Gary Burge laments the poverty of worship in so many evangelical churches and the attraction of worship traditions that bring the worshipers into touch with mystery and the transcendent. Reflecting on his experience of evangelicalism in a variety of traditions, he laments, "Soul-winning, hard-hitting sermons, and revival hymns have become a staple of my diet. And deep inside I know that something is terribly wrong. Something is missing. My friends bravely announce the certainty of evangelical orthodoxy, but somewhere the mystery of God has been lost. . . . I suspect that there is a growing dissatisfaction in evangelical ranks, and nowhere is this pain felt more deeply than in the context of worship."[16]

It is inevitable that we should feel a sense of frustration in worship, irrespective of the style or degree of intensity to which we are accustomed. Human response to the divine disclosure is always inadequate and contains limited perceptions, mixed motives, and partial and conditional commitment. If we stopped to think of the words we sing in our devotional hymns, we would choke on our insincerity. We must either change our hymns or change our ways.

Once again Evelyn Underhill's comments speak with prophetic

precision of both the prosperity motive and anthropocentric tendencies that intrude into so much of our worship. "The tendency of all worship to decline from adoration to demand, and from the supernatural to the ethical, shows how strong a pull is needed to neutralize the anthropocentric trend of the human mind; its intense preoccupation with the world of succession, and its own here-and-now desires and needs."[17]

Return to Ancient Forms: Passing Fad or Permanent Retrieval?
Tradition has been described in the frequently quoted remark of Jeroslav Pelikan of Yale as "the living faith of the dead, whereas traditionalism is the dead faith of the living." The rejection of the latter by a generation weary of empty forms and marginalized by incomprehensible language and ceremonies has also resulted in the neglect of the former, much to our spiritual impoverishment. The words of Evelyn Underhill, addressed to the churches in England in the 1930s, are even more applicable to the church in the context in which I now write in California at the end of the 1990s. "It is plain that the living experience of this whole Church, visible and invisible, past and present, stretched out in history and yet poised on God, must set the scene for Christian worship; not the poor little scrap of which any one soul, or any sectional group is capable."[18]

Our increasingly pluralistic and mobile urban society has created a sense of rootlessness and angst that has contributed to the search for a sense of belonging. We feel the need to be more deeply rooted in a community, rather than being constantly buffeted by a society characterized by ceaseless comings and goings. Pastors are preaching to a parade passing by, rather than to a congregation that has stability and continuity. As Christians our identity and security are in Christ, but we are also members of the body of Christ. Such membership must be viewed in less restrictive terms than the local congregation. In global terms it must be extended to embrace the church militant here on earth and in cosmic terms to embrace the church triumphant in the heavenlies.

The New Testament preserves a balance between the church local and universal. This was important in the first century, as newly established communities of believers were made aware that they were part of a rapidly spreading movement around the Mediterranean world. They also needed the perspective of history, realizing that the God they worshiped was a covenant-keeping God who had watched over his people throughout past centuries. In this regard there is a significant difference in perspective between European and North American evangelicals. Europeans define themselves in terms of their roots, whereas North Americans identify themselves in terms of clearly drawn boundaries. The result is a greater tendency to separatism and fragmentation in the American churches, whereas most European evangelicals have remained within their historic denominations. This difference in perception works out in different approaches to experimentation in worship and church structures.

Radical Experiments
Both in the United States and in the United Kingdom there is a growing number of churches exploring new responses to changing cultural contexts. The models are as varied as their contexts, from suburban to inner-city, from blue-collar to affluent. They may be found in informal house-church settings, in restaurants and bars, or in contemporary worship settings like warehouses, converted movie theaters and churches built purposefully as megachurches.

Graham Kendrick and the annual week-long Spring Harvest conferences, which during the late 1980s and the 1990s attracted more than eighty thousand participants each year at a half dozen locations, have played a significant role in both modeling and marketing creative contemporary worship. An even more radical influence has been the Greenbelt Festival; it has encouraged the arts in worship, challenging the culture that characterizes so much of the evangelical world.

A further significant factor has been the large increase in the number of evangelicals who have emerged from Anglican seminaries (roughly 50 percent today describe themselves as evangelical). The result is that there have not been sufficient evangelical parishes to receive them. Most of those who have gone to churches with Anglo-Catholic parishes have respected the church's tradition and developed a new understanding of ancient rituals and breathed fresh life into them.

David Hilborn has identified a number of the innovative experimental worship forms in England.[19] One of the most widely publicized in the 1980s was hosted by St. Thomas' Crooke in Sheffield: a "Nine O'Clock Service"—p.m., not a.m.! The service attracted many young people who did not emerge from their beds on Sunday mornings until after the traditional hour of morning service.

These services initially drew on the music of the Vineyard Movement in California but then moved on to a heavier and louder style. The youthful, counter-culture leaders told John Wimber that his music echoed the soft rock era of the Righteous Brothers (the group with whom he had worked in the 1960s) and that their God was stronger than that! For a while I kept an edition of the *Sheffield Telegraph* that reported the visit of health inspectors armed with instruments to measure the decibels on the streets around the church, in response to the complaints of neighbors. The front-page headline reported that the noise did not constitute a health hazard. The service attracted such numbers that it moved eventually to larger premises in the Pond's Forge Leisure Centre. A consequent loosening of ties with the parish contributed to a growing lack of accountability, which eventually brought the bold experiment to a disastrous end in August 1995, when the media exposed the improper sexual conduct of the group's leader.

Other examples cited by David Hilborn include the work of Mike Starkey, an evangelical vicar working in an Anglo-Catholic parish in Finsbury Park, North London, and Nick Mercer, who was once a Baptist minister and the vice principal of the London Bible College and is now an ordained Anglican in the Anglo-Catholic tradition.

An even more radical example is that of Dave Tomlinson's
Holy Joe's, a worshiping group that meets in the upper room of a
pub in a cloud of cigarette and pipe smoke and with drinks served
from the bar.[20] Tomlinson's background and spiritual pilgrimage
started in the Christian Brethren movement and went to the
house-church movement, where he became a prominent leader.
He later left it to adopt a controversial "post-evangelical" position, which he articulated in his book *The Post-Evangelical,* pub-
lished in 1995.[21]

The term *post-evangelical* is one that is being used more frequently now in Britain. It does not signify a rejection of foundational evangelical beliefs; rather it denotes a reinterpretation of them
in the light of the changing cultural context of postmodernity. Holy
Joe's attracts disillusioned former evangelicals, as well as seekers
who are not yet prepared to darken the doorway of any church but
who want a place to go where they feel comfortable and can raise
honest questions and demand honest answers.

Here in southern California Barry Taylor, a British pop musi-
cian who was formerly active in the house-church movement and
the annual Greenbelt Festival, is planting a church known as The
Sanctuary among the artistic community and entertainment
industry people in Santa Monica. He has been influenced by
Dave Tomlinson's ministry at Holy Joe's in London and would
identify himself as a post-evangelical. He is exploring a variety
of approaches to communicating the gospel in bars, nightclubs
and poetry-reading groups.

St. James' Newport Beach Episcopal Church in southern California represents a very different but significant ministry among the
affluent communities located around the marinas and artificial
islands. This church holds three services on Sunday mornings. The
first, at 7:30, is a traditional service following the old prayer book.
This is followed at 9:30 with a Eucharist service that uses the current version of the Book of Common Prayer, with a robed choir and
a blend of traditional church music and the contemplative songs

from Taizé. Then at 11:45 is the charismatic service, which is a free-wheeling Eucharist service with a minimal amount of liturgy. A most remarkable feature of this offering of service styles is that two-thirds of the congregation float from one style of service to the other, rather than divide into three separate congregations, each with a preferred worship style.

Entertainment Is No Substitute for Participation

Seeker-sensitive worship is often criticized for fostering a spectator mentality. The assumption behind this criticism is that spectatorism means the absence of involvement through participation. There is some validity to this criticism, especially when the "audience" is simply responding to the stimulus of a single performance and has neither a shared memory nor an ongoing commitment to sustain it. For instance, a movie audience may be so profoundly impacted by an emotionally charged film that the people need to remain in their seats until the last credit is shown and the houselights go up in order to dry their eyes and regain their composure. But once outside in broad daylight, as the crowd disperses, the emotions lift and evaporate like a morning mist.

Their experience is in strong contrast to the emotions demonstrated by the faithful fans supporting their football team from the bleachers week after week and season after season. The fans' level of involvement is of a different order, which is eloquently and perceptively expressed by Nick Hornsby, a die-hard fan of his North London soccer team, Arsenal.

> One thing I know for sure about being a fan is this: it is not a vicarious pleasure, despite all appearances to the contrary, and those who say that they would rather do than watch are missing the point. Football is a context where watching *becomes* doing—not in the aerobic sense, because watching a game, smoking your head off while doing so, drinking after it has finished and eating chips on the way home is unlikely to do you a whole lot of Jane Fonda good, in the way that chuffing up and down a pitch is supposed to. But when there is some kind of triumph, the pleasure does not radiate from the players out-

wards until it reaches the likes of us at the back of the terraces in a pale and diminished form; our fun is not a watery version of the team's fun, even though they are the ones that get to score the goals and climb the steps of Wembley to meet Princess Diana. The joy we feel on occasions like this is not a celebration of others' good fortune, but a celebration of our own. And when there is a disastrous defeat, the sorrow that engulfs us is, in effect, self-pity, and anyone who wishes to understand how football is consumed must realize this above all things. The players are merely our representatives, chosen by the manager rather than elected by us, but our representatives nonetheless, and sometimes if you look hard, you can see the little poles that join them together, and the handles at the side that enable us to move them. I am part of the club, just as the club is a part of me; and I say this fully aware that the club exploits me, disregards my views, and treats me shoddily on occasions, so my feeling of organic connection is not built on a muddle-headed and sentimental misunderstanding of how professional football works. . . . The only difference between me and them is that I have put in more hours, more years, more decades than them, and so had a better understanding of the afternoon, a sweeter appreciation of why the sun still shines when I remember it.[22]

English and Scottish soccer fans turn out no matter what the weather. Win or lose, they remain loyal to the club. Players come and go, but the fans remain. You dare to call in question their depth of commitment and lifelong loyalty at your peril! The die-hard congregation more closely resembles the sporting fans than the moviegoers. These people turn out no matter how boring and predictable the performance. They may complain bitterly and feel harshly treated and unheard, but they will return next week. They were there before the current pastor arrived, and they are determined to outlast him or her. They may look passive, but appearances are deceptive; they are watching every move and catching every voice inflection. Their commitment needs to be affirmed, and they need to be wooed into the drama of worship. Here lies the spiritual gifting of the worship leader or celebrant at the Lord's table.

Graham Kendrick recounts an incident that is both moving and amusing, which occurred during one of the worship services at the Spring Harvest Festival.

Under the orange and blue striped canvas of the enormous marquee, another celebration and teaching evening was in full swing. The sense of God's presence was giving rise to praise of a very enthusiastic nature, there were smiles everywhere, voices rang out, arms were raised, hands were clapped and even some legs got liberated and danced for joy. In the midst of one such group of worshippers sat a severely disabled Christian man in an invalid "buggy". No one would have blamed him for feeling depressed or resentful at those around him who were praising God with agile and healthy bodies, while he could not even stand up. No one would have blamed him for excusing himself from the meeting and trundling off in his electric buggy out into the windy night and back to his room. Apparently nothing of the kind even entered his head, because as the spirit of praise grew stronger those nearby were treated to a lovely example of selfless praise. The buggy was well equipped for street use, and there he sat, flashing headlights, stop lights, indicator lights, warning lights, in fact anything that flashed, moved or made a sound was in use as he gave all he had got in praise to the Lord he loved![23]

Worship leaders are not performers attracting the admiration of the onlookers but prompters who model the act of worship. In order to function authentically in this role they must prioritize worship as the highest form of service to God. Indeed, in Greek *service* and *worship* are the same word. The term *liturgy (liturgia)* means "the work of the people." To return to our sports fan analogy, the players on the field so involve the crowds in the stands that the "field of play" extends to include all present. As those who are not yet believers are surrounded by the worship experience, they themselves become stirred by the Spirit of God, who is nudging and beckoning them to kneel before the cross of Christ as their means of access to the throne of God.

Balancing Word, Emotion and Will

Whatever style of worship is making a significant impact in today's postmodern culture, the crucial need is to maintain the balance of word, emotion and will. We must eschew the tendency to bounce from one extreme to another. Further, God must be seen to be operating in each area. Some power evangelism emphases place too much significance on healing and deliverance, downplaying the power of the Holy Spirit working through the communicated word of God to reveal the mystery of the gospel and to bring about the new birth. The miracle of regeneration is a more comprehensive and permanent miracle than any miracle of physical healing when we pause to consider that every healed person will succumb to further sicknesses and eventually die of some physical malfunction.

However, this argument should not be pressed so far as to de-emphasize the ministries of healing and deliverance, or indeed the ministry of the prophetic word. If worship represents the bringing of our entire being to God, personal and corporate, as a human response to his gracious self-revelation, then God's response is even more holistic. The postmodern person will not tolerate any separation of the body, mind and will. In that, their insistence is a healthy corrective to the cloaked modernity infiltrating the evangelical worldview.

In the course of three chapters we have considered leadership from the standpoint of transitions from bureaucratic hierarchies to apostolic networks. We then focused on issues of the leader's influence on those who follow. Is he or she seeking to be a celebrity who wants adulation or a saint demonstrating the cost of consecration? Finally, we have examined the corporate spirituality of the congregation in relation to its worship. We now change our focus, moving from the inward and upward focus of the church to its outward focus—its mission in the world that is a vital dimension of its very nature.

Implementation

1. In many churches today there is an underlying tension and sometimes open conflict between groups who want church worship to be contemporary or to be traditional; to have a human, need-meeting emphasis or to have a God-directed focus; to emphasize the

immanence of God or the transcendence of God; to be focused on the pulpit or on the table. Ask yourself what it would take in your church to change the either/or mentality into a both/and mentality.

2. Select three churches with very different traditions that are making a significant impact in ministry situations similar to your own. Arrange to visit them as a group. Before each visit pray together for the Lord to speak to you through the people and worship event in that church. Make a report to your church leadership (and to the congregation) on lessons learned.

3. How many individuals participate in the leading of worship (for example, through music, prayers or communicating the message) in your church? How can that group be increased in number, variety and quality of participation?

4. If you have a drama group, provide them with sources that give details of the history of your movement or denomination. Ask them to write and perform a drama that will highlight the vision and concerns of those founders. If you don't have such creative resources, then prepare a seminar on the founding of the movement. Then provide group discussion material to explore how today's situation is similar to or different from those days, how those same concerns need to be addressed in your current context, and what contemporary issues need to be addressed from the standpoint of the values we hold dear as a Christian community.

5. If your church has a historic creedal statement, review it from the perspective of the contemporary and postmodern situation and ask how it needs to be revised. What would you express differently? What issues are no longer as important? Are there any blind spots that are now evident with hindsight? Are there any new issues you would want to include?

seven

From Attracting a Crowd
to Seeking the Lost

T*he changing nature of Western cultures, poised between* modernity and postmodernity, with a powerful tug of war between the two sides as well as a confusing intermingling of presuppositions and values, presents new challenges for the mission of the church in society, which we will explore in the following three chapters.

Whereas in traditional societies the churches have operated on a come-to-us philosophy, this is no longer adequate when the church finds itself marginalized and existing as just one piece in a complex, social, kaleidoscopic mosaic with the pieces constantly realigning. In this chapter we will explore the challenge this presents to the church, requiring it to change its orientation from a centripetal to a centrifugal dynamic. In other words, the church must be not only inviting but infiltrating the groups it seeks to introduce to the Savior.

The so-called seeker-sensitive evangelistic approach is built on the premise that church members are inviting friends who are not yet Christians to accompany them to church and that their friends are prepared to make that journey in order to hear the gospel. There is clear evidence, especially in North America, that many spiritually open, church-orphaned and earnest seekers welcome such an invitation. However, it must not be assumed that the impressive growth of many seeker-sensitive churches is due primarily to the conversion of the unchurched or to the reactivating of the once-churched-but-subsequently-lapsed. The bulk of the growth is more likely to be through the transfer of church members, either because of relocation or because of disillusionment or boredom with their former church.

A growing number of new churches have adopted the seeker-sensitive model from the outset, inspired by the writings and pastors' conferences emanating from Willow Creek Community Church in Barrington, Illinois, and Saddleback Community Church in southern California. Provided that these new churches are located in young, growing suburbs with fairly homogeneous populations, and pastors with a gift of evangelism and the ability to empower others around him in developing need-meeting ministries, such models may have great value.

In the case of existing churches attempting to transition to contemporary worship forms, it is much more difficult to make a significant impact on the community. This is even more the case for a church located in a pluralistic urban environment that considers its community to be its core ministry area. Such a commitment distinguishes it from other churches in urban settings that are located near efficient freeway systems that enable them to function as metropolitan congregations, drawing people of similar backgrounds from a wide area.

The seeker-sensitive approach reflects an honest and determined attempt to provide a welcome home for earnest seekers with no previous church background or with negative experiences of churchgoing. But it will prove an inadequate response to the most recent challenges confronting the churches in North America. The issue facing the church poised between gospel and culture is that it must constantly examine its own self-understanding. Most North American churches have yet to face the challenge of becoming truly *mis-*

sional. Michael Regele makes this assessment when he confesses, "We are even willing to suggest that some of the more popular models of ministry today such as the 'megachurch' concept, the 'seeker church,' and the new 'Cell' church—are only tactical attempts to breathe new life into old structures."[1]

However, seeker-sensitive churches have demonstrated an important point, namely that seekers are prepared to attend a worship service. The weekly gathering of the people of God is a key element in the dynamic of attraction. Yet we are left wondering whether they give enough credit to seekers in regard to their willingness to participate and not simply to remain as observers among a passive audience.

A Spiritual Search Rather Than an Intellectual Quest

In seeking to present the gospel to unbelievers, a strong emphasis has been placed in the past on overcoming intellectual obstacles to faith and on giving reasons to believe. The approach adopted was strongly apologetic in nature, on the assumption that the main reasons keeping people from belief were intellectual. While such an approach is appropriate in many secular and modern settings, in a postmodern cultural environment it may not constitute the starting part in a spiritual discussion. At present increasing numbers of people are already on a personal spiritual search for meaning and a sense of fulfillment.

The significance of worship for the seeker. As we saw in chapters five and six when we discussed spirituality and worship, and as we will see in the following chapter on evangelization, there is a hunger in people's hearts for the transcendent dimension of life. In regard to our present topic the current hunger for God stimulates the attraction that Spirit-filled worship has for some people who are looking for a corporate demonstration of the divine reality rather than wanting to engage in an interminable conversation. In his research into "new paradigm" churches Donald E. Miller discovered:

The routes to conversion are diverse, ranging from solitary religious quests to large group crusades. . . . What might be said is that because Christian symbols are part of the acculturation of most Americans, when there is a strong desire for lifestyle change—accompanied by the right triggering events—individuals readily seize on the Christian story as a guide for interpreting their experience.[2]

Here we note that the barriers to faith were not intellectual so much as experiential and behavioral. The disadvantage is that in trying to relate to a generation hungry for an experience of God, the seeker may simply feed on the experience without working through the life implications of that encounter. Within the Christian fellowship, acceptance and embodiment leads to transformation. If anyone is in Christ, he or she becomes part of Christ's new creation, including the mind and the will, as well as the emotions (2 Cor 5:17). Faith cannot be reduced to a fuzzy feeling.

Where the new growth is coming from in new paradigm churches. Although the majority of megachurch growth may be due to transfer, this does not represent the whole story. There is also a significant 20 percent consisting of persons who were not going to church prior to their affiliation, and there are some megachurches in which the conversion growth is considerably higher than this. Megachurches have made a significant contribution in attracting the dechurched baby boomers. New growth is even more marked in the case of the new paradigm churches, even among those smaller congregations that do not have the resources of the megachurches. Donald Miller's research into the Calvary Chapel and Vineyard fellowships of churches indicates that these movements are fulfilling a significant ministry in reaching the dechurched in considerable numbers.

In our survey we asked what affiliation people had the year prior to attending a new paradigm church. Nearly 30 percent stated that they were unaffiliated (in contrast to 13 percent during childhood). It seems highly possible that these individuals might have completely dropped out of organized religion had they not encountered an expression of it that they found palatable.[3]

Indeed, "if one counts as 'unchurched' those who attended religious services once a month or less during their childhood, then slightly more than a quarter of new paradigm members fit this profile." A surprising factor is the higher percentage of lapsed Catholics (28 percent) among this number, which leads Miller to comment that "new paradigm churches seem to be attracting people who one might not expect to be attending a Protestant church as adults."[4] In one sense the number of Roman Catholics making up the membership is not surprising, considering that southern California has a high percentage of Latinos. On the other hand, there are many other predominantly white congregations that are not proving attractive to boomers. The reason may have to do with the focus on God in worship in the new paradigm churches, which chimes in with the Latin culture, where religious experience is so vital a factor.

Both megachurches and those representing the new paradigm movement now face greater challenges in reaching the dechurched and never-churched segments of the population. They are not as readily accessible and responsive to the evangelical message as they were a decade ago. What are the reasons contributing to this hardening?

The Cresting Wave of Returning Seekers
In the wake of the Vietnam years some of the baby boomers returned to church in search of moral foundations, values and authentic spiritual experience. They were attracted to more conservative and contemporary expressions of Christianity than those in which they were nurtured. They were also the generation shaped by the media with high expectations and a predisposition that "seeing is believing." Seeker-sensitive churches represented a significant response to these returnees, and a small proportion of churches gained a large proportion of the returning boomers.

Yet these gains must be placed in a larger perspective. Only 25 percent of the boomers returned to church. The other three quarters chose to dissociate themselves from the church, and an increasingly large proportion no longer identify with Christian beliefs and values. Also, despite the emergence of more megachurches and the development of the new paradigm networks, overall church attendance has not increased. In fact, the trend has continued to be one of decline. This means either a smaller percentage of the population attends church, or the same percentage attends less frequently.

The wave has subsided and the pool is shrinking. At best the seeker-sensitive approach was a strategy with limited effectiveness, since a considerable number of unchurched boomers did not in fact return to Christian churches but sought spiritual fulfillment in other directions—Zen Buddhism, transcendental meditation, New Age beliefs and quasi-religious militias. Even among those appearing in evangelical churches, many came with a mix-and-match mentality. There is an urgent need for a reality check to examine more carefully the claims made for the seeker-sensitive approach as the main plank in the strategy to evangelize the unchurched at the dawn of a new millennium. One wonders to what extent megachurches are dependent on the feeder system supplied by smaller churches.

Herein lies a significant difference between church growth in the United States and in much of Europe, Canada, Australia and New Zealand. Most of the growth in the United States has been among the "semi-churched." Os Guinness draws attention to the fact that in the United States "most of the 'unchurched' reached would be better described as 'semi-churched.' Most of the newly reached 'unchurched' are really spiritual refugees from the collapse of three groups—legalistic fundamentalism, watered-down liberalism, and overritualistic traditionalism. The United States has yet to see the real unchurched as European Christians have experienced them."[5]

In other parts of the Western world the dechurched population consists not of "refugees" in search of something better but of people who have been turned off by institutional religion and have no interest in looking elsewhere. This is not to imply that the situation is without hope. But for the churches to begin to make any impact, they have to ask some very radical questions about their own identity.

It is not simply a matter of developing better marketing strategies or presenting an updated image. It demands a transforming experience of God and a deeper engagement with Scripture, both in fashioning the internal life of the church and in defining its mission in the world. Churches will need to become genuinely apostolic congregations committed to living out their faith in the world, feeling comfortable operating on the frontlines and prepared to venture into new territory. They will need to recognize that without the sovereign activity of the Holy Spirit, people who are outside of Christ and immersed in a neopagan culture are "dead through the trespasses and sins . . . following the course of this world, following the ruler of the power of the air, the spirit that is now at work among those who are disobedient, . . . following the desires of flesh and senses" (Eph 2:1-3). People who are spiritually "dead" are not aware of any needs until they are "awakened" by the persistent prompting of the Holy Spirit and the glimpses he gives of a more attractive alternative condition.

Seeking in other directions. As we saw in the previous chapter, a significant percentage of baby boomers who returned to church in the 1980s have become disillusioned and departed. According to George Barna the number of people who said that they would definitely attend church if they were invited by a friend has declined significantly in the past fifteen years to the point where only 20 percent of nonchurchgoers are likely to respond to invitations to return to church. Here we see a trend now taking place in the United States that for a much longer time has been evident in Europe. The wave of responsiveness seems to have broken on a rocky shore of pluralism and relativism.

In the early 1990s a greater number of seekers of authentic spirituality began to look elsewhere. George Barna's reports for 1991-1992 and 1994-1995 reveal that in a three-year period boomer attendance dropped by 11 percent. Of those boomers who still attend services, only 33 percent attend four times a month. Twenty-eight percent attend two times or less, and 24 percent of boomers who consider themselves Christians now skip worship entirely.[6]

Although Europe registered a baby boom after World War II, this generation is unlike the boomers of North America. Culturally they are much closer to the Gen Xers in the United States. They did not have the economic advantages enjoyed by their American contemporaries. They were excluded from social advance through the social class system that had not crumbled sufficiently for them to break through in significant numbers. They were influenced by a more radical popular culture and were distanced from the life of the church.

Yet on both sides of the Atlantic young people are engaged in a spiritual search that is unlikely to result in their seeking out local churches on their own initiative. Popular culture is constantly raising questions regarding the meaning of life and the cry for a sense of significance and fulfillment. The problem lies in the inability of most churches to connect with young people in terms they can understand and to which they can relate. There is both an age and culture gap between the two, which Richard Kew and Roger White express regarding their own Episcopal tradition. "While the rootedness of our tradition attracts a significant proportion of these young people, they are hardly likely to feel very much at home in a religious community whose interests and ages are closer to those of their parents or grandparents."[7]

Understanding Worship

Many of the problems with evangelical churches in the United States stem from a fundamental lack of understanding about the true nature of worship. This in turn impacts their spiritual vitality and evangelistic motivation. Worship is not primarily entertainment or instruction, or a morale booster to enable us to face the demands of the coming week, or an exercise in self-realization. Although there may be elements of all of these, they are not the main focus of worship, which is God himself.

Worship must not be subverted to serve other ends. Worship is a worthy end in and of itself. Our highest calling here on earth is to give glory to God in the praise offering of our lips and of our dedicated lives. Evelyn Underhill describes the act of worship with poetic insight.

> It is the implicit, even though unrecognized Vision of God—that disclosure of the Supernatural which is overwhelming, self-giving, and attractive all at once—which is the first cause of all worship, from the puzzled upward glance of the primitive to the delighted self-oblation of the saint. Here, the human derived spirit perceives and moves towards its Origin and goal; even though that perception shares the imperfections and uncertainties of the temporal order, and is often embodied in crude mistaken forms. Here man responds to the impact of Eternity, and in so doing learns the existence of Eternity; accepting his tiny place in that secret life of Creation, which consists in the praise, adoration, and manifestation of God. That is to say, he achieves his destiny.[8]

Under the influence of secularization, with its dismissal of the transcendent, humans have suffered a serious diminution of their powers to worship. It is like the city dwellers whose ears are so accustomed to the noise of traffic that they no longer hear the songs of the birds and, if they did, would be unable to distinguish the call of one bird from the call of another. Consequently, we have to be taught to be still and instructed in how to realize the presence of God. Without learning the disciplines and sensitivity to God's presence, our so-called worship activities will be directed elsewhere. As noted earlier, Underhill laments the "tendency of all worship to decline from adoration to demand, and from the supernatural to the ethical, shows how strong a pull is needed to neutralize the anthropocentric trend of the human mind; its intense preoccupation with the world of succession and its own here-and-now desires and needs."[9]

Worship stimulates evangelism. The connection between worship and evangelism is an intimate one. Although the two activities are closely intertwined, a distinction must be maintained. In the first place, witnesses must be worshipers; otherwise their commending of the faith will be little more than propaganda or salesmanship. Witness flows from our firsthand experiences of God. Morgenthaler emphasizes, "It is difficult to witness convincingly about a God we do not know and love in our inmost being. And when it comes to a worship service, we have already seen that seekers are not the least bit interested in watching us 'go through the motions.' . . . Although evangelism is one of the central tasks of the church, it is worship that 'drives' evangelism, not vice-versa."[10]

When is "worship" worship? Seeker-sensitive evangelism is built on the premise that nonbelievers cannot worship and that when they are brought into a worship service, they are being invited to engage in an alien activity. Therefore, they are present instead in a seeker-sensitive service as an audience to observe the worshipers (primarily a worship team engaging in a minimalist version of worship). The primary task of the worship team is to provide entertainment—not trivial audience titillation—in a more profound way by creatively and attractively addressing issues through songs, drama and well-crafted messages. The issues presented are relevant to the situations and concerns everyone encounters in the course of daily life. Such an approach is commendable pre-evangelism, but it should not be confused with worship and should not be offered as a substitute for worship.

Herein lies a pressing problem for seeker-sensitive churches, namely, if the Sunday service is not primarily for worship but to attract the seeker, when do the believers worship? Some seek an answer to this difficulty by offering a midweek worship service tailored for people who are already Christians. But this is an unsatisfactory response, as is evidenced by the much smaller number of people who are able to meet on this occasion due to midweek scheduling problems. The very timing of the worship services removes worship from its priority place in the life and purpose of the church.

Sally Morgenthaler expresses her concern for "worship deprioritization," commenting that "whatever your introductory orientation is in a church, that becomes your point of reference."[11] Here we see a contrast between the approach of the seeker-driven megachurches and the new paradigm churches that draw the inquirer into the presence of God. Clearly newcomers in the new paradigm churches are not put off by the extended time of worship that typically occupies the first forty-five minutes of the worship service. To the contrary, it is the worshipers' intimacy with God and the genuineness and intensity of their devotion that makes a powerful impact on seekers, preparing their hearts to receive the message that follows. The shift from anonymous observer to relational participant in part represents a change in learning styles between many boomers and Gen Xers. Seeker churches might need to reexamine their approach in the light of changing constituencies.[12] Morgenthaler asks:

> Why would we want to deny unbelievers access to something that is as potentially life-changing, healing, and beneficial as an experience of true worship? If it is because that kind of worship is not happening at our church, we had better admit it and get to work. . . . Worship is the most powerful tool we have for satisfying the hunger of famished, injured souls, for breaking down spiritual strongholds of pride and unbelief, and for ushering in the gift of true joy. How can we refuse to use it?[13]

The essentials of worship evangelism. Worship is not merely a time to speak corporately about God but to speak directly to God and to hear from God. When God speaks and is truly heard, our minds are enlightened and our lives are impacted. Above all else, worship is an encounter with the divine that is hesitant, humbling and exhilarating, or to put it in more theological terms, it generates within us the *mysterium tremendum.* We can sing "Bold I approach the eternal throne" only after we have been humbled and broken at the cross of Christ.

If we attempt to shortcut the pathway in order to avoid the cross, the boldness we proclaim is in reality presumptuous brashness. The outcome of worship is threefold: reconciliation with God and with one another; inspiration through the awareness of God with us in word, sacrament and saving signs; and transformation that results from the encounter with the Divine. Our worship should, in the literal meaning of the word, be characterized by *enthusiasm*—which signifies not simply human exuberance but the divine indwelling *(en-theos).*

Lifeless, meaningless worship will inevitably put off the newcomer who is not yet a believer. But in the heartfelt worship of a people surrendered to him, God is pleased to dwell in the praises of his people. Unbelievers are also likely to sense the presence of God. In England at the present time "celebration evangelism" is assuming a more prominent place, as distinct from the proclamation evangelism of the past. In order to invite unbelievers effectively into the presence of God, worship needs to have the following characteristics, as identified by Sally Morgenthaler:

☐ *Nearness*—A sense of God's presence

☐ *Knowledge*—Worship centered on Christ

☐ *Vulnerability*—Opening up to God

☐ *Interaction*—Participating in a relationship with God and others[14]

Commitment to ongoing evangelism. What needs to be emphasized regarding the ministries of both Bill Hybels (Willow Creek) and Rick Warren (Saddleback) is that both are gifted as evangelists and have a passion for the lost. Lyle Schaller highlights the fact that over the years Willow Creek has succeeded in maintaining its evangelistic priority, something many other churches let slide over the course of time. He writes,

> From the outsider's perspective, a persuasive argument can be offered that the distinctive characteristic of this large independent congregation is not its size or that high energy or the staff or that obsession with quality or their approach to the corporate worship of God. The unique characteristic is that week after week, year after year, and decade after decade, the number one priority has been reaching that audience of unchurched adults.[15]

Seeker-sensitive services do not consist simply of contemporary songs and creative drama but also of a preaching style that is highly relational and topical. It is extremely challenging to remain focused week after week on topics that will truly engage the audience. This approach can all too easily degenerate into pop psychology or social commentary. People come wanting to hear from God. They want to engage in the Christian story. They want a message that is unavailable elsewhere. Preachers face the challenge of communicating the content of Scripture in such a way that the congregation hears it as a fresh word from God addressed to them, not as an ancient message for a people two thousand or more years ago. Clearly the older analytical expository style will need to be modified to communicate in the present cultural context. From his experience of preaching at City Temple in the center of London, David Hilborn comments:

> My suspicion is that to be effective in the postmodern world, evangelical preachers will need much less to show people the expository wheels going round. The exegetical apparatus will still be necessary, but it will function less as the framework of the sermon and more as its scaffolding. It will have to be removed from view before the sermon is preached.[16]

In other words, the preacher shouldn't be parading his or her scholarship but drawing upon it to communicate truth at a popular level.

Rethinking cultural relevance. Eighty-three percent of the adults in the United States were churchgoers at some time in their lives. In fact, a walloping 95 percent of boomers received a religious upbringing. In a recent study, two-thirds of the unchurched said they would prefer to come back to an "informal" church experience.

Leith Anderson, in *Church for the 21st Century,* definitely sees traditional elements making a comeback—people are reacting to change, frightened by losing control and worried about the future. There is a lot of interest in the way things used to be. Nostalgia is in. His view is substantiated by the popularity of Gregorian chant CDs, which sell in the millions. And more recently, interest in Celtic Christianity has been high in much of Northern Europe; it is also beginning to make its presence felt here in North America.

In chapter five we outlined some features that especially appeal to Gen Xers in their search for a historically rooted spirituality. The appeal of both liturgical worship and ancient traditions of spirituality also reflect a reaction to the activism and wordiness characteristic of many evangelical churches today. As a respite from the frenzy and clamor of life, people of all ages are looking for times of calm, quiet and stillness to create a space where they can wait on God and recenter their fragmented and conflicted lives. Sally Morgenthaler observes the disconnection between wordy and high-tech evangelicalism and the multisensory "high touch" approach that is more likely to appeal to today's seekers.[17]

In the second half of this chapter we will focus on the need for the worshiping community itself to become the seeker, fanning out to encounter those who are seeking purpose and fulfillment in their lives. We must not overlook the point that at some stage seekers will be invited into the company of the worshipers. At that point it is critical that they are enveloped by a worship experience in which God is worshiped in Spirit and in truth and that they sense the presence of God dwelling in the worship of his people. Morgenthaler is forthright in her description of the shortcomings of much contemporary worship. She says it fails not only to appeal to seekers in our midst, but it also fails to be a transforming experience for many church members.

> The hour we spend at services like these will most likely be glutted with polished performances and pedestal personalities. Our emotions will be tapped by well-planned musical sequences and segues, culturally correct humor, pithy anecdotes, and well-rehearsed humility. We will have our brains stuffed with information about how to make life work and how to work harder at life. Most likely, we will leave feeling very good about ourselves. But one thing we will not have done: We will not have met with God. A true encounter with God leaves us with a lot more than good feelings. It leaves us with changed hearts and calls us to changed lives. Very simply, to experience God's presence is to be transformed from the inside out.

Where is this transformation today? More and more of us are leaving our worship centers and sanctuaries without even so much as a mar on our glossy finish! We are going out the same way we came in. We may have had an entertainment fix, a self-esteem fix, a self-righteousness fix or a self-help fix, but we have not been changed.[18]

The rhythm of weekly worship provides the opportunity for the seeker to gradually appreciate what is happening and be touched by it. This worship experience is reinforced by conversations with welcoming people who establish warm, respectful friendships. By being exposed to the worshiping community, seekers begin to realize that a vital dimension is lacking from their lives. Worship focuses on the God who is not only *there* but also *here* among us. It becomes an important element in the total process of a person coming to faith.

I agree with Morgenthaler in her assertion that pre-Christians are not blocked off from worship before they have committed their lives to Christ and been born of the Spirit. Who can tell when and how the Spirit of God begins to work in the soul of the seeker? Exposure to worship offered "in spirit and truth" often stimulates the search for God. It whets the appetite. "If we truly believe that all seekers have absolutely no ability to understand spiritual things, then we had better exclude them from crusades and seeker events as well as worship."[19]

In summary, the issue is that seeker-sensitive worship is a valid approach to evangelism when it is seen as part of a total strategy. We cannot assume that there are significant numbers of seekers in the community at large who are ready to take the initiative to visit churches. Certainly there will always be such individuals, but it is safer to assume that many more are not so motivated. And the most effective seeker-sensitive churches, in fact, do not simply work on the services to make them marketable to the unbeliever. Rather, pastors lead them with an evangelistic gift and have congregations sufficiently motivated to share their faith and do the inviting.

From Welcoming the Seeker to Seeking the Lost

The fundamental question raised by the seeker-sensitive approach to evangelism is, Who are the seekers? From the Gospels we learn that it was the "Son of Man [who] came to seek out and to save the lost" (Lk 19:10). The Great Commission entrusted to the church was to go into all the world, not to beckon to the world to come to it. The

Good Shepherd does not stand by the gate of the sheep pen calling for lost sheep to return but goes out in search of lost sheep. The churches in the West, and especially in the United States, have increasingly relied on a strategy of "welcome evangelism." Perhaps this has been in order to distance themselves from confrontational evangelistic strategies that were so prevalent from the 1960s to the 1980s. Relying on seeker-sensitive services as the main strategy for evangelism as we go into the new millennium means substituting the Good Shepherd approach for a Little Bo Peep approach. In the children's nursery rhyme:

> Little Bo Peep has lost her sheep
> And doesn't know where to find them,
> But leave them alone, and they will come home
> Wagging their tails behind them.

On the world mission scene Donald McGavran in the 1960s railed against mission agencies and churches because they had adopted what he termed "search theology." By this he meant a token search, which was often fruitless or meager in results, instead of a vast and continuous searching until the lost sheep were found and brought safely to the fold.[20] He expressed his concern that effective strategies be used to reach potentially responsive populations and employed the term "harvest theology." This is a concept that needs to be reinterpreted in light of the current challenge facing the churches in the West. Harvesting is done in the fields, not in barns. But the problem facing the contemporary churches is that in preparing the people of God for ministry, the main focus has been barn-based activities, rather than equipping and sending out teams of fieldworkers. Seeker-sensitive worship is an inadequate evangelistic strategy in a nonchurched culture in which 80 percent of evangelism must be conducted outside the sanctuary. In other words, the church needs to move from the *Constantinian* model—which presumed a churched culture—to an *apostolic* model designed to penetrate the vast unchurched segments of society.

Philip Kenneson and James Street draw attention to the inadequacy of relying on designing and advertising seeker-sensitive worship services as an effective evangelistic strategy:

> The unexamined assumption that the weekly worship service or the church building itself should be the centerpiece of the church's evangelism program stems from certain ways of thinking that presume a Christendom model. Within mainstream American culture, one could at one time assume a certain affinity between the culture of the church and the wider culture. In other words, one could assume a certain overlap between the language, convictions, practices, and narratives of the church and the language, convictions, practices, and narratives of the wider society. Within such a framework, evangelism often entailed little more than getting people to "come to church," for once there, much of what was happening was relatively understandable. But with the collapse of Christendom and the increasing secularization of American culture, things have changed dramatically. No longer can one assume that any overlap exists. The language, convictions, practices, narratives of the church are all but completely alien to the unbeliever in our society. This is why many Christians today speak of the need for "pre-evangelism."[21]

Seeking the Seeker

When Paul declared that he was prepared to become all things to all people in order that he might by every means save some, he was thinking not in *marketing* but in *missional* terms. His strategy was to make the transformation not on the security of his own familiar turf but on the turf of those he was endeavoring to win for Christ, which was a much more risky and demanding task. This dynamic is clearly brought out in Eugene Peterson's paraphrase of 1 Corinthians 9:19-23:

> Even though I am free of the demands and expectations of everyone, I have voluntarily become a servant to any and all in order to reach a wide range of people: religious, nonreligious, meticulous moralists, loose-living immoralists, the defeated, the demoralized—whoever. I didn't take on their way of life. I kept my bearings in Christ—but I entered their world and tried to experience things from their point of view. I've become just about every sort of servant there is in my attempts to lead those I meet into a God-saved life. I did all this

because of the Message. I didn't just want to talk about it; I wanted to be *in* on it.[22]

The apostle Paul's strategy was not one of extraction but of incarnation. According to Kenneson and Street, "Paul could do this precisely because he was out among these different people, trying to figure out how to communicate the gospel to them in their own terms. He was not trying to figure out how to design a worship service or ministries that would attract them to a building."[23]

Donald McGavran developed the "people group" approach to evangelism, not as a device for segmenting the "market" to invite people like us but as a strategy for penetrating the mission fields of the world. He was interested in meeting people on their own turf and identifying with the seeker. As we have seen, McGavran's emphasis went beyond seeking lost sheep to finding and enfolding them. He was concerned that the seed be sown as widely and plentifully as possible, with a view to achieving a maximum harvest through carefully cultivating the fields that had been sown. In the process of sowing their seed, farmers come to recognize which is the receptive soil. It is futile to sow seed on hard, stony soil. Hard work and great patience are needed to prepare the soil to receive the precious seed.[24]

Moving Beyond Seeker-Sensitive Strategies

The challenge of reaching the lost is more radical when the worship service is seen from a missional and not simply a marketing perspective. The so-called seeker-sensitive approach will remain significant as long as there are seekers out there who are coming to the church for answers. Yet I do not think that we can rely on a seeker-sensitive approach as our main strategy for urban evangelism in the coming decades. Leighton Ford sees beyond the seeker-sensitive approach in trying to reach the unchurched.

> After World War II, the Sunday school emerged as a powerful evangelistic tool in most churches. From the mid-1960s to the 1980s, the Sunday Worship Service—especially the Willow Creek-style "seeker service"—was the principal point of entry.

But as we move through the 1990s, we are seeking a proliferation of entry points, especially non-weekend events such as cell groups and home Bible studies, retreats, support and recovery groups, and affinity groups.[25]

There is increasing evidence that disillusioned boomers are now looking outside of Christianity and that a disturbingly large number of Gen Xers has given up on church. In their case the church must become the seeker, following the example of Jesus.

I believe there is an increasing need to distinguish between various categories of seekers. In addition to "returning seekers" there are "disillusioned seekers," "despairing seekers" and "deluded" or "diverted seekers." More and more seekers may be looking not in the direction of Christian churches that regard themselves as seeker-sensitive but for alternative forms of religious experience.

As I reflect on the application of Donald McGavran's insights to the situation in the United States, I am concerned that we may have substituted marketing for mission and thereby seriously compromised the church-growth paradigm. A market-driven approach can lead to superficial responses to deep issues. It can lead to the promotion of a distorted form of the gospel that appears to meet needs yet does not challenge priorities and assumptions.

Evangelization as an Invitation to Companionship

In practical terms what will it mean for the church to become the seeker? In the first place it will entail the church coming to a fresh understanding that it is called to live not for itself but for the world that the Lord came to save. The church will need to review all its activities in the light of the great objective to be a sign and a servant of the kingdom of God in the world. It will mean facing a long list of hard questions, headed by the challenge, "Is there sufficient evidence within the confessing community that the King is indeed in residence among his people?"

Darrell Guder raises the issue of the priority of the church's internal mission to live out its calling within its own ranks. The reign of God is given; it is received; we are invited to enter. The reign of God also embraces the eschatological tension of God's reign being a present fact and an anticipated future. "The [church's] first mission is always the internal mission: the church evangelized by the Holy Spirit again and again in the echoing word of Jesus inviting us to receive the reign of God and to enter it."[26]

In engaging in the task of evangelizing others, the church itself is constantly being evangelized. Its own members cannot present the gospel to others without themselves continually facing the promises, claims and challenges of the gospel afresh. The gospel is good news even after it has been heard a thousand times. It never becomes mere platitudes from history. When the church addresses itself at the same time it addresses others, its approach is more believable and winsome.

Good news sharing is not a declaration from people who have all the answers and have appropriated all that the gospel conveys. Rather we share as much about God as we have come to understand, and we invite others to join us in our pilgrimage through life. In joining us they will enrich our fellowship by the questions they ask, the enthusiasm they demonstrate and the freshness they bring. The presence of seekers and new believers provides a necessary reality check that at times will be discomforting as well as invigorating. Darrel Guder emphasizes the importance of companionship in the journey.

> Evangelism would move from an act of recruiting or co-opting those outside the church to an invitation of companionship. The church would witness that its members, like others, hunger for the hope that there is a God who reigns in love and intends the good of the whole earth. The community of the church would testify that they have heard the announcement that such a reign is coming, and indeed is already breaking into the world. They would confirm that they have heard the open welcome and received it daily, and they would invite others to join them as those who also have been extended God's welcome.[27]

In the next chapter we will explore the outworking of these attitudes in the task of enfolding seekers into the confessing community. Seekers are invited to participate fully in order to examine the fellowship of Christians at close quarters as insiders. They may ask whatever questions they wish and may hold the members accountable by pointing out inconsistencies and compromises. The seeker has a right to test our profession of faith to see to what extent it is lived out in an authentic lifestyle.

Implementation

1. Assess the effectiveness of your church in attracting visitors. Invite visitors to share what attracted them to the church and what their first impressions were. Did members of the congregation welcome them? Was the service meaningful and easy to follow? Was their experience a positive one?

2. What is the level of expectation of (a) the church leaders and (b) the congregation in terms of their awareness of the presence of visitors? Do they anticipate the presence of visitors who will be drawn to Christ through the presentation of the gospel?

3. What changes would need to be made in your style and pattern of worship in order to lead Gen Xers into the presence of God?

4. What significant segments of the population is your church failing to reach? Are other churches proving more effective in reaching them? If not, what steps are you prepared to take in order to meet with them on their turf?

eight

- -

From Belonging
to Believing

n societies where there is widespread suspicion of exaggerated claims, ploys for power, manipulative marketing techniques and organized religion the church will have to adopt different communication strategies to avoid suspicion. Its stance must be less confrontational and programmatic, and more relational and contextual. We will argue that we have a lot of unlearning to do if we are to relate to a growing segment of the population that has either given up on church or for which church has never been part of its life. In this regard churches in the United States are increasingly experiencing the same degree of alienation among young people that has been true for several generations of young people in Europe.

Evangelism in the United States has been influenced strongly by revivalism, that is, the restoration to personal faith of former church members or of those who were nurtured within a churchgoing culture. Because of the social strength of churches and the high percentage of the population reared in the evangelical tradition, we have in the past been able to assume that people in the United States had quite a bit of background knowledge about the Bible and the content of the gospel. We could assume that a person was culturally compatible with the Christian church.

This assumption, historically, influenced the approach of the visiting evangelists. They would arrive in town for a week of special meetings designed to restore the spiritually and morally wayward. It is significant that the evangelistic meetings were generally billed as "revival meetings," which reflects the fervor of the occasion. Rodney Clapp states, "The most prominent American evangelistic paradigm from the eighteenth century right into our day [is] revivalism," and observes that "revivalism aims to revive or revitalize the preexisting but now latent faith of birthright Christians."[1] In the context of the United States, the most widely adopted evangelistic strategy was a brief presentation culminating in an invitation to respond immediately to the gospel. As with many a salesperson, the sales pitch of the preacher consisted of a "one shot, hot sell, close the deal" presentation.

We will examine in this chapter the proposition that such a strategy is increasingly inappropriate for the boomer, buster and mosaic (millennial) generations in the United States. It has proven even more inappropriate and ineffective in the European context. Consequently there has been a swing away from confrontational toward relational approaches, which has in turn highlighted serious problems. Many Christians have few non-Christians with whom they are in contact and feel comfortable sharing their story and explaining the gospel. The lone ranger, entrepreneurial approach is inadequate and needs to be replaced by teams and communities of witnesses scattered and strategically placed in the many segments of our fragmented postmodern world.

From Believing to Belonging and Behaving

One problem with confrontational forms of evangelism, whether in a mass meeting or person-to-person, is that people will acquiesce only under duress. There is a great deal of truth in the old saying, "A person persuaded against his will, is of the same opinion still." As fallout to this method, there are many people who claim a "born again" experience whose lives do not evidence any change of heart or ways. Furthermore, lone-ranger evangelistic encounters can lead to people making a decision without ever getting involved in a community of believers. Premature, intrusive procedure can result in the aborting of a potential new birth.

In a secular society that individualizes and privatizes faith, self-confessed Christians delude themselves into thinking that they can survive alone. They revert to their accustomed manner of life, secure in the belief that they now hold an eternal life insurance policy.

The strengths of the confrontational approach. When I point out the limitations of the confrontational approach, some would say that I am really dealing with the abuses of the method. As a corrective, it is only fair to acknowledge the strengths of confrontational evangelism. Mark McCloskey, who worked for Campus Crusade for Christ, provides one of the most lucid and balanced arguments regarding confrontational and relational strategies. He writes that those who adopt a confrontational strategy do so in the belief that "as many as possible should hear as soon as possible, as clearly as possible."[2] This strategy emphasizes the theological and missiological urgency of the task. Our responsibility is to communicate the gospel as widely, quickly and efficiently as possible so that as many people as possible might have the opportunity to hear and respond to Christ. People who use a confrontational approach also operate under the conviction that there is inherent power in the message and that with each gospel presentation, the supernatural power of the Spirit is able to achieve God's purposes in the life of the unbeliever quite independently of the presenter. Therefore, they are prepared to embrace all means that are ethically appropriate in order to reach all people.

The weaknesses of the confrontational approach. To the drawbacks which we have already mentioned we need to add that it can be intrusive when there is an overbearing manner or insensitivity in regard to timing. Bad experiences make it more difficult to subsequently reach people who have been put off by such approaches.

The confrontational person often gives the impression that he is setting himself above the other individual.

Those who criticize the confrontational approach of evangelists and other Christians who are eager to share their faith with all who cross their path must beware lest their opposition be, in reality, a cover for their own lack of evangelistic concern. When Dwight L. Moody was criticized for his evangelistic methods, he is reported to have replied the he didn't care much for them himself. But "on balance, I prefer my way of doing it to your way of not doing it!" Indeed some defend the use of the confrontational method on the grounds that it must be resorted to because the vast majority of believers are not accepting their responsibility to witness to people around them. It must be admitted that they have a valid point.

The confrontation method characterized by both mass meetings and by armies of Christians trained to present the gospel following a simple outline is still effective in many areas of the world. This is especially the case where there is spiritual awareness in the culture and an eagerness to hear and to respond to the good news that they are hearing for the first time. However, such openness does not characterize the prevailing spiritual climate in the West. Here many people who are resistant to unsolicited approaches feel they know too much already about the church and its message. Or else they consider that religion in general is irrelevant and thus reject Christianity as intolerant of other faiths. Intrusive and insensitive approaches simply confirm people's stereotypes and prejudices. Once people have been scarred by such a confrontation, it is all the more difficult to gain a considered hearing.

Communicating Through the Christian Community

In a world where the church exists as a minority movement in an increasingly hostile culture, the church needs the strength of community to reinforce its message. Donald Posterski expresses this in terms of Christian communities becoming "meaning-makers."

The world needs to see what the Christian life looks like. People who think God is unnecessary, or just optional in life, need fresh images of how life is meant to be lived. They need hard evidence that following Jesus really makes a difference.

In order to engage today's world with a credible Christianity, contemporary followers of Jesus will need to be strategic. Injecting fresh meaning into the old gospel will not be achieved by buying more prime-time television or by handing out colored tracts. Rather, the gospel will be perceived as a feasible alternative when those who do not know God have some positive personal experiences with people who do know him.[3]

From belonging to believing. The never-churched need to be enveloped by small communities of believers so that they can see the impact of the gospel in their relationships and experience some of the benefits through intentional spillover. Such was the dynamic that made the pre-Constantinian church so effective. Within the context of the Christian communities the disillusioned, cynical and disinterested are respected and accepted, and are converted into "awakened seekers," to employ John Wesley's significant description.

Willow Creek Community Church provides an impressive contemporary model for applying a strategy by which unchurched people are invited to a seeker-friendly service, where they can listen without being pressured. As outlined here, "Unchurched Harry" has the opportunity to hear multiple presentations that relate the gospel to his needs while in the company of tens of thousands of people like himself.

1. A friendship develops between Harry and a Willow Creek attender.

2. The attender shares a verbal witness with Harry.

3. Harry visits a Willow Creek weekend meeting, which is designed for unchurched individuals.

4. Harry begins attending "New Community," a midweek worship and teaching meeting.

5. Harry joins a small group.

6. Harry uses his gifts in serving.

7. Harry becomes a good steward of his finances.[4]

A common problem with such a strategy is trying to move people from step two to step three because many people want the benefits of the message without having to get too personally involved. The challenge is even stronger when the seeker is surrounded by friends who regard strongly held religious beliefs as alien to their culture. As Donald Posterski has pointed out, in today's world we Christians are a minority, and the non-Christians' way of life is the norm.[5] "In subtle whispers and with bold accolades the culture chants, 'You do not need God. You do not need God.' And when you hear the same message over and over again, at least at an unconscious level, you begin to believe it."[6] Confessing Christians soon begin to feel the impact of their marginalized status, which Posterski describes as "social demotion."[7]

To ensure that the third step in the seeker-sensitive strategy does not constitute so great a hurdle, an alternative approach is needed to provide a series of attractive evangelistic presentations to which individuals are invited. These presentations involve them in relationship building. They come as part of a crowd, sit among friends at a meal, then hear a talk about an aspect of the gospel. Then everybody forms smaller groups with trained discussion facilitators. During this time everyone is invited to express what he or she felt about the message. Without a doubt the most significant application of this dynamic in operation is the Alpha Course, which originates in Holy Trinity Brompton Church, an Anglican church in London, England. To date the course has attracted a million or more participants! Within the context of the supportive, healing, informing and inviting community, the implications of "power evangelism" need to be considered.

The use of the term *belonging* does not imply that the unbeliever is spiritually incorporated into the body of Christ, for that cannot occur apart from the regenerating work of the Holy Spirit. We must recognize that if we do not have the spirit of Christ, we do not belong to him. Here I am using the term *belong* to mean full acceptance as a human being made in the image of God even though that image is marred by sin.

A sense of belonging places seekers in the position of observer-participant so that they can learn what the gospel is all about. They can observe at close quarters how it impacts the lives of individuals and shapes a community. Through this process the seeker comes to know when he or she is ready to make a personal decision to fully identify both with the Lord and the body of Christ.

In a fragmented and pluralistic society it is even more important than ever for the church "in each time and place to embody and communicate the life of Christ exactly where it is. . . . Christians are called to live the story, not restate it in the forms of universalized propositions. . . . Christianity is not an ideology to be recovered or a philosophical system to be remembered."[8] As communities of believers are scattered throughout every segment of society, non-believers will find those fellowships accessible. They will discover people like themselves working out the implications of their faith in every area of life, people whose lifestyles and occupations closely correspond with their own.

In other words, nonbelievers will be exposed to the gospel in a highly contextualized form. They will not be confronted with a generic, propositional message, but one in which the big story of salvation history as recorded in Scripture is worked out in the little stories of the lives of each individual and at the micro level of the local group of believers. What's more, they will not be presented with an idealized version of the story that will later lead them to become disillusioned. Instead they will engage in open and honest dialogue with people they know well and consider credible witnesses.

Great preaching and high-quality music may be able to draw a crowd, but they do not build an *organism* in which all have a functional role. In a phrase, the gospel is about the restoring and building of relationships with a holy God and with one another in the body of Christ, as well as with the wider community we serve. We receive one another with unconditional love. But that does not mean the church is a society in which anything goes. The goal of acceptance is to work toward transformation, not that people should feel more comfortable about their sins. Bruce and Marshall Shelley underscore this point when they insist that change requires belonging as well as believing:

> We change not only from capturing some new idea or experiencing some emotional crisis but by accepting a new view of reality and entering into new relationships. A conversion alone means little until it is reinforced by a community that makes sense of the new life we have entered. That is why the early North African Christian Tertullian, said, "Christians are made, not born."[9]

In a bureaucratic secular society, the individual is reduced to the level of a nonperson. Against this the postmodernists react strongly—and rightly so.[10] For, from the perspective of biblical theology, people are made in the image of God, and the vestiges of that image remain despite the Fall. Consequently, every person has intrinsic worth and must not be reduced to a statistic or turned into a dispensable functionary—a human resource—who will eventually wind up on the human scrapheap.

Among boomers and Gen Xers there is an apprehensive craving for community—apprehensive because people are wary of becoming overly committed and because these two generations have already experienced abuse and betrayal. They do not want to be exposed to further hurt and harm. Yet they still want to keep their options open. As Rodney Clapp observes, we live in a culture that is not community-friendly.

> This is a world system that rewards and promotes novelty over the familiar, reservation of options over commitment, an "open" future over an accepted past, functional over substantive relationships, what works over doctrine, independence over interdependence and quantitative measures of worth over qualitative measures of worth. None of this bodes well for community.[11]

This is a special challenge for churches both large and small. Large churches face the challenge of ensuring that individuals do not get lost in the crowd but are gently and persistently wooed into supportive and accountable relationships. Small churches risk forming an exclusive group that is difficult for newcomers to penetrate because they cannot get past the "gatekeepers." Misfits have nowhere else to go in a single-cell church. They disappear to try their luck elsewhere, or they resign themselves to going nowhere.

Welcoming unbelievers into the fellowship puts believers on notice that their personal lives and corporate interaction are under close scrutiny. By the ways in which we interact, do we make it easier or harder for the visitor in our midst to believe in a gracious God? Making it easier to believe will only happen as we learn to treat one another in the same way that the Lord treats us—with generosity and long-suffering. "Effective evangelization is the saying of the gospel in full harmony with the being and doing of the witness. Within the community of faith, we need to hear the gospel in ever-renewed readiness to have it confront and convict us as believers, whose faith is as yet too small."[12]

Full of grace and truth. Having been with Jesus during the three-year period of his earthly ministry, John could write, "We have seen his glory, the glory as of a father's only son, full of grace and truth" (Jn 1:14). "Grace" speaks of the costly generosity of God toward the undeserving, and "truth" refers to the reliability of all that Jesus taught and his personal authenticity. In other words, he was for real. Furthermore, Jesus did not just display these qualities, he imparted them to his followers. The first disciples bore witness to the fact that "from his fullness we have all received, grace upon grace" (Jn 1:16).

The apostle Paul made the same point as someone who had never had the privilege of knowing Jesus as had the other disciples. "And all of us, with unveiled faces, seeing the glory of the Lord as though reflected in a mirror, are being transformed into the same image from one degree of glory to another; for this comes from the Lord, the Spirit" (2 Cor 3:18).

Yet we need to frankly acknowledge the shortcomings of the church. Critics of Christianity excel in pointing out the wide credibility gap, which is plainly evident, between what the gospel espouses and what the church actually is and does. We cannot emphasize the incarnational nature of the church and its work and then deny that incarnation by making the "true church" into an ephemeral, spiritual entity that is neither historical nor experiential.

The strengths of the relational approach. Being exposed to the gospel within the context of a Christian group emphasizes the importance of the friendship factor. God's way of speaking to us and of ministering to our needs is through a Person: "God so loved the world that he gave his only Son" (Jn 3:16). Each friendship constitutes a bridge, both to further understanding and into the network of relationships. Small groups provide a quality context in which the new Christian can grow. They offer a ready-made opportunity for several people to share their stories and explain the gospel in a variety of ways.

In a small-group setting, unlike a one-time encounter, there is no time constraint to pressure people into a premature decision. Individuals who have little prior knowledge of the gospel or exposure to Christian community especially need time to grow in understanding before they are ready to commit themselves. Group members can get to know such an individual, coming to appreciate his or her personality, background and current situation, which helps them to speak the gospel with a closer application. Time needs to be allowed for the "courtship" to develop. While it is true that for some couples it is "love at first sight," this remains the exception rather than the rule.

The weaknesses of the relational approach. As with the confrontational approach already discussed, there are also potential weaknesses when people argue for the relational approach as the only legitimate way to present the gospel. An exclusive relational focus can result in our never going out of our way to reach those out of touch with Christians and may deaden us to the potential significance of chance encounters. There can be an overemphasis on relationship building to the point that there is an unhealthy shift of focus from the message to the personality and experience of the witness. Also, those who stress relational evangelism over confrontational evangelism tend to display an aversion to methodology, tools and systematic strategy. Where there is an absence of training, usually there is a lack of effective evangelistic outreach.[13]

Factors influencing our approach. A number of factors influence the approach that people adopt in evangelism. First, there are theological presuppositions regarding the present condition and eternal destiny of the lost. Second, there is the contrast between the itinerant and the more localized ministry. Contrast the relational ministry model of Jesus, whose movements were confined to a small geographical area in which he frequently retraced his steps, with the confrontational approach of the apostle Paul, who traveled over a vast area. Third, there is the influence of personality. Whatever our personality type, we must be prepared to step outside our comfort zone. People who have extrovert personalities take the initiative in opening up conversations, while introverts are far more guarded and must make great efforts to initiate a conversation. Fourth is the area of our gifting. People with the evangelistic gift tend to be more confrontational, driven by a sense of urgency and compassion for the lost.

From a Prepackaged Presentation to a Person-Centered Approach

This is the nub of the problem with regard to training in evangelism. Previously evangelism training was based on a single approach and a fixed gospel outline. It is questionable whether this strategy was adequate in the past, and increasingly we are finding that one particular approach is not appropriate for many individuals who are open to God. People do not want to be processed in a propaganda machine; each person wants to be treated as an individual who is listened to, as a unique person whose opinion is respected and whose knowledge is weighed fairly. This present-day aversion to prepackaged presentations is especially strong among Gen Xers.

Those who witness in a Gen X context need to be less dogmatic and confrontational and must resist dividing the world into "haves" and "have-nots." It is much more helpful to use the language of journey. We need to remind ourselves that God always got there before we did and that the listeners are already on their spiritual journey and have their story to relate. While many may be dangerously off course, others may be moving toward Christ, even though they do not recognize him as yet.

Kevin Ford advocates an evangelistic approach that emphasizes narrative rather than propositions. For many Gen Xers life has become meaningless; therefore, "the very storylessness of this generation is our opportunity! Because not only do we have the story—the gospel itself—but we also offer an alternative community, a narratable world in which human meaning can be discovered and lived out. That narratable world is the church."[14]

Another problem associated with learning a gospel presentation is that we can make an outline too complicated, with the result that believers are inhibited rather than enabled in expressing their testimony. They are even more hesitant to start a gospel presentation for fear of getting the steps out of order or forgetting a crucial memory verse needed to substantiate a point.

Sometimes too much is assumed in a gospel outline. The presentation doesn't start far enough back; it takes for granted that people believe in a personal God, the deity of Christ, life after death, and the existence of heaven and hell. There is the temptation to say too much at one time. We move ahead too rapidly for people to assimilate what we are saying. As a consequence we are still speaking long after they have stopped listening.

Recognize the value in developing a variety of approaches. Our approach must be flexible because individuals are so different from each other in their personalities, life experiences, perceptions and levels of spiritual awareness and interest. We must also be dependent on the Holy Spirit, not only in terms of when and to whom we should speak but also in regard to what we say. We must come to terms with the fact that there is no evidence of a "canned" approach in Jesus' dealing with individuals, although no doubt he repeated himself on many occasions. He had to deal with similar issues when speaking with smug Pharisees at various times. Yet he had a completely different agenda when in company with religious outcasts, tax collectors or prostitutes.

It is helpful to think about specific individuals or groups of people we know work out how we might present the gospel in each situation. What ideas and choice of words would make sense or arouse their curiosity? Think of a variety of ways in which the Scriptures approach the gospel. List the key ideas with appropriate Bible passages and verses. Then represent the idea visually in the form of a simple diagram. Remember, you don't necessarily have to explain *all* of the gospel in any one presentation. There is value in a multiple approach, coming at the gospel from a variety of angles.

Start with one particular approach but don't get locked into it. As in learning any new skill, the best approach is to learn a little and practice a lot, rather than learning more and more with little or no opportunity to put into practice what we have been taught. This is how we master any skill, whether it be playing a sport or learning how to use a computer. In evangelism, use one approach until you can present the gospel with clarity and confidence. Practice with your Christian friends through role play. Hear yourself saying it until it no longer sounds hesitant or forced. Another golden rule is that you should not say anything that you don't feel comfortable saying. If that's not how you speak, then don't say it that way. We have to learn our own way to explain the gospel in order to "own" the message.

When we have gained confidence in witnessing on a number of

occasions using one particular approach, we are then ready to begin developing others. It is often helpful to try out ideas with a group of Christian friends who are also eager to improve their effectiveness in presenting the gospel. The person with whom we are endeavoring to share the good news about Jesus can also provide helpful feedback. We should not hesitate to ask whether what we are saying is making sense to them.

Developing Alternative Ways of Presenting the Gospel

Neither in the four Gospels nor in the account of the expansion of the early church in Acts do we find a "standard" gospel presentation. C. H. Dodd argues that there were six basic elements in the *kerygma* in the early church. They covered the birth, death, burial, resurrection, exaltation and return of Jesus Christ and were followed by a closing appeal to repent of sin, to be baptized and to receive the gift of the Holy Spirit. Each of the significant events in Jesus' life and ministry was interpreted in the light of the Old Testament prophecies concerning the dawning of a messianic age.[15] However, the explanation and contextualization of these concepts cannot be achieved in the course of a brief gospel presentation. Furthermore, it must be recognized that most of the messages recorded in Acts relate to Paul's ministry among Jews, where he could assume a comprehensive knowledge of the Old Testament. Thus Paul framed his message in terms of the Jewish context. Note that his approach is very different among the Gentile audiences in Lystra (Acts 14:15-17) and in Athens (Acts 17:22-31).

More recently a number of New Testament scholars have argued that C. H. Dodd made the *kerygma* far too wooden and fixed, notwithstanding the fact that the key elements must always stand at the heart of the gospel.[16] Robert C. Worley points out that "there was a basic core but also a wide variety in the way it was presented. Evangelism is never proclamation in a vacuum; but always to people, and the message must be given in terms that make sense to them."[17] Dodd has also been taken to task for creating too sharp a distinction between proclaiming the gospel to unbelievers and teaching believers in the church meeting, because in New Testament times teaching was not restricted to believers alone but was addressed to all who were ready to listen. The terms teaching and preaching in the book of Acts are used interchangeably.[18]

In seeking to communicate the core of the gospel among people who have little or no knowledge of who Jesus is or of the biblical stories and concepts, much more time and patience is required. The same missionary principles must be applied in a Western context as in other parts of the world, whether pre-Christian or post-Christian. In both scenarios a great number of misconceptions may need to be cleared away in order for the message to be heard. In any situation the following suggestions should be kept in mind:

☐ Provide a variety of approaches applicable to different situations in which we have an opportunity to express our hope in Christ.

☐ Keep each approach as simple as possible by basing it on one biblical concept and utilizing one visual picture.

☐ Practice in order to gain confidence in using each approach to explain the gospel in everyday language.

☐ Provide Bible references that support the key concept you are using as a basis of your gospel presentation.

☐ Recognize that all of the gospel can never be encapsulated in one presentation.

Based on the above considerations the following examples demonstrate different ways of introducing the gospel, each for a specific context. Each presentation is based on one key concept and refers to just one passage of Scripture from which the gospel can be explained. Sometimes alternative versions of the Scripture passage will prove helpful because they render a clearer translation than the version normally used. The list does not pretend to be exhaustive but is offered as a basis for developing further approaches appropriate for other contexts.

To those who say that God seems remote from their lives. For people to whom God seems remote, the well-known "bridge over the chasm" illustration is particularly appropriate. The chasm represents the separation from a hóly God created by the sin in our lives. That chasm cannot be bridged from our side, whether by good works, religious knowledge or our spiritual experiences. They key verses in this presentation are Romans 3:23-24, *"Since all have sinned and fall short of the glory of God; they are now justified by his grace as a gift, through the redemption that is in Christ Jesus."* Rather than jumping from this verse to other texts dealing with other "steps" to salvation, it is preferable to spend time discussing each of the key terms—*sinned, glory, justified, grace, redemption* and *Christ Jesus.* We cannot assume that the person with whom we are speaking has a clear understanding of each of these key terms. It is more likely that the listener will misinterpret them on the basis of the misinformation he or she already has.

It is also helpful to open the Bible so people can see the verses for themselves and place the phrases quoted in the context in which they were written in Paul's letter to the Romans. Supporting texts such as Isaiah 59:2 and Ephesians 2:13 might also be referred to in order to reinforce the separation image.

To overachievers determined to reach the top of the ladder at any cost. The gospel of Christ presents a radical challenge to those who believe that fulfillment in life flows from human achievement. A life of ruthless competitiveness and self-centered ambition destroys relationships and ultimately the individual. The key verse here is found in 2 Corinthians 5:15: *"And he died for all, so that those who live might live no longer for themselves, but for him who died and was raised for them."* Here the contrast is made between Jesus' life of sacrificial self-giving and our self-centered attitude to life. We can then turn to Jesus' teaching in the Gospels that provide the basis for Paul's way of life. For instance, in Matthew 16:26 Jesus speaks of the futility of gaining the whole world at the price of losing one's soul. In Luke 9:23 Jesus insists that following him entails self-denial and self-surrender as an attitude that needs to be renewed each day. Paul sought to practice what Jesus preached, as we see in Romans 14:8 and Philippians 1:21.

To those who feel that their lives are so messed up that they are beyond help. People whose lives are in a mess need to be helped to realize that the Christian life does not consist either in simply a course correction or in trying to bring order. Rather it offers the necessity of a brand-new start through forgiveness, reconciliation and the impartation of God's own presence in our lives through the person of the Holy Spirit. Here the key verse is 2 Corinthians 5:17: *"So if anyone is in Christ, there is a new creation; everything old has passed away; see, everything has become new!"* The gospel emphasizes not only the need for reconciliation but also the possibility of transformation arising out of a continuing relationship with God as his child and as a member of his family, the church.

In making this point, the main thrust of 2 Corinthians 5 needs to be kept in mind, namely, that believing, belonging and behaving are inextricably linked. In the absence of a supportive community, the world is likely to have the greatest influence in molding a person's life. This is made clear in Romans 12:2, which is vividly paraphrased by J. B. Phillips. "Don't let the world around you squeeze you into its own mold, but let God remold your minds from within, so that you may prove in practice that the plan of God for you is good, meets all his demands and moves toward the goal of true maturity." Supporting texts include 2 Corinthians 12:9, Philippians 4:13 and Colossians 1:27.

To those crushed by a sense of guilt. A key passage on working through guilt is Psalm 51:1-12. It reflects David's anguish as a man of God who has fallen into grievous sin of adultery—then murder to conceal his immorality. With this understanding of the background to the Psalm, we can appreciate more fully the strength of the sentiments expressed. David offers no excuses, he simply throws himself on the mercy of God. By verse 17 he is able to say, *"The sacrifice acceptable to God is a broken spirit; a broken and contrite heart, O God, you will not despise."*

Two other references highlight the removal of guilt. The first speaks of blood-red stains being removed beyond trace so that the cloth is snowy white (Is 1:18). The other refers to forgiveness in terms of distance: *"As far as the east is from the west, so far he removes our transgressions from us"* (Ps 103:12). Satan is in the habit of reminding us of the sins God has already erased from his memory. When people have come to the point where they want to know how God can forgive them, then we can go on meaningfully to speak of Christ's substitutionary death. We can explain that in his death on the cross Christ bore the penalty of sin and removed the stain and broke the chains of sin. Guilt-ridden people often need to linger in the company of forgiven people to help them to claim those promises of forgiveness.

To those overwhelmed by anxiety. Anxiety occurs when we always expect the worst and feel apprehensive about all the circumstances outside of our control. At times anxiety builds up when we know we have taken too much upon ourselves. We pretend to be stronger and wiser than we are, but we are too proud to come to terms with our limitations. Two key verses that apply when we are in this state of mind are Luke 12:22-31 and 1 Peter 5:6-7, which says, *"Humble yourselves therefore under the mighty hand of God, so that he may exalt you in due time. Cast all your anxiety on him, because he cares for you."*

To those who are afraid of death. Sooner or later fear of death becomes a big issue for many Westerners because our culture is a death-denying one. Consequently, when we can no longer avoid the topic as a loved one dies or when we are faced with the issue of our own mortality, we are ill-equipped to deal with it. A Christian perspective on death is provided in Romans 8:35-39. This passage makes the point that nothing can separate us from the love of Christ, not even death itself.

> Who will separate us from the love of Christ? Will hardship, or distress, or persecution, or famine, or nakedness, or peril, or sword? As it is written,
>> "For your sake we are being killed all day long;
>> we are accounted as sheep to be slaughtered."

No, in all these things we are more than conquerors through him who loved us. For I am convinced that neither death, nor life, nor angels, nor rulers, nor things present, nor things to come, nor powers, nor height, nor depth, nor anything else in all creation, will be able to separate us from the love of God in Christ Jesus our Lord.

None of the above examples represents a complete statement of the gospel. Instead each is a way of beginning to speak about essential aspects of the new life in Christ. Often the most fruitful witness is in response to questions that individuals raise because either their curiosity has been aroused or a trust level has been created that triggers the question. The above examples may be used in the context of one-on-one or group interaction, allowing for open discussion and sharing as much of the gospel as the person is able to relate to.

One of the secrets of effective communication is to tell people less than they want to know, rather than overload them with information they are not ready to receive. One person is not *lecturing* to the other from the text, but rather both are *listening* afresh to the Word and allowing it to speak to them. The witness needs to learn to sit back and let the Word and Spirit of God do their own work. The word of the human witness is always ancillary to the Word of God (see figure 8).

☐ Realize that God got there before you did.

☐ Find out where people are in their experience and understanding of God.

☐ Take time to establish relationships and built trust.

☐ Be open to the possibility that God may have something significant to say to you through the other person.

☐ Focus on Jesus Christ: who he is, what he accomplished and your relationship to him.

☐ Tell people only as much as they are able to hear.

☐ Realize that people need multiple opportunities to hear the gospel, expressed in a variety of ways by different people.

☐ Allow time for people to process that they have heard.

☐ Assume people know nothing about the Bible and the Good News until you have evidence to the contrary.

☐ Believe in the power of the gospel to bring about a radical and permanent change in people's lives.

☐ Realize that some people come to faith by belonging before believing.

☐ Help people through the trauma of postdecision uncertainty.

Figure 8.1. Guidelines for sharing the good news

From Propositional Truth to Dialogue and Story

In the postmodern culture there is strong resistance to propositional statements dropped from above, as it were, that have to be accepted without examination and questioning. We need to recognize that many of the propositional statements about God recorded in Scripture were hammered out on the anvil of human experience. Revelations are not given in a disconnected dream world. They are given as we cry out to God in our extremity or wait upon him with an issue turning over in our minds and churning up our emotions. Propositions become platitudes when they are presented as statements without a context.

The Word of God arose out of particular cultural contexts and out of episodes in the corporate life of the people of God and of individuals in their personal struggles. So also in our witness we need to begin with our small stories to which people relate. In gathering a variety of such individual experiences, we can see common themes, which in turn can be related to the big story. Concerning the prevailing attitude among most Gen Xers influenced by postmodernism, Mike Regele writes:

> Every story is equally valid; therefore no story is eminently valid. There is tremendous cultural resistance to *any* singular story, because a story bestows power and influence on some and takes them away from others. With the growing diversity of people and belief systems, it is easy to understand the stake that various smaller stories have in resisting a great story. Furthermore, we have opted for protecting the right of individuals to hold their own story, at the expense of our unified American story. Much of the cultural warring that has marked the end of the twentieth century reflects the tug-of-war between those who want to conserve the grand American story and those who want to finally break free of its "tyranny."[19]

The task facing the church is not to attempt to remake the story of the United States (or anywhere else, for that matter), but to see beyond that story to the good news of the breaking into history of God's kingdom. It is that reality that passes judgment on every human story, whether national myths or personal journeys through life. When any nation or society loses sight of that big picture, it loses momentum and faces disintegration. Diogenes Allen draws attention to the consequences of losing the big picture:

> To see our life as part of a larger pattern carries tremendous moral power; such narratives not only enable us to retrieve and draw upon past achievements, but also put us in contact with the sources of good in our universe and their transcendent source in God. When a story or narrative involves human growth and flourishing, it treats life as if it were a journey. A person, or group, or the race itself moves from a worse to a better condition. This understanding of life is shared by most of the great philosophers of the past, such as Plato, Aristotle, Plotinus, Descartes, Spinoza and Hegel, as well as the great theologians of Christianity and other religions of the world. All of them see life as a movement away from illusion, error, or sin toward enlightenment, truth, or renewal.[20]

Mike Regele asks, "What happens when a grand story fails? Morality, leadership and institutions begin to languish."[21] All believers are called to be witnesses to the truth revealed to them in Jesus Christ and to testify to the impact that he has had upon their lives. Every witness must be honest and avoid exaggeration, remembering that every statement made is open to cross-examination.

God's big story is not one that we can impose arbitrarily. Rather we must emphasize the fact that it has an inner coherence; and it is a story that holds attention because it provides the vital clues by which to interpret *our own* story (whether personal, societal, national or global). Rodney Clapp emphasizes the role of the Christian community in communicating this story. "A faith narrative is more worthy of our consent if it is able to encompass a variety of life experiences, and need not deny experiences that persistently present themselves [poverty, illness and death]."[22]

Christian testimony contains a number of elements. We witness or attest to what Christ has done on our behalf on the cross. We give full credit to Christ for all that he is doing in our lives through the Holy Spirit and our various responses to his working. We acknowledge what Christ is doing through us in the lives of those with whom

God has brought us into contact. We draw people's attention to what Christ is doing around us through his church and outside of his church. And we witness to what Christ holds before us as our future hope, which he has guaranteed to us through the witness of his Spirit in our lives.

We witness to the unique gospel as recorded in the four Gospels. The four Gospels (Matthew, Mark, Luke and John) are the foundation of the Christian faith. They provide a reliable record of the words and actions of Jesus Christ himself. They are the authoritative, public and divine revelation of God for all people and times. They cannot be replaced, added to or subtracted from. The Gospels provide the evidence of the objective grounds for our salvation. Thus to the question, "When were you saved?" we can reply, "When Jesus died on the cross and rose again!" Easter provides the objective basis for our witness.

We witness through relating our story to God's Story. Joseph G. Healey, a Roman Catholic missiologist working in Tanzania, wrote a book in 1981 titled *A Fifth Gospel: The Experience of Black Christian Values.* Seven years later in response to criticisms he wrote a follow-up article in *Missiology* titled "A Fifth Gospel: The Experience of Black Christian Values: Our Stories as Fifth Gospels."[23] He there explained that he had used the term *fifth gospel* as a metaphor to describe the different kinds of faith stories that illustrate the good news. He gave as examples of fifth gospels the testimony of the prophet Isaiah and the accounts of the early believers recorded in the Acts of the Apostles.

There are many fifth gospels in Healey's use of that term. None can claim to represent a normative account, because God deals with each person and situation in ways that are appropriate for that individual and context. Contemporary good news is being written in many different forms expressing the reality and dynamism of the living, ongoing, unfolding gospel. In every faithful fifth gospel the primary point of reference is always God communicating in our contemporary experience and the events of daily life through Christ who is present with us by the Holy Spirit. The "Emmanuel Experience," the history of Jesus, the living Christ, continues in our own history as a living Christology. In this manner Paul reminded the believers in Corinth that they were letters of Christ, written by the Spirit of the living God (2 Cor 3:3). In down-to-earth language Billie Hanks presents the challenge: "You will win no more people and exert no more influence for the Savior than the quality of your life allows."

We witness to the final gospel that will be consummated with the return of the glorified Christ. The gospel will reach its full realization with the second coming of Christ. Therefore each of us who bears witness for Christ must keep in mind that there are three tenses in salvation. I *have been* saved, because of an unrepeatable event in history. I *am being* saved, as I live out the day-to-day implications of my salvation in the power of the Holy Spirit. And I *will be* saved. I will be saved when I go to be with the Lord and am changed in the twinkling of an eye, and I will then know as I am known.

Our testimony not only looks back and witnesses to Christ's death on our behalf on the cross, it not only speaks of our present experience of God's grace, but it also expresses our future hope. Not until that great day arrives can we express *all* of the gospel. Thus in my present witness, I can only say as much as I understand of the gospel and have experienced in my stumbling obedience.

Implementation
1. Encourage people to tell their story within the supportive atmosphere of the church. Often people feel awkward and struggle to find the words to express their experience of Christ, whether at the time of an initial encounter or as an ongoing relationship. They also labor under the misapprehension that their story is so ordinary that it is unlikely to be of interest to anybody else. They are encouraged when they discover that other people are in fact intensely interested in what they have to say and that their testimony strengthens others in faith. People needed repeated opportunities to tell their story so that

they can get used to hearing themselves and gain sufficient confidence to tell their story to those who have not yet become Christians.

2. Facilitate a group gathering where the gospel is shared and people are invited to tell their stories. This might be a low-key recreational event or an evangelistic program such as an Alpha Group.

3. Identify your witnesses and pair them with people who want to share their faith but are too nervous to launch out on their own. Pray together for opportunities in which the issues of life and the gospel can be discussed in an open and spontaneous manner. Ask each other not only what you were able to say but what you heard from the other persons. What did God have to say to you through the encounter? In light of that experience what would you do differently if a similar situation presented itself?

nine

From Generic Congregations
to Incarnational Communities

This final chapter reviews and endeavors to integrate the insights derived from the previous chapters. It discourages churches from basking in the success of highly publicized megachurches only to discover that they represent models that are not readily transferable. Such churches, which are touted as models for the future, are usually the product of a convergence of favorable factors, including gifted leadership emerging in a context of growing, homogeneous communities with upwardly mobile populations (see figure 9.1). When a vital component is missing for those seeking to build their churches along similar lines, then frustration occurs, eventually resulting in disillusionment. These models do not transfer into older communities, especially in urban and multiracial locations.

☐ Led by entrepreneurial founding pastors
☐ Located in suburban settings
☐ Serve metropolitan areas
☐ Profile their target populations
☐ Are able to operate programs at a high standard
☐ Attract leaders with strong commitment and great ability
☐ Have access to the necessary financial resources
☐ Have space to expand their facilities

Figure 9.1. Characteristics of most high-profile church models

The burden that runs through this book is that evangelical churches in the new millennium must expand from their suburban strongholds to impact urban, rural and corporate America. In addition, they must move beyond their preoccupation with baby boomers to give more attention to reaching those under thirty-five, referred to as baby busters or Generation X, without whom there will be no church of tomorrow. In contemporary society, which is increasingly permeated by postmodern thinking, maintenance-minded churches need to be transformed into missional communities, which will entail decentralizing their operations. Church leaders will need to facilitate this transition by giving higher priority to working outside the institution, functioning as teams of believers located in a highly polarized and pluralistic world. From a strategy of *invitation* the churches must move to one of *infiltration,* to being the subversive and transforming presence of Jesus.

Understand the Mission Challenge

In chapter two we observed that the church in North America is no longer regarded as one of the central institutions that bonds society. Finding themselves marginalized in the context of a pluralistic world, churches today increasingly resemble those of the first three centuries of the Christian movement, prior to the conversion of Emperor Constantine. In the Roman world the communities of believers had neither social prestige nor political influence. They owned no real estate. They were a movement, not an institution. Such must be the mindset of the church today in most of the Western world.

The church's ministry must be modeled after that of Jesus himself. John's Gospel records that when the Greeks sought Jesus out at the Passover festival, he apparently interpreted this approach from the Gentiles as a further sign that his earthly ministry was drawing to its climax. In response to the message, relayed by Philip, that they wanted to see him, he replied, "The hour has come for the Son of Man to be glorified. Very truly, I tell you, unless a grain of wheat falls into the earth and dies, it remains just a single grain; but if it dies, it bears much fruit. . . . Whoever serves me must follow me, and where I am, there will my servant be also. Whoever serves me, the Father will honor" (Jn 12:20-26). For the Greeks to "see" Jesus entailed his dying and rising, which was the Father's way of glorifying his Son.

The apostle Paul, writing to the Philippians, sets forth the ministry of Jesus as the model for all subsequent ministry. He exhorts them, "Let the same mind be in you that was in Christ Jesus" (2:5). He who renounced the splendors and security of heaven, emptying himself to be born in human likeness, became obedient to the point of death—even the excruciating death meted out to a common criminal. The results of that ministry were totally in the hands of the Father to vindicate him through raising him from the dead and exalting him to his right hand (Rom 1:4; Phil 2:1-11).

In regard to his own life and ministry, Paul also prayed that he might know not only the power of Christ's resurrection but also the sharing of his sufferings (Phil 3:10). He recognized that you couldn't have one without the other. The truth of these verses is borne out in the experience of the church engaged in mission across the centuries. They provide a salutary reminder that in speaking of the church in mission we are not speaking simply about new emphases and programs. The issue is not simply one of ecclesiastical reengineering. Rather we are talking about a radically different way of being the church. For the incarnational presence of the church in the world demands our dying to self—to our self-reliance, self-centered promotion and selfish concerns—in order for Christ to be glorified among his people. The seed that is sown must first be buried to make possible the miraculous process of germination and multiplication.

At the outset we reiterated the caution that mainline churches throughout the Western world—including the United States—must be prepared to face the seismic changes shaking apart old structures and the assumptions on which they were built.

Get Missionary Training

A missionary perspective reflects the dynamic interplay of gospel, church and culture, that is represented by the diagram in figure

9.2. In this diagram the church does not enjoy immunity from the influence of culture, as Rodney Clapp discerns in his critique of Richard Niebuhr's classic work *Christ and Culture*.[1] Clapp argues that the author failed to appreciate the fact that the church does not stand above culture. Niebuhr's work was the creation of a time when few Christians could conceive of the church as itself being a culture.[2]

Churches in the Western world are poorly equipped to face the current missional challenge, in that they have a truncated view of the gospel and a weak doctrine of the church. And their leaders are largely oblivious to the extent to which secular cultural presuppositions have permeated their own worldview. As we saw in chapter two,

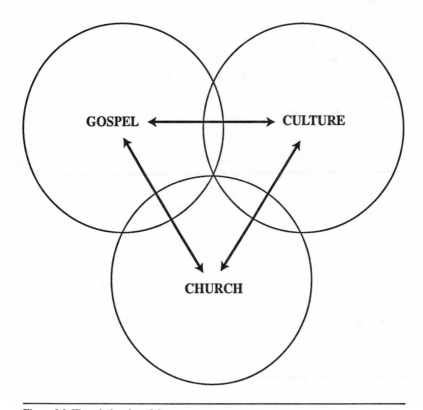

Figure 9.2. The missional model

church leaders who lack missiological training resort to marketing strategies. This has serious, largely unrecognized, long-term consequences. George Hunsberger argues that the church operates within cultural frameworks. He warns us "against conceiving the 'gospel and culture' encounter as one that is merely a matter of audience analysis, as though it has only to do with sizing up the thoughts, feelings, and values of the target population to make our communication of the gospel sharper."[3] Taking this approach allows church leaders to duck the more radical challenge that the gospel presents to the church-in-mission, namely, the extent to which it has itself been subverted by those same cultural influences.

Become a Counter-Culture Movement

Instead of becoming a church that is simply absorbed by culture or that vainly endeavors to be a church that exists in isolation from the broader culture, the church must engage in a dynamic interaction with the culture in which it is immersed. The church must resist the temptation to define itself by its culture. Rodney Clapp describes how the *church on the left* has relinquished its identity to culture through sentimental capitulation, whereas the *church on the right* has retrenched and fought a rearguard action. Finally, *the radicalizers* seek to present an alternative scenario as true followers of the way seeking to express the values of the kingdom of God in response to God's surprising and suspenseful grace.[4]

The gospel judges each culture according to its compatibility with the focus, values and goals of the kingdom of God. Due to the operation of the grace of God outside the sphere of the church, there will be aspects of culture that the gospel will affirm. There will be unfulfilled cultural aspirations that the gospel will bring to fruition. There will be demonic elements in every culture on which the gospel passes judgment.

The gospel also reveals to what extent the church has itself become enculturated by accommodating to cultural aspirations contrary to the reign of God, thereby denying its prior allegiance. In our contemporary Western setting that denial would certainly include our materialism, excessive individualism and self-reliance. The church must constantly turn to the Scriptures, humbly seeking the illumination of the Holy Spirit to receive the necessary correctives and encouragement to sustain its transforming presence in society.

Churches tend to focus on one of the four areas illustrated in figure 9.3. Some churches emphasize contending for the faith that was once for all entrusted to the saints (Jude 3). A second group is concerned with preserving its ecclesiastical heritage and liturgical tradition. A third group emphasizes relevance to the contemporary setting in terms of its worship style and need-related ministries, while a fourth group is characterized by a triumphalist anticipation of the imminent coming of the Lord.

The missional church must embrace *all four* emphases, with the inevitable tensions that this brings. Such tension is inescapable, not only because of our human limitations but because the church exists in the time between the times—the time between the inauguration and the consummation of the kingdom of God.

The church is called to be faithful to the gospel, but it must be alert to the fact that it reads and interprets the Scriptures through its own cultural lens. It is a church with a long heritage that can either enrich or encapsulate it. As the church faces new challenges, it needs to have learned well the lessons from past periods when it faced equally momentous, although different, challenges. As the old adage goes, if we forget our history, then we are in danger of repeating it. At the same time, the missional church must recognize its responsibility before God to witness faithfully by demonstrating both the relevance and the the power of the gospel within its contemporary setting.

The "baton" of the Great Commission mandate—to disciple all peoples of the world—has to be passed from one generation of discipling apostles to the next. Each generation is responsible for reaching those with whom it identifies. The prophetic task of the church is to speak the word of God, using understandable language and appropriate means,

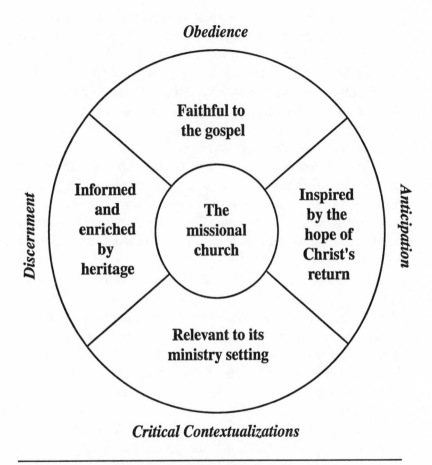

Figure 9.3. Reference points for the missional church

into a world of rebellion and confusion. It cannot take refuge either in castles of dogmatic assertions or in museums of fossilized ecclesiastical structures and liturgical antiquities. The church is also inspired by the hope of Christ's return. Indeed, as an anticipatory sign of that event it is learning to live God's future now.

Work from the Margins
In the opening chapter we traced the witness of the church from tradi-

tional settings to the self-assured world of modernity, then to the fragmented and fragile world of postmodernity. The church, as just one
segment in that fragmented world and characterized by polarization
and conflict in which each segment is fighting for its right of self-
determination, can assume no privileged position (see figure 9.4). As
it finds itself marginalized in a pluralistic world, it can draw fresh
inspiration from the situation of the church in New Testament times
up until the conversion of Constantine.

In many churches today the process of developing a new mindset
appropriate to the present time is complicated by the fact that the
members (and to some extent the leaders) comprise a mix of people
with traditional and modern mindsets. Therefore, the tensions and
turmoil that are so prevalent in churches today should not come as a
surprise.

If the church found itself marginalized under modernism, it must
not now expect that it can return to the position it once held under
the Constantinian model. A fragmented world means that there is no
longer either a center or a circumference. The church of the twenty-
first century is in a different situation from that of the first century,
for there is now no equivalent of the Roman Empire with the *pax*
that it endeavored to impose. Today's world is a balkanized world of
warring factions.

In addressing today's context the insights of Alan Roxburgh are
particularly valuable. Regarding the decentered context of North
American churches he writes:

> The fourth and twentieth centuries form bookends marking transition
> points in the history of the church. Just as the fourth century adoption
> of Christianity by Constantine forced the church to struggle with its
> self-understanding as the new center of the culture, twentieth century
> Christians must now struggle to understand the meaning of their
> social location in a decentered world.[5]

> The church's minority experience is not, therefore, that of periphery to
> center but a more generalized, pervasive embeddedness in a complexity
> and fragmentation that renders center-margin language obsolete.[6]

Traditional Position

Modern Position

Postmodern Position

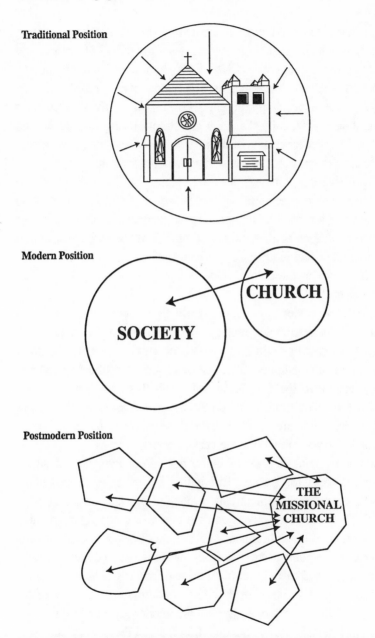

Figure 9.4. The changing position of church in society

The turbulence and turmoil created by the contended transition from modernity to postmodernity creates a great deal of anxiety and defensiveness throughout society. This in turn spills over into the church. As the turbulence increases, concerns over our ability to survive become increasingly urgent. "For many, ministry roles have changed so dramatically that they are simply trying to hold on and survive. The precariousness of these realities makes it difficult for pastors to discuss questions of missionary encounter models."[7]

The typical response of the modern mindset is to discover and develop some new technique by which we can stabilize our situation and secure a future. "Guiding pastoral strategy are the cultural values of instrumental rationality, expressed in 'if it works and is successful then it is true.' Technique is the primary method for reestablishing the church's place in the culture. God is but a legitimating footnote of ecclesiology."[8]

In order to understand more clearly the process of cultural and social marginalization and reentry, Roxburgh uses the model of *liminality* developed by anthropologist Victor Turner.[9] The first stage of separation from the larger culture causes a loss of confidence and certainty, leading to the questioning of much that had been taken for granted for a long time. To be on the margins *(limen)* is to be in turmoil, which the church handles either by denial and protective introversion or by warfare among the various constituencies.

Liminality is not a state of limbo but one of dynamic transition. According to Victor Turner, "Liminality is a term that describes the transition process accompanying a change of state or social position."[10] "It is the conscious awareness that as a group (or individual) one's status-, role-, and sequence-sets in a society have been radically changed to the point where the group has now become largely invisible to the larger society in terms of these previously held sets."[11]

Throughout this book we have been addressing the issue of the church's response to modernity and postmodernity in relation to the principal dimensions of its ongoing life. Each of these mindsets (modern and postmodern) constitutes a distinct type of liminality. They exist alongside each other in many churches, creating an internal tension that inhibits churches' ability to address the broader cultural contexts outside their own communities. The first form of liminality concerns "the long-term change in relationship between Church and modern culture. . . . Modernity functioned on the moral and spiritual fragments of Christendom."[12] The second form, according to Roxburgh, constitutes a more fundamental transition from modernity to postmodernity, for "in contrast to pre-industrial societies and much of modernity, there no longer exist norms that provide coherence and frameworks for the change processes through which we are moving."[13]

Due to the stress generated by external changes and internal tension, there is the tendency to understand liminality in terms of negation, not potential.[14] Yet given the fragmented nature of the postmodern world, the church cannot hope to regain its former position in society. Instead, it must learn to work as just one piece in the cultural mosaic, but a piece that is called to act as salt, leaven and light, bridging and permeating other pieces of the mosaic. The church's reentry into the world (or "reaggregation" in Turner's liminality model) entails immersion in cultural contexts that may be unfamiliar and too readily perceived as hostile.

Provide Pastoral Care, Leadership and Outreach Among Each Generation That Makes Up the Congregation

We live in a world in which we are experiencing changes at an ever-increasing pace. Moreover those changes are impacting every area of life, and many are global in extent. Such instability creates defensive anxiety, hyperactivity, social fragmentation and conflict. Wounded people bring that stress into the church, either to find answers or merely to vent their feelings. Precisely because religion deals with the fundamental issues of life, the church becomes a place of tension. It is the place where deep-seated anxieties are most likely to surface. The raising of contentious issues provides the occasion rather than the cause for an emotional outburst.

The escalating pace of change has divided the population in North

America into at least five generations, each characterized by a prevailing attitude. Pastors of established churches face the challenge of shepherding people in their flocks in every one of these age bands. They have the added challenge that the sheep within their flocks do not always gather in the same groupings, and, as is the way with sheep, have a tendency to wander off on their own to bleat alone on the hillside. They do not have the luxury of establishing a new church with a clearly defined, homogeneous target population. Each generation is likely to respond in a fairly predictable way to issues of faith.

The builders (born between 1901 and 1924) tend toward defensiveness. They have lived through as much change as they can emotionally handle. Everything in life has changed around them, and their one remaining anchor is their church, which they do not want to see change with the times. This is especially true if they have lost a spouse who shared their faith and sat next to them in church. For this generation, church leadership needs to provide a secure and familiar base that will see them safely into the presence of the Lord. At the same time, among their number you can find some adventurous types who welcome experimentation, considering that it will be their final fling in life and that they won't have to live with unpleasant results for very long!

Seniors are often overlooked in our youth-oriented, age-sensitive and death-denying culture. But as people live longer, and as the number of seniors swells as the boomers age, ministry to seniors will become increasingly important. Further, many are discovering that living longer does not always mean enjoying carefree golden years. The aging process can be a discomforting experience, with failing strength and faculties, and increased health problems that drain financial resources. The fragmentation of the family means that churches will be called upon to provide increasing support. The seeker-sensitive church will also have to be senior sensitive.

The silent generation (1925-1942) is characterized by resentment. This generation is labeled "silent" because it became the overlooked or in-between generation. It lacked creativity, being intimidated by the achievements of the previous generation, and did not adapt easily when the industrial age gave way first to the high-tech and then to the information age. It is this generation that is most intimidated by computers and the Internet. They demonstrate a defensiveness, insecurity and conservatism that is reinforced when their children leave home and they become empty nesters. In many ways the silent generation is more resistant to change than the builders; they are less entrepreneurial, have been victims of change and don't want to face the prospect of having to live with unwelcome change again.

The legalism and formalism of their parents' religion frustrated members of the silent generation. The charismatic movement that broke out within the mainline denominations in the 1960s, and was especially influential in liturgical traditions, attracted some who grew up within traditional liturgical churches. In addition to freeing up worship, the charismatic movement also stressed every-member ministry through the discovery and exercise of spiritual gifts. The proliferation of small groups provided the context in which these gifts could be explored in a supportive environment.

The silent generation presents the greatest challenge to the younger, entrepreneurial church leader, largely because they enjoy the benefits of the church renewal they experienced beginning in the 1960s. They are suspicious of anything more radical, especially when it is expressed in the music styles of their offspring, which they resisted strongly, complaining that the music was too loud and they couldn't hear the words. Perhaps the most effective way to challenge them is by asking them why their children left the churches that meant so much to their parents and what it would take for their children to want to return to church.

Insecurity and the desire to achieve characterize the boomer generation (1943-1960). They are the products of an age of experimentation in which some sought new ways of personal fulfillment through the use of drugs that enhanced sensory experiences, in meditation techniques and by seeking the wisdom of the ages distilled in Hinduism and Buddhism. Others found meaning through encountering Christ in the Jesus Movement. Some were eclectic in their spiritual pilgrimage, adopting a mix-and-match approach. Religious experience and belief became a means to personal fulfillment. As they grew older boomers shed their radicalism and became more materialistic and supportive of the establishment.

Resentment and suspicion characterize the Generation X (1961-1981). They present the greatest challenge facing the churches in the Western world. For the most part they are not looking to Christian churches to meet their spiritual needs. They are the first generation in North America to search outside of the church. They will incorporate elements of Christianity, but they are equally likely to turn to New Age beliefs, Native American religions, Eastern religion and paganism.

Following the Gen Xers are the bemused millennials (1982-). This generation is still largely a mirror image of its parents, the boomers. It has not had time to develop distinctive characteristics. It represents the increasing socioeconomic polarization taking place with the erosion of the middle class due to business relocation and the failure of some to learn the new skills required to make the transitions to new jobs created by advances in technology.

Develop Contemporary Models of Discipleship Through Building Authentic Community

If believers are to make an impact in today's fractured and disoriented society, they will need to learn survival skills and themselves be transformed by the message they seek to communicate. Discipleship simply means the imitation of Christ (1 Thess 1:6). Through the first-century Thessalonian believers the gospel spread as imitators of Christ became examples to others, so that in every place their faith in God became known (vv. 7, 8). Eugene Peterson sums it up in his paraphrase, "The news of your faith in God is out. We don't even have to say anything anymore—*you're* the message!"[15]

A disciple is one who embodies the message he or she proclaims. It was to people who were themselves disciples that Jesus gave the Great Commission to disciple the nations. The implication is clear—it takes a disciple to make a disciple. We reproduce after our own kind

Undiscipled church members present one of the greatest challenges facing the church, not only in the West but around the world. Rodney Clapp reminds us that "Christianity is not an ideology to be recovered or a philosophical system to be remembered. Christians are called to live the story, not restate it in the form of universalized propositions."[16]

Within the evangelical tradition there has been an undue emphasis on the conversion *event*, to the neglect of an understanding of conversion as a lifelong *process*. Conversion is a swivel point, a turning around to head in a new direction, but many other course corrections will be necessary in the process of life's journey. If we don't know where we are headed, we are in danger of simply rotating. Discipleship entails a path to be walked and a goal to be reached. Having turned around to take our position at the starting line, we are not to remain for the rest of our lives at that location, even with the laudable aim of helping as many people as possible undergo the same reorientation. As the Gospels, Acts and the Epistles make clear, reorientation is to lead to transformation. How is this all-encompassing change to come about?

It is evident that education and exhortation are not sufficient to accomplish this goal. In seminaries there is increasing recognition of the need for spiritual formation alongside theological education. Diogenes Allen, professor of philosophy at Princeton Seminary, remarks on the fact that it is only in recent times that spiritual theology became isolated from dogmatic theology, to the neglect of the former, and that "for most of the history of theology, they interacted richly. To make progress in doctrinal theology it was essential to mature in one's spiritual life, because theological understanding and spiritual progress went hand-in-hand."[17]

The mission of the church in North America today to an alien culture around it requires much more than adapting existing structures. Rather, it requires the creation of new forms of common life. This point is argued by E. Dixon Junkin in the following terms:

> Instead of continuing to expend such energy trying to make outworn patterns of institutional life serve us, it seems appropriate to devote

more attention to the task of creating new forms of common life that may, over time, allow a new consensus to emerge. . . . Let us imagine thousands of communities whose members in an intentional, disciplined fashion do the following six things:

1. Pray together.
2. Share their joys and struggles.
3. Study the context in which they find themselves.
4. Listen for God's voice speaking through Scripture.
5. Seek to discern the obedience to which they are being called.
6. Engage in common ministry.[18]

For such a vision to be realized, church leaders will have to make a number of significant changes, including the pruning of programs, which have become ends in themselves. It is the very programmatic mindset of the church that has led to departmentalization and fragmentation. In other words, many churches have any number of specialized programs for different interests and age groups. The Scriptural models of the church call for a more holistic approach, which is also the heart cry of most postmodern people.

We are not here reemphasizing the need for small groups, which have often been overlaid on already over-full and over-demanding church calendars. Rather we are arguing for basic communities to become the very building blocks on which the church is built and is able to expand. Dixon Junkin makes a crucially important point when he states that "in such communities the participants might learn in a new way the coherence of their lives before God. All too often congregational life as we experience it encourages a kind of compartmentalization."[19]

The modern tendency to separate the spiritual from the practical is played out in the church when decision-making groups are divorced from the disciple-making groups.

The difficulty is that, at present, many decision-making groups within the church appear to discipline their lives according to secular models, rarely if ever attempting to practice significant discernment, while groups that exist for such purposes as mutual support, education, mission, or fellowship often go about their task in ways that finally serve to further the compartmentalization of their members' lives. Therefore we should certainly encourage people of faith, in addition to forming new communities, to reshape existing communities along the lines of some such integrating discipline.[20]

In chapter three we explored the significance of networks in the modern world and saw that they have worked to undermine the power of hierarchies. The disadvantage of some networks is that they are a poor substitute for community. As part of a network you come and go as you please. You "work" the net in order to achieve your personal and group goals. The network does not require commitment or accountability, and this same mentality is brought into small groups. Members weigh up their options before promising to attend the next meeting, and that promise is promptly broken if a better offer comes along. The individual reigns supreme. The assumptions behind this mindset must be firmly challenged. As Rodney Clapp observes, "We must *recognize that we are inescapably communal creatures*. We really can't—contra the modern myth—create ourselves."[21]

Develop an Apostolic Commitment

Groups that promote discipleship tend to focus on the personal, spiritual growth aspects. Their concern is more with the inward journey of faith than the outward venture of communicating that faith in all its dimensions. In contrast to this introspective model, we find in the New Testament that discipleship was linked to apostleship. Learning together from the Lord leads to going out into the world in his name.

Churches living out the apostolic paradigm define themselves in missional terms and are prepared to embark upon risk-taking initiatives. This bold willingness to take new missionary risks is their distinctive feature and gifting that challenges the great majority of churches stuck in a survival mode.

The vision of local churches for lay ministry is not restricted to activities in the church community itself but has the apostolic vision to venture into new territory to reach hitherto unreached people who have been either overlooked or deliberately avoided. For a ministry to be apostolic does not necessarily entail crossing an ocean; it may simply mean crossing the street or the railroad tracks or riding an elevator. Apostolic churches resist the temptation to get willing laypersons absorbed and sidetracked in committee work. Resisting the institutional pressures, they ensure that a high percentage of laypeople are engaged in ministry and outreach activities. Some churches insist that every person occupying a board position must also be involved in a specific area of ministry and outreach, and must bring regular reports to the board for its prayer support and evaluation. Rick Warren cautions against creative church bureaucracies that preoccupy members to the neglect of ministry.[22]

Such decentralization not only releases more potential, but it allows for a quicker response because it does not first require committees to deliberate and then to look for volunteers. Bottom-up initiative taking "encourages ministry to be delivered any time, any place, by anyone, no matter what. . . . . The shorter the time lag between discovering a spiritual need and putting it into an actual ministry, the more effective the church will be in the Quantum Age."[23]

Be Strong on Envisioning but Flexible in Strategizing and Planning
The church began as a movement driven by a vision. It consisted of small groups of people who believed that Jesus was the Son of God and who had committed themselves totally and unreservedly to him as Lord and Savior. These groups replicated themselves throughout the Mediterranean world and beyond. They had no real estate. Their leaders were, for the most part, local people whom the apostles appointed and empowered. The movement had no social prestige or influential patrons. It operated from the margins and succeeded in infiltrating every level of society and department of life.

The church of the twenty-first century must recapture this same dynamism and must not fight to try to regain the prestige it enjoyed in past days. It can assume no special rights or privileges but exists and thrives only through the grace of God. As the church of today looks to the risen Lord and into the future, it is informative to compare the characteristics of "global learning organizations" today, as identified by Michael Marquardt and Angus Reynolds, with the church in its global mission. Uncertainty becomes an occasion for growth, not a cause for paralysis. It is a church prepared to take risks, which learns from its failures and mistakes. It is a church able to embrace change. It is a church that encourages accountability at every level. It is a church that decentralizes decision making and is prepared to empower people in ministry. It is a church that does not live for itself but lives out its life in the broader community.[24]

The vision driving the church is not simply a clever slogan. It is an integrative vision that inspires all that the church does and everybody involved. The Great Commission provided that vision, despite the fact that it took approximately fifteen years for the church to break out of its cultural cocoon and fly into the wide world beyond Judea and Samaria. It is significant that the Great Commission was given in Galilee-of-the-nations rather than in Jerusalem, the holy city and gathering point for the nations.

The Great Commission was concerned with making disciples, not precipitating decisions. Unfortunately, over time it has become compartmentalized and marginalized from the life of the church, partly because the relevant verses are treated as if they were in isolation from the rest of Matthew's Gospel. We have been prone to overlook the fact that the teaching of Jesus throughout Matthew spells out clearly and comprehensively what it means to become and to function as one of Jesus' disciples.

Keep in Touch with the Frontline

As we saw in chapter three, rapid change, the electronic communication highway, diversification in the marketplace and suspicion toward centralized bureaucracies all contribute to a widespread trend in government, industry, education and the church to flatten organizational pyramids and get rid of layers of middle management. A trend of equal significance is the inclusion of the grassroots and frontline people—those who are actually in the trenches, so to speak, doing the ministry—in the decision-making process. Denominational hierarchies must recognize that the churches do not exist to support them; they exist to facilitate local churches.

In a complex world of rapid and discontinuous change, it is the people on the frontlines who are most acutely and promptly aware of the nature of the changes taking place around them. They sense how deep-rooted and widespread the changes are. They see their implications for the mission of the church. These changes may signal the winding down of old ministries and the starting up of new ones. Andrew Grove, as the CEO of Intel, appreciated the need to step outside of corporate culture, with its institutional constraints and tunnel vision, in order to discover what was happening in the world. He observed that it was not senior managers but middle managers—especially those who dealt with the outside world, such as those in sales—who were often the first to realize that what worked before doesn't quite work anymore, that the rules are changing.[25]

Transition from Being an Inviting Church to Becoming an Infiltrating Church

We conclude where we began, with the need for churches in the Western world to undergo a profound reorientation, turning around from a survival mode to a mission mode. The church will need to be turned inside out in order to bring those outside in. It will not suffice to simply invite the seeker to come to us to hear the gospel on our turf. Instead the church will have to be the church in the world—gathering for worship in order to go out in mission. Its programs must be geared to equip and support the people of God in the strategic locations where the Lord has already placed them to serve as his representatives.

Be Prepared to Live Adventurously with Diversity and Paradox

As we venture into the world, we will soon discover that it is a confused and messy place, which is to be expected of a society in rebellion against God. And yet we will discover that God has not abandoned his world. He is present everywhere behind the scenes. He is always there before we arrive! The task of the believer is not to valiantly witness to a distant Lord, endeavoring to bring a hostile world to him. Rather the task is to take Christ to the world; for wherever the people of God are found, there also is Jesus, living through their individual and corporate lives.

The gospel does not provide instant answers to everything. In mission the church will have to learn to walk by faith, trusting God to be there by his Spirit to guide along the way. There is no schedule prepared ahead of time. There is no step-by-step guide to instruct us how to handle every eventuality. Precisely because the world is in a fallen and broken state, we have to learn to live with diversity, ambiguity and paradox. There is no mission without mess. As Eugene Peterson has noted, much of life consists of "mucking out."[26]

The uncertainty that plagues so many church leaders today is evidenced by their frustrating search for clear answers and step-by-step, fail-safe plans. This mindset represents our succumbing to the temptation to walk by sight and not by faith. It signifies our dependence on our own ability to produce answers and fix things. We must learn to admit that when we have done all that we know how to do, it will not be adequate to solve all the problems. The fragmented, fearful and fractious world of postmodernity presents a daunting challenge. Yet it also provides a fertile environment in which the flower of faith can flourish.

We are moving beyond the day when books on management and leadership emphasize long-range planning, centralized organization and firm control. That style of leadership might have been appropriate in the assured world of modernity, but it is woefully inadequate in a postmodern world of unpredictable change.

Inability to live with paradox will result in paralysis. As we engage in the task of mission, we will gain a greater awareness that the whole creation continues to groan in labor pains until now (Rom 8:22-23).

Paradox is grounded in theology—in the "now" and the "not yet" of the kingdom—and there is no escaping that tension until the Lord comes and we are face to face with him.

Transitioning to the New Paradigm

As we review the churches that are engaging with the culture to make a significant missional impact, we find that a new paradigm is emerging. The churches and networks comprising the expression of this new paradigm do not represent models to be replicated in identical form. But they do provide principles to be contextualized, recognizing that some situations will yield results far more quickly than others. The lessons in the Parable of the Sower remind us that we sow the seeds of the gospel in various kinds of soil with differing results: the same sower and the same seed, but different levels of receptivity and results.

New paradigm churches have a leadership that recognizes the centrality of worship and emphasizes a transformational encounter with the living God. Their leaders are concerned with equipping the people of God for mission in the world. They are committed to identifying, training, granting peer support to and mentoring their fellow leaders. They empower emerging leaders and are ambitious for them. Leaders of new paradigm churches are accessible and vulnerable, and they have earned the authority that they exercise. They minister on the frontline alongside their people. They are aware of cultural values and trends, and relate the gospel to the community outside their walls. They are as comfortable mingling with the unchurched as with church people and are able to gain their confidence and trust. Lastly, they are assured of the presence of the Lord with them, in continuing fulfillment of his promise to his original band of disciples, "I am with you always, to the end of the age" (Mt 28:20).

Implementation

1. Review the ministries of your church and the deployment of your members-in-ministry. What percentage of your ministries is directed to maintaining the institution and to meeting the needs of existing

members (both of which are important)? What percentage is directed to serving the community at large and to sharing the good news through incarnational witness?

2. How are laypersons in your church trained, equipped and supported in their witness in the world? Are they left to survive as lone operators? Or do they enjoy the companionship of those in similar situations who share their sense of calling to ministry where God has placed them?

3. Pray with a group of people who are concerned for the church that it may be revitalized and that it may be reoriented to become increasingly a transforming presence in the world.

Notes

Introduction

[1]I use the term *Majority World* in reference to the non-Western world in place of the more common term, *Third World,* which is now anachronistic with the collapse of the Eastern and Western alignments, and its successor, *Two-Thirds World,* which seems contrived.

Chapter 1: From Living in the Past to Engaging with the Present

[1]Lesslie Newbigin, *Foolishness to the Greeks* (Grand Rapids, Mich.: Eerdmans, 1986); and *The Gospel in a Pluralist Society* (Grand Rapids, Mich.: Eerdmans, 1989).

[2]Mike Regele with Mark Schulz, *The Death of the Church* (Grand Rapids, Mich.: Zondervan, 1995), p. 11.

[3]Ibid., p. 182.

[4]George Barna, *The Second Coming of the Church* (Nashville: Word, 1998), p. 5.

[5]Lyle E. Schaller, *Innovations in Ministry* (Nashville: Abingdon, 1994), pp. 65-66.

[6]See Normal Shawchuck and Gustave Rath, *Benchmarks of Quality in the Church* (Nashville: Abingdon, 1994), p. 12.

[7]Richard Kew and Roger White, *Toward 2015: A Church Odyssey* (Cambridge, Mass.: Cowley, 1997), p. 94. The authors cite the example of the Episcopal diocese of Ohio, which went from seven congregations being served by part-time clergy to thirty-three congregations— 30 percent of all its parishes—being served by part-time clergy. These churches have bivocational priests or are served by part-time clergy or ministry clusters.

[8]Kew and White speak in terms of the need for "Great Commission congregations" (ibid., p. 81) in response to "a new world being born." They describe today as representing "the dawn of a new apostolic age" (ibid., p. 75).

[9]Tony Campolo, *Can Mainline Denominations Make a Comeback?* (Valley Forge, Penn.: Judson Press, 1995).

[10]William M. Easum, *Sacred Cow Makes Gourmet Burgers* (Nashville: Abingdon, 1995), p. 19.

[11]Regele, *Death of the Church,* p. 15.

[12]Ibid., p. 23.

[13]"What Is Modernity? Historical Roots and Contemporary Features," ed. Philip Sampson, Vinay Samuel and Chris Sugden, in *Faith and Modernity* (Oxford: Regnum Books, 1994), pp. 16-17.

[14]Ibid., p. 25.

[15]Quoted by Philip Sampson, "The Rise of Postmodernity," in *Faith and Modernity,* p. 30.

[16]Ibid., p. 40

[17]Roger Lundin, *The Culture of Interpretation* (Grand Rapids, Mich.: Eerdmans, 1993), p. 15.

[18]See Stanley J. Grenz, *A Primer on Postmodernism* (Grand Rapids, Mich.: Eerdmans, 1996), pp. 167-74; and David Hilborn, *Picking Up the Pieces* (London: Hodder & Stoughton, 1997), chap. 2.

[19]*Newsweek,* October 6, 1997, p. 64 (emphasis mine).

[20]Roger Lundin, *Culture of Interpretation,* p. 148.

[21]Andrew Walls, "Western Society Presents a Missionary Challenge," in *Missiological Education for the Twenty-first Century,* ed. Dudley J. Woodberry et al. (Maryknoll, N.Y.: Orbis, 1996), p. 19. This assessment did not originate with Walls but goes back to Hendrick

Kraemer in *The Communication of the Christian Faith* (Philadelphia: Westminster Press, 1956), pp. 100-101. It was further reiterated by Lesslie Newbigin on his return to England after decades of serving the Church of South India (*Foolishness to the Greeks*, p. 20). It is significant that all three write from overseas mission experience.

[22]Lundin, *Culture of Interpretation*, p. 41.

[23]Ibid., p. 203.

[24]George Steiner, *Real Presences* (Chicago: University of Chicago Press, 1989), p. 120.

[25]Ibid., p. 93.

[26]Ibid., p. 99.

[27]Ibid., p. 133.

[28]Lundin, *Culture of Interpretation*, p. 25.

[29]Tom Beaudoin, *Virtual Faith* (San Francisco: Jossey-Bass, 1998), p. 13.

[30]Andrew S. Grove, *Only The Paranoid Survive* (New York: Currency Doubleday, 1996), p. 32.

[31]Ibid., p. 3.

[32]Ibid., p. 31.

[33]Ibid., p. 34. I have adapted Grove's points to apply them more directly to the church situation.

[34]Ibid., pp. 92-93.

Chapter 2: From Market Driven to Mission Oriented

[1]George Barna, *The Second Coming of the Church* (Nashville: Word, 1998), p. 99.

[2]Philip Kotler, *Marketing Management: Analysis, Planning, Implementation, and Control*, 6th ed. (Englewood Cliffs, N.J.: Prentice Hall, 1988).

[3]Philip D. Kenneson and James L. Street, *Selling Out the Church* (Nashville: Abingdon, 1997), pp. 97-106.

[4]G. A. Pritchard, *Willow Creek Seeker Services* (Grand Rapids, Mich.: Baker, 1996), p. 242.

[5]Donald McGavran, *Understanding Church Growth*, ed. C. Peter Wagner, 3rd ed. (Grand Rapids, Mich.: Eerdmans, 1990), p. 163.

[6]Donald E. Miller, *Reinventing American Protestantism: Christianity in the New Millennium* (Berkeley: University of California Press, 1996), p. 28.

[7]Os Guinness, *Dining with the Devil* (Grand Rapids, Mich.: Baker, 1993), p. 16.

[8]Ibid., p. 35.

[9]Pritchard, *Willow Creek Seeker*, p. 246.

[10]Ibid., p. 256.

[11]Kenneson and Street, *Selling Out*, pp. 73-74.

[12]Guinness, *Dining with the Devil*, p. 65.

[13]Ibid., p. 67.

[14]Norman Shawchuck et al., *Marketing for Congregations: Choosing to Serve People More Effectively* (Nashville: Abingdon, 1992), p. 21.

[15]Kenneson and Street, *Selling Out*, p. 47.

[16]I would not go as far as Kenneson and Street, who believe that "this tool should not be placed in the service of the church's unique mission, for to do so does serious damage to the church's self-understanding" (*Selling Out*, p. 129).

[17]Lesslie Newbigin, *Foolishness to the Greeks* (Grand Rapids, Mich.: Eerdmans, 1986), p. 26.

[18]Pritchard, *Willow Creek Seeker*, p. 256.

[19]Ibid.

[20]Kenneson and Street, *Selling Out*, p. 48.

[21]Ibid., p. 60.

[22]Rodney Clapp, *A Peculiar People* (Downers Grove, Ill.: InterVarsity Press, 1996), chaps. 1-3.

[25]George R. Hunsberger, "Missional Vocation: Called and Sent to Represent the Reign of God," in *Missional Church: A Vision for the Sending of the Church in North America*, ed. Darrel Guder (Grand Rapids, Mich.: Eerdmans, 1998), p. 78.

[24]Ibid., p. 79.

[25]This is the dilemma posed in Bruce Shelley and Marshall Shelley, *The Consumer Church* (Downers Grove, Ill.: InterVarsity Press, 1992).

[26]See Rodney Clapp's critique of H. Richard Niebuhr's *Christ and Culture* in this regard. He writes that Niebuhr's work "was the creation of a time when few Christians could conceive of the church as itself a culture" (*Peculiar People*, p. 59).

[27]Based on Darrel Guder, *Missional Church* (Grand Rapids, Mich.: Eerdmans, 1998), pp. 11-12 and pp. 4-5; see also David Bosch, *Transforming Mission: Paradigm Shifts in Theology of Mission* (Maryknoll, N.Y.: Orbis, 1991), p. 390.

[28]See "Empirical Indicators of a 'Missional Church,' " in *The Gospel and Our Culture* 10, no. 3 (1998).

[29]Guder, *Missional Church*, p. 14.

[30]Newbigin, *Foolishness to the Greeks*, p. 20.

[31]In the Gospel of Matthew the emphasis is placed on the *objective* of the task, which is to *make disciples* (Mt 28:19). Mark draws attention to the *extent* of the task. The gospel must be preached to the whole creation, and the preaching will be reinforced by miraculous signs and wonders (Mk 16:15-18). In Luke the *means* are the focus of attention; namely, evangelization necessitates the preaching of the gospel, and that task can only be effectively undertaken as the disciples receive *the promise of the Father*, which is the empowering of the Holy Spirit (Lk 24:46-49). Not until the Lord was risen could his ministry become their ministry. Last, John stresses Jesus' emphasis on the *continuity* of the disciples' mission with his own (Jn 17:18; 20:21) and that his departure would be to their advantage in that he would then send another to be their advocate, teacher and encourager (Jn 14:26; 15:26; 16:13).

[32]McGavran, *Understanding Church Growth*, pp. 23-30.

[33]See the enlightening exposition of the Great Commission in the context of Matthew's Gospel in David Bosch, "Matthew: Mission as Disciple-Making," in *Transforming Mission* (Maryknoll, N.Y.: Orbis, 1991).

[34]Johannes Verkuyl, *Contemporary Missiology* (Grand Rapids, Mich.: Eerdmans, 1978), p. 166.

[35]S. Pearce Carey, *William Carey* (London: Hodder & Stoughton, 1923), pp. 71-72, 84.

Chapter 3: From Bureaucratic Hierarchies to Apostolic Networks

[1]See Lyle Schaller, *Innovations in Ministry* (Nashville: Abingdon, 1994), p. 65.

[2]Tony Campolo, *Can Mainline Denominations Make a Comeback?* (Valley Forge, Penn.: Judson Press, 1995), p. 157.

[3]Wade Clark Roof, *A Generation of Seekers* (San Francisco: HarperSanFrancisco, 1993), pp. 41-45.

[4]Leith Anderson, *A Church for the Twenty-First Century* (Minneapolis: Bethany House, 1992), pp. 28-30.

[5]Donald Miller, *Reinventing American Protestantism: Christianity in the New Millennium* (Berkeley: University of California Press), p. 32.

[6]William Easum, *Sacred Cow Makes Gourmet Burgers: Ministry Anytime, Anywhere by Anyone* (Nashville: Abingdon, 1995), p. 36.

[7]Lyle E. Schaller, *The New Reformation: Tomorrow Arrived Yesterday* (Nashville: Abingdon, 1995), pp. 13-14.

[8]Ibid., p. 20.

[9]Campolo, *Can Mainline Denominations,* p. 146.

[10]Ibid., p. 149.

[11]C. Peter Wagner, ed., *The New Apostolic Churches* (Ventura, Calif.: Regal, 1998), pp. 18-25.

[12]Ibid., p. 20.

[13]David Cannistraci, *The Gift of Apostle* (Ventura, Calif.: Regal, 1996), p. 35.

[14]John R. W. Stott, *Baptism and Fullness,* 2nd ed. (London: Inter-Varsity Press, 1975), pp. 99-100.

[15]See Peter Brierley, *Future Church* (Crowborough, East Sussex, U.K.: Monarch, 1998), chaps. 3, 4 and 5.

[16]Nominalism should not be regarded as a recent problem. For instance, during the morally decadent and spiritually dry eighteenth century an influential network of spiritual leaders arose, including Isaac Watts, William Law, Philip Doddridge, John and Charles Wesley, Lady Selina (the countess of Huntingdon), George Whitefield, John Newton, William Cowper, Hannah More, and William Wilberforce, to name some of the most prominent individuals. Each challenged in a different way the conventional Christianity of the period, calling for the renewal of spiritual life and the reform of society, including the provision of education, the reform of prisons and the abolition of slavery. See David Lyle Jeffrey, ed., *English Spirituality in the Age of Wesley* (Grand Rapids, Mich.: Eerdmans, 1994; original title: *A Burning and Shining Light: English Spirituality in the Age of Wesley,* 1987).

[17]See Donald A. McGavran, *Understanding Church Growth,* ed. C. Peter Wagner, 3rd ed. (Grand Rapids, Mich.: Eerdmans, 1990), p. 287.

[18]See Peter Brierley, *Towards A.D. 2000: Current Trends in European Church Life* (London: MARC Europe, 1984).

[19]Easum, *Sacred Cow,* pp. 22-23.

[20]Tom Beaudoin, *Virtual Faith* (San Francisco, Calif.: Jossey-Bass, 1998), pp. 56-57.

[21]Miller, *Reinventing American Protestantism,* p. 149.

[22]Easum, *Sacred Cow,* pp. 110-11.

[23]Ibid., p. 111.

[24]Ibid., p. 55.

[25]Robert Slocum, *Maximize Your Ministry* (Colorado Springs: Navpress, 1990), p. 170.

[26]Ibid., pp. 171-72.

[27]Easum, *Sacred Cow,* p. 53.

[28]Miller, *Reinventing American Protestantism,* p. 156.

[29]Leith Anderson, *Church for the Twenty-First Century,* pp. 47-49.

[30]Easum, *Sacred Cow,* p. 102.

Chapter 4: From Schooling Professionals to Mentoring Leaders

[1]Lyle Schaller, *Innovations in Ministry* (Nashville: Abingdon, 1994), p. 21.

[2]"The current method of clergy recruitment is not conducive to attracting people with exceptional leadership skills; seminaries may even dull the vision and passion of those who might lead the church in the twenty-first century. Specifically, the radical decentralization of clergy training within new paradigm churches should be examined as a possible model for mainline churches. When it is time to hire a new staff member, for example, perhaps someone should

be selected from the ranks of the laity. Why? Because that person has proven his or her leadership abilities and fully understands the vision and culture of the institution. Restructuring the clergical vocation in such a radical way would be deeply threatening to many ministers who have been trained more traditionally, but simply tinkering with the organizational structure of mainline Christianity will serve little purpose" (Donald Miller, *Reinventing American Protestantism: Christianity in the New Millennium* [Berkeley: University of California Press, 1997], p. 188).

[3]Alan Roxbugh, *The Missionary Congregation: Leadership and Liminality* (Harrisburg, Penn.: Trinity Press International, 1997), p. 17. The same point is made by Vinoth Ramachandra: "Under the influence of television and advertising, Christian gatherings in affluent societies have experienced major shifts from Word to Image, from passion for truth and righteousness to cultivating intimacy and 'good feelings,' from exposition to entertainment, from integrity to novelty, from action to spectacle. The reduction of knowledge to information, and the growth of a specialized, esoteric 'knowledge class,' . . . are evident in church-affiliated theological seminaries no less than in university faculties of theology. Many seminary graduates are now skilled in management techniques, or counseling skills and even 'church planting' methodologies, but lack any integrating *theological* vision. Even mission has come to be a specialized discipline of professional study—'missiology'—an item of consumer choice and subject to all the fashionable computer gimmickry and statistical qualification beloved by the new mandarins. That *all* study and life should, for the Christian, be motivated by, and orientated around, a sense of mission, seems too radical a thought for the modern seminary" (Vinoth Ramachandra, *Gods That Fail: Modern Idolatry and Christian Mission* [Downers Grove, Ill.: InterVarsity Press, 1996], p. 18).

[4]Richard Kew and Roger White, *Toward 2015: A Church Odyssey* (Cambridge, Mass.: Cowley, 1997), p. 49.

[5]Ibid., p. 47.

[6]Ibid.

[7]Mike Regele with Mark Schulz, *Death of the Church* (Grand Rapids, Mich.: Zondervan, 1995), p. 96.

[8]Leith Anderson, *A Church for the Twenty-First Century* (Minneapolis: Bethany House, 1992), p. 46.

[9]Ibid., p. 47.

[10]Miller, *Reinventing American Protestantism*, p. 188.

[11]George Barna, *The Second Coming of the Church* (Waco, Tex.: Word, 1998), p. 29.

[12]Kew and White, *Toward 2015*, p. 66.

[13]See Thomas Allan Smail, *Reflected Glory* (London: Hodder & Stoughton, 1975), pp. 94-95.

[14]See John Adair, *Training for Leadership* (London: Macdonald, 1968).

[15]Lyle Schaller, *The New Reformation: Tomorrow Arrived Yesterday* (Nashville: Abingdon, 1995), pp. 62-64.

[16]Ibid., p. 63.

[17]Ibid.

[18]Philip Kenneson and James Street, *Selling Out the Church: The Dangers of Church Marketing* (Nashville: Abingdon, 1997), p. 107.

[19]Ibid., p. 108.

[20]Max De Pree, *Leadership Jazz* (New York: Bantam Doubleday Dell, 1992), pp. 8-9.

[21]Kenneson and Street, *Selling Out*, p. 116.

[22]Ibid., p. 119.

[23]Ibid., p. 117.

[24]Barna, *Second Coming*, p. 107.

[25]Richard Farson, *Management of the Absurd: Paradoxes in Leadership* (New York: Touchstone Simon & Schuster, 1996), p. 38.

[26]Barna, *Second Coming*, p. 35. Barna provides a helpful contrast between the characteristics of the leader and the teacher, although he unfairly caricatures the teacher on some points.

[27]Richard John Neuhaus, *Freedom for Ministry*, rev. ed. (Grand Rapids, Mich.: Eerdmans, 1992), p. 219.

[28] For a profile of the new paradigm church leader, see Miller, *Reinventing American Protestantism*, pp. 169-70.

[29]Ibid., p. 170.

[30]Farson, *Management of the Absurd*, p. 122.

Chapter 5: From Following Celebrities to Encountering Saints

[1]Os Guinness, *Dining with the Devil* (Grand Rapids, Mich.: Baker, 1993), pp. 18, 62.

[2]See, for instance, Tom Smail's emphasis on the Spirit in Christ and the Christian in *Reflected Glory* (London: Hodder & Stoughton, 1975); and on the neglect of the Father in *The Forgotten Father* (London: Hodder & Stoughton, 1980).

[3]George Barna, *The Second Coming of the Church* (Waco, Tex.: Word, 1998), p. 68.

[4]Wade Clark Roof, *A Generation of Seekers* (San Francisco: HarperSanFrancisco, 1993), pp. 30-31.

[5]Tom Beaudoin, *Virtual Faith* (San Francisco, Calif.: Jossey-Bass, 1998), p. 26.

[6]Ibid., p. 41.

[7]Roof, *Generation of Seekers*, p. 243.

[8]Ibid., pp. 4-6.

[9]Leith Anderson, *A Church for the Twenty-First Century* (Minneapolis: Bethany House, 1992), p. 21.

[10]Roof, *Generation of Seekers*, p. 54.

[11]Donald Miller, *Reinventing American Protestantism: Christianity in the New Millennium* (Berkeley: University of California Press, 1997), p. 91.

[12]Ibid., pp. 87-88.

[13]Ibid., p. 96.

[14]Barna, *Second Coming*, pp. 73-77.

[15]Ibid., p. 76.

[16]Beaudoin, *Virtual Faith*, p. ix.

[17]Diogenes Allen, *Spiritual Theology* (Cambridge, Mass.: Cowley, 1997), p. 100.

[18]See William E. Diehl, *The Monday Connection* (San Francisco: HarperSanFrancisco, 1993).

[19]Allen, *Spiritual Theology*, p. 86.

[20]Thomas Merton, *Contemplation in a World of Action* (Garden City, N.Y.: Doubleday, 1971), p. 345.

[21]Michael Casey, *Sacred Reading: The Ancient Art of* Lectio Divina (Liguori, Mo.: Triumph, 1996); Thelma Hall, *Too Deep for Words: Rediscovering* Lectio Divina (New York: Paulist, 1988); Sam Anthony Morello, *Lectio Divina* (Washington, D.C.: Institute of Carmelite Studies, 1996).

[22]Allen, *Spiritual Theology*, p. 150.

[23]I am indebted to Esther de Waal, *The Celtic Way of Prayer* (New York: Doubleday, 1997); which provides a scholarly and concise overview of Celtic spirituality.

[24]Ibid., p. 2.

[25]Ibid., p. 3.

[26]Ibid., p. 97.
[27]Ibid.
[28]Ibid., p. 17.
[29]Ibid., p. 95.
[30]Ibid., p. 113.
[31]Ibid., p. 145.
[32]Ibid., p. 144.
[33]Ibid., p. 142.
[34]Ibid., pp. 145-46 (summary, not direct quotation).
[35]Ibid., p. 164.
[36]Ibid., p. 166.
[37]See Dallas Willard, *The Spirit of the Disciplines* (San Francisco: HarperSanFrancisco, 1988).
[38]Allen, *Spiritual Theology,* pp. 16-18.
[39]See David Lyle Jeffrey, *English Spirituality in the Age of Wesley* (Grand Rapids, Mich.: Eerdmans, 1994; original title *A Burning and Shining Light: English Spirituality in the Age of Wesley,* 1987). This book provides an illuminating essay about the social and spiritual conditions of the time and an anthology of the writings of some of the most influential figures, each introduced with a brief biography.
[40]Miller, *Reinventing American Protestantism,* p. 122.
[41]Richard J. Foster and James Bryan Smith, *Devotional Classics: Selected Readings for Individuals and Groups* (San Francisco: HarperSanFrancisco, 1993).

Chapter 6: From Dead Orthodoxy to Living Faith

[1]Bill Hybels, "Willow Creek Community Church and the Willow Creek Association," in *The New Apostolic Churches,* ed. C. Peter Wagner (Ventura, Calif.: Regal, 1998), p. 77. Hybels identifies these seven steps as (1) become a friend of sinners; (2) share a verbal witness; (3) provide a place every week where people can bring their spiritually seeking friends; (4) participation in the mid-week worship service; (5) join a small group; (6) perform ministry according to spiritual giftedness; and (7) biblical stewardship, which is more than just giving of one's finances but being completely committed, at a heart level, to building the church both locally and internationally, through the church's extensive missions efforts (pp. 78-83).
[2]Sally Morgenthaler, *Worship Evangelism: Inviting Unbelievers into the Presence of God* (Grand Rapids, Mich.: Zondervan, 1995), p. 26.
[3]Peter Brierley, *Future Church* (Crowborough, East Sussex, U.K.: Monarch, 1998), p. 184. See also Eddie Gibbs, *In Name Only: Tackling the Problem of Nominal Christianity* (Wheaton, Ill.: Bridgepoint/Victor, 1994), pp. 287-88.
[4]Martin Robinson, *The Faith of the Unbeliever* (Crowborough, East Sussex, U.K.: Monarch, 1994), p. 175.
[5]Wade Clark Roof, *Generation of Seekers: The Spiritual Journey of the Baby Boomer* (San Francisco, Calif.: HarperSanFrancisco, 1993).
[6]George Barna, *Barna Report 1994-1995* (Ventura, Calif.: Regal, 1994), pp. 259, 308.
[7]Roof, *Generation of Seekers,* pp. 236, 78.
[8]Morgenthaler, *Worship Evangelism,* p. 17.
[9]Robert Webber, *Evangelicals on the Canterbury Trail* (Waco, Tex.: Word, 1985), p. 40.
[10]Morgenthaler, *Worship Evangelism,* p. 40.
[11]Evelyn Underhill, *Worship,* rev. ed. (Guildford, Surrey, U.K.: Eagle, 1991), p. 4.
[12]Ibid., p. 14.

[13]Ibid., pp. 11-12.

[14]See Webber, *Evangelicals*.

[15]Peter E. Gillquist, *Becoming Orthodox: A Journey to the Ancient Christian Faith* (Ben Lomond, Calif.: Conciliar Press, 1992). See also Charles Bell, *Rediscovering the Rich Heritage of Orthodoxy* (Light & Life, 1994).

[16]Gary M. Burge, "Missing God at Church? Why So Many Are Rediscovering Worship in Other Traditions," *Christianity Today*, October 6, 1997, p. 22.

[17]Underhill, *Worship*, p. 14.

[18]Ibid., p. 67.

[19]David Hilborn, *Picking Up the Pieces* (London: Hodder & Stoughton, 1997), pp. 124-42.

[20]Ibid., pp. 79ff.

[21]David Tomlinson, *The Post-Evangelical* (Nashville: Abingdon, 1995).

[22]Nick Hornsby, *Fever Pitch* (London: Penguin Books, 1992), pp. 186-87.

[23]Graham Kendrick, *Learning to Worship as a Way of Life* (Minneapolis: Bethany House, 1984), p. 99.

Chapter 7: From Attracting a Crowd to Seeking the Lost

[1]Mike Regele with Mark Schulz, *The Death of the Church* (Grand Rapids, Mich.: Zondervan, 1996), pp. 183-84.

[2]Donald Miller, *Reinventing American Protestantism: Christianity in the New Millennium* (Berkeley: University of California Press, 1997), pp. 72-73.

[3]Ibid., pp. 161-62.

[4]Ibid., p. 79.

[5]Os Guinness, *Dining with the Devil* (Grand Rapids, Mich.: Baker, 1993), p. 82.

[6]See George Barna, *Barna Report 1991-1992: What Americans Believe* (Ventura, Calif.: Regal Books, 1991), p. 308; *Barna Report 1992-1993: America Renews Its Search for God* (Regal, 1993), p. 277; and *Barna Report 1994-1995: Virtual America* (Regal, 1995), p. 259.

[7]Richard Kew and Roger White, *Toward 2015,* (Boston: Cowley, 1997), p. 97.

[8]Evelyn Underhill, *Worship*, rev. ed. (Guildford, Surrey, U.K.: Eagle, 1991), p. 4.

[9]Ibid., p. 14.

[10]Sally Morgenthaler, *Worship Evangelism: Inviting Unbelievers into the Presence of God* (Grand Rapids, Mich.: Zondervan, 1995), pp. 40-41.

[11]Ibid., p. 44.

[12]Ibid., p. 45. Morgenthaler believes that if the seeker churches were to reinstate worship as their primary identity, their impact on the unchurched community and influence in evangelicalism would be greatly enhanced.

[13]Ibid., p. 84.

[14]Ibid., chap. 5.

[15]Lyle Schaller, *Innovations in Ministry* (Nashville: Abingdon, 1994), pp. 49-50.

[16]David Hilborn, *Picking Up The Pieces* (London: Hodder & Stoughton, 1997), p. 60.

[17]Morgenthaler, *Worship Evangelism*, p. 135.

[18]Ibid., p. 52.

[19]Ibid., p. 90.

[20]Donald A. McGavran, *Understanding Church Growth*, ed. C. Peter Wagner, 3rd ed. (Grand Rapids, Mich.: Eerdmans, 1970), pp. 15, 32-48.

[21]Philip Kenneson and James Street, *Selling Out the Church* (Nashville: Abingdon, 1997), p. 142.

[22]Eugene Peterson, *The Message* (Colorado Springs: NavPress, 1993), p. 352.

[23]Kenneson and Street, *Selling Out,* p. 145.

[24]McGavran, *Understanding Church Growth,* chap. 17.

[25]Leighton Ford and Jim Denney, *The Power of Story* (Colorado Springs: NavPress, 1994), p. 132.

[26]Darrell L. Guder, ed., *The Missional Church* (Grand Rapids, Mich.: Eerdmans, 1998), p. 96.

[27]Ibid., p. 97.

Chapter 8: From Belonging to Believing

[1]See Rodney Clapp, *A Peculiar People: The Church as Culture in a Post-Christian Society* (Downers Grove, Ill.: InterVarsity Press, 1996), p. 163.

[2]Mark McCloskey, *Tell It Often—Tell It Well* (San Bernardino, Calif.: Here's Life, 1986), p. 186.

[3]Donald Posterski, *Reinventing Evangelism* (Downers Grove, Ill.: InterVarsity Press, 1989), pp. 31-32.

[4]G. A. Pritchard, *Willow Creek Seeker Services* (Grand Rapids, Mich.: Baker, 1996), pp. 23-24.

[5]Posterski, *Reinventing Evangelism,* p. 18.

[6]Ibid., p. 55.

[7]Ibid., p. 61.

[8]Clapp, *Peculiar People,* p. 188.

[9]Bruce Shelley and Marshall Shelley, *The Consumer Church* (Downers Grove, Ill.: InterVarsity Press, 1992), p. 52.

[10]For a penetrating analysis of bureaucracy, which is "the rule of nobody and is therefore experienced as tyranny," see Lesslie Newbigin, *Foolishness to the Greeks* (Grand Rapids, Mich.: Eerdmans, 1986), pp. 32-33,

[11]Clapp, *Peculiar People,* p. 194.

[12]Darrell Guder, *Be My Witnesses* (Grand Rapids, Mich.: Eerdmans, 1985), p. 149.

[13]See McCloskey, *Tell It Often,* p. 182.

[14]Kevin Ford, *Jesus for a New Generation* (Downers Grove, Ill.: InterVarsity Press, 1996), p. 243.

[15]C. H. Dodd, *The Apostolic Preaching and its Developments* (New York: Harper & Row, 1936).

[16]See Robert C. Worley, *Preaching and Teaching in the Earliest Church* (Philadelphia: Westminster Press, 1967), pp. 35-36; Michael Green, *Evangelism in the Early Church* (London: Hodder & Stoughton, 1970), pp. 60ff; William J. Abraham, *The Logic of Evangelism* (Grand Rapids, Mich.: Eerdmans, 1989), pp. 43-51.

[17]Quoted in Lewis A. Drummond, *The Word of the Cross* (Nashville: Broadman, 1992), p. 209.

[18]Worley, *Preaching and Teaching,* pp 35-36.

[19]Mike Regele with Mark Schulz, *Death of the Church* (Grand Rapids, Mich.: Zondervan, 1995), p. 83.

[20]Diogenes Allen, *Spiritual Theology* (Cambridge, Mass.: Cowley, 1997), p. 22.

[21]Regele, *Death of the Church,* p. 87.

[22]Clapp, *Peculiar People,* p. 184.

[23]Joseph Healey, *A Fifth Gospel: The Experience of Black Christian Values* (Maryknoll, N.Y.: Orbis, 1981); and "A Fifth Gospel: The Experience of Black Christian Values: Our Stories as Fifth Gospels," *Missiology* 16, no. 3 (1988): 305-20.

Chapter 9: From Generic Congregations to Incarnational Communities

[1]Richard H. Niebuhr, *Christ and Culture* (New York: Harper & Row, 1952).

[2]Rodney Clapp, *A Peculiar People: The Church as Culture in a Post-Christian Society* (Downers Grove, Ill.: InterVarsity Press, 1996), p. 59.

[3]George R. Hunsberger and Craig Van Gelder, eds., *The Church Between Gospel and Culture* (Grand Rapids, Mich.: Eerdmans, 1996), p. 289.

[4]Clapp, *Peculiar People,* chap. 1.

[5]Alan J. Roxburgh, *The Missionary Congregation: Leadership and Liminality* (Harrisburg, Penn.: Trinity Press International, 1997), pp. 7-8.

[6]Ibid., p. 12.

[7]Ibid., p. 16.

[8]Ibid., p. 20.

[9]Alan J. Roxburgh, "Pastoral Role in the Missionary Congregation," in *Church Between Gospel and Culture,* ed. Hunsberger and Van Gelder, pp. 323-24.

[10]Ibid., p. 23.

[11]Ibid., p. 24.

[12]Ibid., p. 37.

[13]Ibid., p. 38.

[14]Ibid., p. 30.

[15]Eugene Peterson, *The Message* (Colorado Springs: NavPress, 1993), p. 429 (emphasis in the original).

[16]Clapp, *Peculiar People,* p. 188.

[17]Diogenes Allen, *Spiritual Theology* (Cambridge, Mass.: Cowley, 1997), p. 19.

[18]E. Dixon Junkin, in *Church Between Gospel and Culture,* ed. Hunsberger and Van Gelder, p. 312.

[19]Ibid., p. 314.

[20]Ibid.

[21]Rodney Clapp, *Peculiar People,* p. 194.

[22]See Rick Warren, *The Purpose Driven Church* (Grand Rapids, Mich.: Zondervan, 1995), pp. 376-79. See also William Easum, *Sacred Cow Makes Gourmet Burgers: Ministry Anytime, Anywhere by Anyone* (Nashville: Abingdon, 1995), p. 51.

[23]Easum, *Sacred Cow,* p. 53.

[24]Michael Marquardt and Angus Reynolds, *The Global Learning Organization* (Burr Ridge, Ill.: Irwin, 1994), p. 23.

[25]Andrew S. Grove, *Only the Paranoid Survive* (New York: Doubleday, 1996), pp. 21-22, 109.

[26]Eugene Peterson, *Under the Unpredictable Planet?* (Grand Rapids, Mich.: Eerdmans, 1992), p. 16.

Index of Names

Index of Subjects